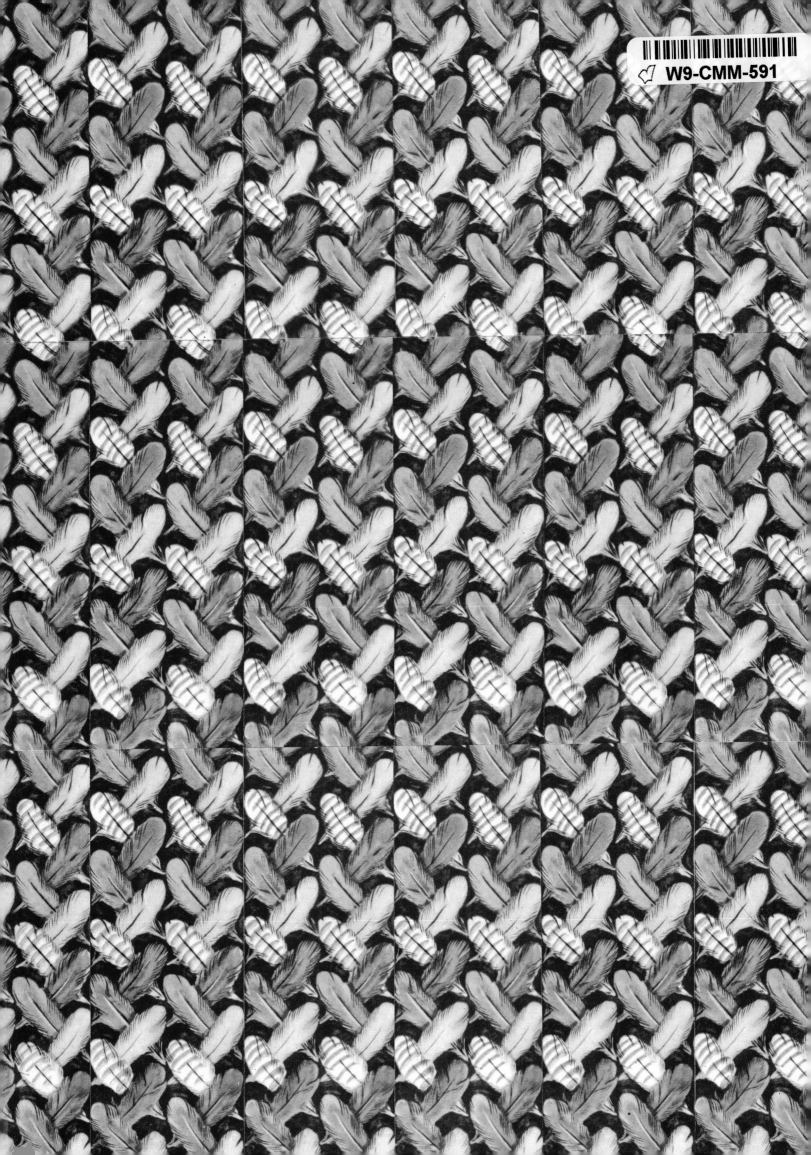

THE BIRDS OF AMERICA

FROM THE PAINTING BY F. CRUICKSHANK

THE BIRDS OF AMERICA

John James Audubon

With a Foreword by Robert McCracken Peck

Introduction and Descriptive Captions
by William Vogt

MACMILLAN PUBLISHING COMPANY
New York
COLLIER MACMILLAN PUBLISHERS
London

Macmillan Publishing Company
866 Third Avenue, New York, N.Y. 10022
Collier Macmillan Canada, Inc.

Library of Congress Cataloging in Publication Data

Audubon, John James, 1785–1851.
The birds of America.

1. Birds—North America—Pictorial works.
I. Vogt, William, 1902–1968. II. Title.
QL681.A97 1985   598.2973   85-3030
ISBN 0-02-504450-8

Macmillan books are available at special discounts for
bulk purchases for sales promotions, premiums, fund-raising,
or educational use. For details, contact:
Special Sales Director
Macmillan Publishing Company
866 Third Avenue
New York, New York 10022

10 9 8 7 6 5 4 3 2 1

Printed in the United States of America

TYPOGRAPHY BY PETER BEILENSON
LITHOGRAPHED IN THE UNITED STATES OF AMERICA BY DUENEWALD LITHOGRAPH COMPANY, INC.

FOREWORD
By Robert McCracken Peck

The history of American art is filled with figures whose reputations have waxed and waned with the cycles of taste. John James Audubon is one whose popularity and critical reputation have defied the averages and increased exponentially since the issue of the first "double elephant" folio plates of *The Birds of America* in the spring of 1827. The bicentennial of Audubon's birth —marked by Macmillan's reissue of *The Birds of America,* the issue of a U.S. postal commemorative, and a spate of special exhibitions, symposia, and television documentaries about the artist and his work—provides an opportunity to reflect on the remarkable phenomenon of Audubon's achievement.

Never one for false modesty, Audubon himself described *The Birds of America* as an "extraordinary work." So it was: 435 plates with life-size depictions of 1,065 individual birds, sold by subscription in groups of **5 plates,** or volumes of 100 and more, over an eleven-year period. Never before had such an ambitious project been attempted. That it was carried off so well and by a man with no formal training in art, natural history, or publishing seems little short of miraculous.

Everything about *The Birds of America* was large: the scope of the work, the years of research involved, the extent of supervision required for its production, and of course, the dimensions of the book itself. Each of the 435 plates measured 39½ by 26½ inches, and each had to be individually hand-printed and hand-colored, a monumental undertaking by any standard. Nevertheless, the final number of complete sets was small—probably under two hundred. How then did the book have such a huge impact, and why has its fame increased with time?

Of the many factors that contributed to the initial success and continuing influence of *The Birds of America,* its scientific value, artistic strength, popular subject, remarkable size, and strategic distribution were among the most crucial.

The bibliographical history of North American ornithology prior to Audubon is surprisingly spare. Mark Catesby's *Natural History of Carolina, Florida, and the Bahama Islands* (1731–1743) was the first book to contain a significant number of detailed color plates depicting North American birds. The 220 hand-colored etchings that illustrate the volume include 109 bird species, each with a plate and accompanying text.

The next major advance in information on North American birds came in 1791, with the publication of William Bartram's *Travels through North and South Carolina, Georgia, East and West Florida,* an influential book in which the naturalist-author chronicled a four-year trip through the wilds of southeastern North America (1773–1776). *Travels* did not contain any illustrations of birds, but it did include some new behavioral descriptions, important information on distribution, and a listing of 215 bird species—almost double Catesby's total.

With Bartram's encouragement and help, Alexander Wilson, a Scottish-born weaver, schoolteacher, and aspiring poet, wrote and illustrated the first book devoted exclusively to North American birds, *American Ornithology* (1808–1825). This nine-volume work contained pictures and detailed descriptions of 279 bird species. Wilson's book, later supplemented by Charles Lucien Bonaparte, was the most complete work on the subject until Audubon's *The Birds of America* (1827–1838) and its later, textual companion, *Ornithological Biography* (1831–1839), which contained 489 bird species.

The many insightful, firsthand observations that Audubon included in his *Ornithological Biography* would have given this publication—and Audubon—lasting importance even without the plates of *The Birds of America,* but it was certainly the paintings that brought Audubon to the attention of the world and maintain his reputation today. In both books Audubon provided valuable information in a style that could excite even those with no prior interest in birds. The combination assured attention; the quality of presentation guaranteed lasting success.

In an attempt to gain artistic (and social) credibility and thereby increase subscriptions for his book, Audubon sometimes claimed to have studied with the great French neoclassical painter Jacques Louis David. Although there is no evidence to support this claim, and most of Audubon's biographies have discounted it, it is often repeated in cameo accounts of his life. Ironically, through his self-aggrandizement Audubon gave some of the credit for his own artistic genius to another artist. In fact, it was his departure from the prevailing neoclassical taste that has given Audubon such an important place in the history of American art.

In depicting the birds of his adopted land, Audubon went well beyond the clinical profiles dictated by scientific and artistic tradition. His compositions had strength and power, his birds had personality and life, and his botanical and landscape backgrounds, often painted with the help of assistants, conveyed a sense of grandeur that captured the excitement of a new, Romantic age.

Audubon's brilliant departure from the long tradition of scientific illustration ruffled some feathers in the scientific community. His critics considered the emotional content of his paintings incompatible with objective scientific analysis. They cited several of his predator-prey subjects (particularly the Mockingbird [21], Brown Thrasher [116], and Bob-white [76]) as being scientifically inaccurate or unnecessarily anthropomorphic.

Of course, some of the criticism Audubon received was valid, but much of it was petty and inconsequential, growing from the personal animosity and jealousy of a small group of contentious naturalists who had tried to discredit the project from the very start. Fortunately, most of Audubon's patrons were willing to overlook or tolerate these relatively minor points of scientific disagreement. They recognized *The Birds of America* as the watershed work that it was.

Despite the overwhelmingly positive reception of *The Birds of America,* Audubon's companion volume on mammals, *The Viviparous Quadrupeds of North America* (1845–1849), never achieved the same level of success. This may have been due in part to Audubon's declining powers as an artist and his decreased level of direct involvement with the project. With a text by the Reverend John Bachman, and more than half of the 150 lithographic plates drawn by Audubon's sons, Victor and John, the book fails to convey the intense personal interest and enjoyment Audubon expressed so eloquently in *The Birds of America* and *Ornithological Biography.*

Another, more compelling explanation for the difference in public response, however, involves the subject matter of each work. Even if it had been entirely written and illustrated by John J. Audubon, *The Viviparous Quadrupeds of North America* probably would have remained in the shadow of his earlier ornithological achievements—for of all natural subjects, birds and flowers have traditionally had the broadest public appeal. That Audubon's were American birds and flowers (the latter usually portrayed in his plates by his collaborators Joseph Mason, Maria Martin, and others) has added immeasurably to the long-term interest in, and demand for, his work.

At the time of the first publication of *The Birds of America,* North American subjects were of special fascination to amateur naturalists in England and Europe, many of whom had the financial resources to provide the badly needed sponsorship for the enterprise. Of the 308 original subscribers for *The Birds of America,* almost half came from overseas. Since that time, increased American interest has resulted in the sale of some of Audubon's English and European folios to American collectors and institutions. Unfortunately, the seemingly insatiable demand for Audubon's work has also encouraged the breakup and sale of bound sets of *The Birds of America* on both sides of the Atlantic. Today, fewer than 134 double elephant folios survive intact.

From the very beginning, the remarkable size of *The Birds of America* has played a role in its success. The physical dimensions of the double elephant folio immediately set it apart from the scores of other beautifully illustrated bird books that enjoyed such popularity in the nineteenth century. Robert Havell, Jr., and the other engravers who worked with Audubon pushed the printing technology of the day to its limit, producing life-size aquatint engravings of even the largest American birds. While the tremendous size of the plates made the volumes unwieldy to handle and difficult to store, it also made them the conspicuous focal point of any library. As volumes have been split up and sold, the individual prints have continued to command special attention and preferential display at least in part because of their size.

When Audubon left the United States for England in 1826 to arrange for the publication of *The Birds of America,* he hoped to secure a total of five hundred subscribers to finance the undertaking. In numbers, he fell short of his goal, but the subscribers he did enlist were an impressive and extremely influential group, running the political gamut from Daniel Webster and Henry Clay to the kings of France and England, and included many of the most important institutional libraries in the Western world. Their patronage went a long way toward guaranteeing the acceptability, visibility, and lasting fame of his work.

Audubon could have started his publishing career with a smaller, less expensive book than the double elephant folio. The popularity of his octavo edition (1840–1844), which incorporated the text from *Ornithological Biography,* suggests that there was a market for such a publication, but Audubon was determined to see his "great work" produced on a scale befitting the scope of the undertaking and in a manner worthy of his magnificent subjects. The great cost associated with the double elephant folio of *The Birds of America* ($1,000 per set) meant that only the wealthiest and most influential individuals and organizations could afford it. By thus limiting his initial audience, he was assuring a selective distribution, which would eventually give the book its greatest impact. Later, Audubon's own octavo edition and Julius Bien's full-sized chromolithographs of plates from *The Birds of America* further increased the book's popularity. In the twentieth century, an abundance of less expensive reproductions, the first of which was Macmillan's volume in 1937, made Audubon's previously rare images accessible to households all over the world.

Time, the greatest test of any work of art or science, has added luster to *The Birds of America* and changed forever the way we see its magnificent plates. To some, these once-novel perceptions of a wild, young America have become a moving visual requiem. The Carolina Paroquet [26], Passenger Pigeon [62], and Ivory-billed Woodpecker [66]—some of Audubon's strongest, most memorable plates—represent species now gone forever. Yet, in many ways, the vision and masterful artistry of these and other Audubon images transcend the subjects they depict. Like great paintings, great writing, or great music from any age, Audubon's birds, abundant or extinct, will live forever as the masterworks of one of America's most gifted artists.

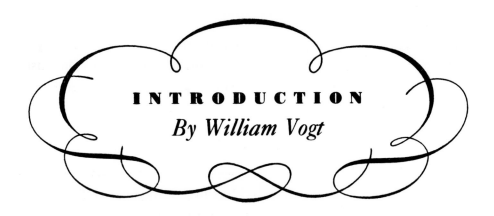

INTRODUCTION
By William Vogt

JOHN JAMES AUDUBON
—"The American Woodsman"—was born April 26, 1785, at Aux Cayes, the son of a French naval officer and a *créole de Saint-Domingue*. Dr. Francis H. Herrick has published strong documentary evidence of this romantic, if humble, origin. Those who would identify Audubon with one of the numerous Lost Dauphins that ubiquitously popped up, like prairie dogs, after the French Revolution have been able to adduce no testimony more eloquent than a fancied Bourbon resemblance and several cryptic statements by the naturalist himself. It is easy to discount Audubon's own hints when his capacity for self-dramatization is remembered, and when one considers how bitterly his pride and ambition would have suffered had the true circumstances of his birth been made known.

Like that other famous West Indian illegitimate, Alexander Hamilton, he adopted his North American home whole-heartedly. Although his speech retained, to the end, a Gallic seasoning, and his use of a dagger in self-defense seemed objectionably "furrin" to many of his fellows of the frontier, he nowhere felt himself at home except among the birds of America. His devotion to the swamps of the Mississippi valley, the forests of the Ohio, the rich coast of South Carolina, was little short of a passion. With the wilderness everywhere at his back door he turned without regret from more lucrative and humdrum ways. He has been romanticized, and all but canonized, as one possessed by a noble ideal. Actually, like many a biology professor and game warden since, he was thoroughly—and selfishly—enjoying life in the woods, fields, and marshes.

This is not the place to dilate on Audubon's extraordinary life. Though one may be inclined to challenge Stanley C. Arthur's statement, in his admirable new biography, "As a man he is far more interesting than aught he accomplished," this is only because of the sweep of Audubon's accomplishments. His rise to fame, after vicissitudes that to most men would have been heart-breaking, parallels other American success stories; and his climb was aided, like that of thousands of Americans before and since, by his very American cultivation of the art of salesmanship. Ben Franklin knew the effectiveness of plain Quaker garb at the French court. P. T. Barnum built a fortune on hyperbole. The American Woodsman clung to his unfashionable dress in London—though he had been eager enough to dress well in New Orleans—and allowed his long, bear-greased locks to be shorn only after many importunities by his friends.

Few of the men who wrested its virgin fruits from this continent dealt so fairly with it as Audubon. He compounded its riches to his own benefit; but, unlike most pioneers of his period, he contributed far more than he took away. Others fouled the rivers, destroyed the soil, pillaged the forests, and slaughtered the wild creatures. Audubon, loving that rich land as few men have loved it, before or since, captured within his books, and saved for us who must painfully correct our ancestors' mistakes, the essence of America that was.

The stature of Audubon the artist can best be judged by an examination of his work. Posterity has established him among the American immortals. The prices of his original plates have placed them beyond the reach of the ordinary man. Set after set has been broken up—the number of sets issued was under two hundred—and sold over the counter. For the first time this volume makes the 435 plates of the Elephant Folio available at a price within reach of the general public.

Audubon vowed he would never paint stuffed specimens, and took ornithological art out of its glass case, for all time. If some of his realism—as in the gory-beaked Duck Hawk—now seems overtheatrical, it should be remembered that he was in vigorous revolt against the stodgy methods of painters of his day. The dramatic always appealed to him, and his ability to dramatize his subjects brought forth an instant response from scientists and connoisseurs. Most of the bird paintings they had seen resembled mummies rather than living birds. A Gordon Craig would probably damn Audubon as a truckler to mere effectiveness; had his work been less startling, however, it is doubtful if it—or he—would have survived.

Audubon the naturalist has, in the recent revival of appreciation, been overshadowed by Audubon the artist. His scientific abilities are less striking than his skill with the brush, and he was preceded in America by another eminent ornithologist, Alexander Wilson; but his *Ornithological Biography* (written with the help of William MacGillivray) still has far more value than many a bird book issued in the twentieth century! There have been thousands of bird students, professional and amateur, since he floated down the Mississippi; but among his accounts of North American species are still some of the most complete and accurate that have ever been published. And his wide-ranging, vigorous mind anticipated by a century the experimental investigation of bird behavior that plays an increasingly prominent part in American ornithology.

* * * * * *

In the brief text that accompanies these plates, this general plan has been followed: The modern names, both vernacular and scientific, are given. The ranges, based on the *Check-List* of the American Ornithologists' Union, will suggest in which *parts* of the country the various species should be expected. Under *Habitat* an attempt has been made to indicate in what *sort* of country one should look for the birds, especially in the breeding season. During migration, of course, birds may appear in all manner of places. Not long ago a Woodcock dropped, exhausted, on a roof outside the Audubon Society offices in New York City, and considerable difficulty was experienced in convincing interested people it had not been planted as a publicity stunt! Under *Identification,* conspicuous, diagnostic characteristics have been suggested, as far as space permits. There are exceedingly few North American birds that cannot be readily and certainly recognized in the field, and it is by the natural tags—white outer tail-feathers in the Vesper Sparrow, for example—that students know them. Relatively few attempts have been made to describe songs, since in most cases this cannot be done in English syllables. Readers are urged to consult Aretas A. Saunders' *Guide to Bird Songs,* which provides a system without the use of musical notation.

Largely, no doubt, as a result of Audubon's influence, the birds of North America have been portrayed and described far better than those of most other parts of the world. A small ornithological library, as a key to the world of birds, will repay the investment many times over. For identification in the field, Roger Tory Peterson's *A Field Guide to the Birds* and the more recent *Field Guide to Western Birds* have no equal. We are also fortunate in having superb state publications on birds; it is well for the student to add one of these to his library. He need not wait for his own state to publish, if a near-by state has produced a good book. For example, Arthur H. Howell's *Florida Bird Life* will be found extremely useful throughout most of the Southeast. No finer regional bird books have been produced than T. S. Roberts' *Birds of Minnesota* and E. H. Forbush's *Birds of Massachusetts and Other New England States*. In this same category are William Leon Dawson's *The Birds of California*, Florence Merriam Bailey's *Birds of New Mexico*, W. E. Clyde Todd's *Birds of Western Pennsylvania*, and P. A. Taverner's *Birds of Canada*. Frank M. Chapman's *Handbook of Birds of Eastern North America* is all but indispensable in the region covered (his bibliographies are invaluable), and Mrs. Bailey's western *Handbook* occupies approximately the same niche on the opposite side of the continent.

To one making the acquaintance of birds, the local list (usually costing only a few cents) is most helpful in telling what birds are where, and when. Usually the nearest natural history museum library can give information concerning these lists.

Identification, in natural history, is only the beginning of wisdom. While it is pleasant to recognize birds, wherever one may be, and while thousands of bird-lovers the world over eagerly compete in the effort to acquire the largest possible day, year, and life lists, birds are worth far more attention than a casual glance, a certain identification, and a check on a field card. Indeed, there is evidence that increasing numbers of bird students realize this fact, and that they are turning from a quantitative to a qualitative approach.

Few fields have benefited more from amateur effort than natural history. This is especially true of ornithology, in which some of the brightest names are those of non-professionals. Everyone interested in birds may, by a constructive use of his time, contribute materially to the advance of the science. In the process, the bird watcher will find birds far more fascinating than he has dreamed, and will correspondingly enjoy his hobby. To anyone who has spent a few hours in close observation of birds at their nests, or during their courtship period, these creatures will provide unending delight.

To make such a study, and to make it significant, requires no equipment beyond notebooks and knowledge of what has already been published; though a pair of binoculars, and bird banding apparatus, will speed the explorer on his way. As an introduction to the world of the living bird, I strongly recommend *How Birds Live* and *The Art of Bird-Watching*, by E. M. Nicholson; *Bird Behavior*, by F. B. Kirkman; *Wild Birds at Home*, by F. H. Herrick; *The Book of Bird Life*, by A. A. Allen; and the opening pages of Chapman's *Handbook*. Since the life stories of only four American species have been adequately written, this particular form of bird study challenges the ingenuity, skill, and knowledge of everyone who has been stirred by a Red-wing's February song.

To the beginner, there is one further suggestion: make the acquaintance of fellow hobbyists, and join the local bird study group, if possible. Bird watchers are, generally, friendly folk who are more than willing to share their experience and knowledge. Much bird study is carried on as a social avocation, and one of its pleasantest rewards is the memory of days afield with co-workers. They not only help one to find and know the birds of one's region; they give the beginner the confidence in his powers that he probably lacks. The ability to recognize birds is within reach of anyone. Among the quickest and most accurate field students I have known are boys and girls in their teens. I have an eleven-year-old friend who, like a veteran, names the Ducks and shore-birds on the wing. Her only unusual intellectual equipment is a complete unconsciousness that such identification is difficult.

One more matter should be stressed: conservation. It is inconceivable that any book about Audubon today could ignore this important activity, with which his name has almost come to be synonymous. In no aspect is his prescience more remarkable than in his early understanding of conservation. His bird biographies show a comprehension of wild life similar to that which has been achieved by modern ecological research; much of his defense of the Crow, for example, might have been written by a researcher of the 1930's.

Only eleven years after Audubon's Labrador trip, the Great Auk was exterminated—at least, the last recorded specimen was taken. Twenty-six years after his death, the Labrador or Pied Duck vanished. From that day to this, other species have been wiped out, or driven down into the twilight zone. Some of this destruction of America's wild life has been incidental to destruction of habitats by advancing civilization. Much of it, however, has resulted from direct killing for profit or sport. The Passenger Pigeon and the Eskimo Curlew were recklessly slaughtered by market hunters. Colonial sea birds, and plumed Egrets, were all but wiped out over much of their range, for the profit of a few dealers in millinery supplies. The Bald Eagle, the symbol of a proud, free nation, has been exterminated from much of the country largely because it is a big, tempting target. Hawks have been destroyed by hundreds of thousands in the mistaken belief that they are responsible for the almost universal scarcity of game. Herons, Cormorants, White Pelicans, Terns, and Kingfishers are butchered by fishermen on a similar false assumption that they are the cause of the lack of food and sport fishes.

Opposed to this destruction there has been a public-spirited body of conservationists, who find life more worth living because it includes birds. Through their support, lost ground **has been regained,** and birds that a third of a century ago seemed doomed have been restored to something like their normal numbers. Even the ravages of civilization, which a few years ago seemed inevitable, have been assayed by scientific investigation, and by a broad social evaluation that counts more than today's dollar. Forests, grasslands, soil, water and —above all—marshes, that are the necessary habitats of our wild life, are now coming to be recognized as indispensable in our land economy if this nation is to continue to prosper. The conservation education that, alone, can save the land on which this democracy depends for its existence, still has far to spread. The very fact that it has a vigorous existence, however, keeps alive the hope that yesterday's America may still persist tomorrow.

Acknowledgments: Dr. T. S. Roberts, author of *The Birds of Minnesota,* Mr. Roger Tory Peterson, author of *A Field Guide to the Birds,* and Mr. Arthur H. Howell, author of *Florida Bird Life,* have generously given me permission to quote from their important works, and Mrs. William Leon Dawson has granted me the privilege of drawing on *The Birds of California* by her late husband. I have also turned frequently to Ridgway's *The Birds of North and Middle America,* and to A. C. Bent's unequalled *Life Histories.* Mr. Leon F. Kelso of the U. S. Biological Survey, and Mr. Richard H. Pough, Mr. Joseph J. Hickey, Mr. John T. Zimmer, and Dr. Robert C. Murphy, have given valued advice and criticism. Mr. Peterson has read the entire text and made invaluable suggestions and corrections; all responsibility for errors, however, remains mine. Mr. Charles Banks Belt has considerably smoothed my way by lending me his octavo edition of Audubon's *Birds.* The librarians of the American Museum of Natural History have been characteristically helpful in making the Museum's library available to me. And throughout the planning and preparation of this text, my wife has given indispensable advice, criticism, and assistance. To all these I express my sincere appreciation and thanks.

THE BIRDS OF AMERICA;

from

ORIGINAL DRAWINGS

By

JOHN JAMES AUDUBON,

Fellow of the Royal Societies of London & Edinburgh and of the
Linnæan & Zoological Societies of London
Member of the Natural History Society of Paris, of the Lyceum of New York,
&c. &c. &c.

LONDON.

Published by the Author.

1827_30.

NOTE

THE 435 plates in this volume were originally published by Audubon, in London, during the years 1827–1838. A superb set of these original "Elephant Folio" plates—a set believed to be the finest in uncut state in America—has, through the courtesy of the owner, been followed in making the present reproductions.

The bird names accompanying the present reproductions are those adopted in the *Check-List* of the American Ornithologists' Union.

Further information about the original plates is to be found in the *Transcript of Legends on the Original Plates* in the back of the present volume.

1. WILD TURKEY

(MELEAGRIS GALLOPAVO)

Range: Pennsylvania and Oklahoma to central Mexico. Formerly to South Dakota and Maine. *Habitat:* Forests, swamps, especially where mast is available. *Identification:* Resembles the familiar domestic bird, except that it has chestnut tail-tips, instead of white. In many places, however, the wild and domesticated forms have hybridized and discrimination is virtually impossible. *Nesting:* In leaf-lined hollows in the ground. Ten to fifteen, and sometimes twenty, eggs. *Food:* Insects and other arthropods, nuts, seeds, fruits.

2. YELLOW-BILLED CUCKOO
(COCCYZUS AMERICANUS)

Range: Breeds from British Columbia and New Brunswick to Mexico and the Florida Keys. Winters in northern South America. *Habitat:* Brush, clearings, orchards. *Identification:* Its extreme slenderness. Known from the Black-bill (Plate 32) by the light area at the base of the flight feathers; the large amount of white in tail; and yellow on lower mandible. Length, 11½ inches. *Voice:* Loud *kow-kow-kow-kow. Nesting:* Two to six eggs on flat nest. *Food:* Caterpillars—especially the hairy ones.

3. PROTHONOTARY WARBLER
(PROTONOTARIA CITREA)

Range: Breeds from Nebraska and Maryland to Texas and Florida. Winters from Nicaragua to Colombia. *Habitat:* Swampy woods, where there are dead trees. *Identification:* The almost incandescent golden yellow of head and breast, with *unbarred* bluish wings.

Length, about 5¼ inches. *Voice:* Loud, clear, *peet, peet, peet.* *Nesting:* In holes in dead stumps; preferably in natural cavities. Also nests in gourd bird-houses, and deserves the encouragement of bird-lovers. Four to six eggs. *Food:* Primarily insects.

4. PURPLE FINCH

(CARPODACUŚ PURPUREUS)

Range: Breeds from British Columbia and Newfoundland to Lower California, New Mexico and Long Island. Winters from well north of the southern boundary of its breeding range to Florida and Mexico. *Habitat:* Most frequently spruce, pine, etc. forests. Often, however, in more open cultivated country. *Identification:* Male not likely to be confused with anything but much larger Pine Grosbeaks. Female, *with very heavy bill,* more heavily streaked than Sparrows. Length about 5¾ inches. *Food:* Mostly weed seeds.

5. CANADA WARBLER

(WILSONIA CANADENSIS)

Range: Breeds from Alberta and Newfoundland to Minnesota and, along the Alleghenies, Georgia. Winters in Ecuador and Peru. *Habitat:* Wet woods and swamps. A bird of the lower vegetation. *Identification:* The narrow band of dark stripes across breast. Length, about 5½ inches. *Voice:* A rolling, buzzing warble. *Breeding:* Four to five eggs in nest on or close to the ground. *Food:* Like most other Warblers, it feeds primarily on insects. Many of these it takes on the wing, Flycatcher-fashion.

6 · WILD TURKEY
(MELEAGRIS GALLOPAVO)

The former abundance of this bird is vividly shown by Audubon's words: "At the time when I moved to Kentucky . . . Turkeys were so abundant that the price of one in the market was not equal to that of a common barn fowl now. I have seen them offered for the sum of three pence each, the birds weighing from ten to twelve pounds." The familiar barnyard Turkey is descended from Mexican stock, that was taken to Europe by the Spaniards, and exported to the United States. See Plate I.

7. PURPLE GRACKLE
(QUISCALUS QUISCULA)

Range: Breeds from Long Island and the lower Hudson Valley to Georgia, Alabama and Tennessee. Winters mainly south of the Delaware Valley. *Habitat:* Swampy woods, farmlands, city parks. *Identification:* The long tail, shaped like a blunt spear-head, dis-

tinguishes the Grackles from other Blackbirds. The iridescent barring on the back distinguishes this bird from the Bronzed race. Length, about 1 foot. *Voice:* A deep *check;* squeaky, creaky calls. *Food:* Insects, seeds, eggs and young birds.

8. WHITE-THROATED SPARROW

(ZONOTRICHIA ALBICOLLIS)

Range: Breeds from Mackenzie and Newfoundland to Montana and Massachusetts. Winters from Missouri and Massachusetts to Mexico and Florida. *Habitat:* Abandoned pastures, brushy second-growth. *Identification:* Striped top of head, *white throat and yellow* *before eye.* Length, about 7 inches. *Voice:* A lovely series of clear notes descending in approximate half-tones. *Breeding:* Four to five eggs in nest on or near ground. *Food:* The White-throat is a tame bird that readily accepts the hospitality of our feeding stations.

9. HOODED WARBLER

(WILSONIA CITRINA)

Determination as to which species Audubon intended to portray in this plate is more difficult than field identification of the immature Hooded Warbler it seems to represent. Plate 110 gives an excellent idea of the bird. Females, and especially young birds, are variable; there is usually a foreshadowing of the hood pattern in young males, but this may be indefinite. The *yellow forehead* is a good clue.

10. AMERICAN PIPIT

(ANTHUS SPINOLETTA)

Range: Breeds from Siberia and Greenland to Great Slave Lake and Quebec; in high western mountains, to New Mexico. Winters from California and the Delaware Valley, to Guatemala. Other races are found in Europe, Asia and North Africa. *Habitat:* On migration, and in winter, when we see it, on beaches, plowed fields, areas of short grass. *Identification:* It walks and wags the tail, which has conspicuous outer white edges. Length, about 6½ inches. *Voice:* A characteristic but indescribable *cheep.*

11. BALD EAGLE

(HALIAEETUS LEUCOCEPHALUS)

This species, which is portrayed in all its adult magnificence on Plate 31, offered difficulty to Audubon who clung to the belief that the immature bird in this dark plumage represented a new species. Many an amateur ornithologist has padded his list of "rarities" by calling it a Golden Eagle. Young of the latter species have considerable white in the wings; at all ages the light and dark in the tail are more contrasted than in the maturing Bald Eagle. Golden Eagle extremely rare in East. See Plate 181.

12. BALTIMORE ORIOLE

(ICTERUS GALBULA)

Range: Breeds from Wyoming, Alberta and Nova Scotia to Texas and Georgia. Winters from southern Mexico to Colombia. *Habitat:* Farms, villages, roadsides, parks. *Identification:* Size and coloration make males distinctive. Females difficult to tell from female Orchard Orioles, though somewhat brighter. Length, about 7½ inches. *Voice:* Clear, rich, varied whistles. *Breeding:* Four to six eggs in hanging nest at end of topmost branches, usually elms. *Food:* Insects, and some fruit. A common resident in the trees of villages.

13. SLATE-COLORED JUNCO
(JUNCO HYEMALIS)

Range: Breeds from Alaska and Quebec to Minnesota and (in the mountains) Georgia (Carolina race). Winters throughout eastern United States to the Gulf coast. *Habitat:* In woods, pastures—where there is brushy shelter. *Identification:* Slate color, *white outer tail* *feathers.* Length, about 5¾ inches. *Voice:* A rolling trill, as though someone were beating a rapid tattoo on a taut wire. *Breeding:* Four to six eggs, on or near ground. *Food:* Insects and weed seeds. An habitual visitor at winter feeding stations.

14. PRAIRIE WARBLER

(DENDROICA DISCOLOR)

Range: Breeds from Nebraska and Massachusetts to Alabama and Florida; also in the Bahamas. Winters from Florida through the West Indies. *Habitat:* Usually on poor land, such as abandoned, worn-out farms and pine barrens. *Identification:* The characteristic facial pattern, stripes on the flanks, *reddish markings on back*. Length, about 4 2/3 inches. *Voice:* About seven high-pitched buzzes, the last usually markedly higher. *Breeding:* Three to five eggs, often so low that one may readily look into the nest.

15. PARULA WARBLER

(COMPSOTHLYPIS AMERICANA)

Range: Breeds from Nebraska and Cape Breton Island to Texas and Florida. Winters in Florida, West Indies, Mexico and Nicaragua. *Habitat:* Wet woods, where Spanish moss or *Usnea* lichen is available for nests. *Identification:* Audubon's name gives a clue to the most definite field mark—the yellow patch on the back. The colorful breast-band marks the male, but cannot be depended on in the female. Length, about 4½ inches. *Voice:* "A sizzling trill" (Chapman).

16. DUCK HAWK
(FALCO PEREGRINUS)

Range: Breeds from Alaska and Greenland to Lower California, Mexico and Tennessee. Winters from Vancouver Island and Massachusetts to the West Indies and Panama. *Habitat:* Crags and cliffs, especially near rivers, lakes, the sea. In the winter it frequents city skyscrapers where it helps to keep down the numbers of semi-domestic pigeons. *Identification:* Long tail and *pointed*, falconiform wings; large size; contrast between dark back and light underparts; "moustache" on face. Length, about 17½ inches.

17. MOURNING DOVE
(ZENAIDURA MACROURA)

Range: Breeds from British Columbia and New Brunswick to Mexico and the Bahamas. Winters south to Panama. *Habitat:* Ubiquitous—though very likely to be found on cultivated lands, near houses. Often found on grain fields in fall and winter. *Identifica-tion:* A small Dove—length about 12 inches—*with pointed, white-edged tail.* Rises with clear whistle of wings. *Voice:* Soft *croo-ah, croo-croo.* *Breeding:* Usually two eggs in a poor apology for nest. Often shot at seasons when young are in nest.

18. BEWICK'S WREN
(THRYOMANES BEWICKI)

Range: Breeds from British Columbia and Pennsylvania to Lower California and Georgia. Winters from near the northern limit of its range to California and Florida. *Habitat:* Almost anywhere there is a nesting hole, especially near houses and other buildings. *Identifica-*tion: Large size, light line over eye, long tail, *containing much white.* Length, about 5¼ inches. *Voice:* ". . . suggesting that of a Song Sparrow" (Howell). *Food:* Insects, spiders, lizards, frogs. Races are known as Texas, Baird's, Vigors's, San Diego Wren, etc.

19. LOUISIANA WATER-THRUSH
(SEIURUS MOTACILLA)

Range: Breeds from Nebraska and New England to Texas and Georgia. Winters from Mexico to Colombia, and in the West Indies. *Habitat:* Wooded swamps and rocky valleys. *Identification:* Teetering walk; striped underparts; *white* line over eye. (In Northern Water-Thrush this line *yellowish.*) Length, about 6 inches. *Voice:* A loud, wild, and varied series of notes, startlingly beautiful in the retirement of its breeding territory. *Breeding:* Four to seven eggs, often in hollow under stream bank.

20. BLUE-WINGED WARBLER
(VERMIVORA PINUS)

Range: Breeds from Minnesota and Rhode Island to Alabama and Georgia. Winters from Mexico to Guatemala. Migrates across the Gulf of Mexico. *Habitat:* Abandoned, brushy pastures, edges of woodlots, etc. Usually to be found in low trees and brush. *Identifica-* *tion:* Black line from eye to bill, mostly yellow, with pronounced barring on blue-gray wings. Length, about 4¾ inches. *Voice:* A lazy-sounding, insect-like *sweee-chee*. *Breeding:* Four to five eggs in ground nest.

21. MOCKINGBIRD

(MIMUS POLYGLOTTOS)

Range: Chiefly from California, Wyoming and New Jersey to Mexico and Florida. Introduced into Bermuda. *Habitat:* Brushy areas, most commonly near farms, gardens, etc. *Identification:* Gray and white coloration; long tail; white wing patch, which is shared with Shrikes; these, however, carry black facial masks. Length, about 10 inches. *Voice:* An indescribable potpourri of originality and imitation—a night song that equals the Nightingale's. *Breeding:* Three to six eggs in bulky nest, in brush-pile, etc.

22. PURPLE MARTIN

(PROGNE SUBIS)

Range: Breeds from Alaska and Nova Scotia to Mexico and Florida; also, Lower California. Winters in Brazil. *Habitat:* Largely in the vicinity of man's dwellings—even in cities. *Identification:* The largest of our Swallows; males blue-black, females brownish on throat, light below. Length, about 8 inches. *Voice:* A rich, deep, sweet, and varied chirruping. *Breeding:* In hollow trees and caves, but principally in man-erected houses. Often difficult to lure to a nesting box, its presence justifies the effort.

23. MARYLAND YELLOW-THROAT

(GEOTHLYPIS TRICHAS)

Range: Breeds from Alaska and Newfoundland to the Gulf. Winters from California and North Carolina to the West Indies and Costa Rica. *Habitat:* Usually near water in thickets, heavy weed patches, briar-tangles, etc. *Identification:* Male, by his black dom- ino; female, by her whitish belly—and the propinquity of the male. Length, about 5 inches. *Voice:* A bright, quick, *witchery, witchery, witchery,* subject to some variation. *Breeding:* Three to five eggs, on or near ground.

24. MARYLAND YELLOW-THROAT

(GEOTHLYPIS TRICHAS)

Although the A.O.U. *Check-List* recognizes six forms—Northern, Maryland, Florida, Western, Salt Marsh and Tule—of the Yellow-throat, the Maryland name seems destined to remain the almost universal label among bird enthusiasts. Whatever the bird may be called, it is a perennial favorite, and its black mask makes it one of the first to be identified in that—needlessly—puzzling group, the Wood Warblers. Virtually all of them can be learned by two hours of study. See Plate 23.

25. SONG SPARROW

(MELOSPIZA MELODIA)

Range: Breeds from Alaska and Cape Breton Island to New Mexico and Georgia. Winters from Massachusetts to Florida and Mexico. *Habitat:* Near thickets and tangles, especially adjacent to wet places. *Identification:* Long, *unforked* tail, streaked breast *with prominent* *dark spot.* Length, about 6¼ inches. One of the most notable studies of any bird has been made of this species by Margaret Morse Nice, published by the Linnaean Society of New York. Every serious student of birds should be familiar with it.

26. CAROLINA PAROQUET

(CONUROPSIS CAROLINENSIS)

Range: Formerly from Gulf states to Colorado, Nebraska and New York. This beautiful bird, the only Parrot of eastern North America, has not been taken since 1904. As in the case of other birds that have vanished from North America in historic times, it was brutally and needlessly persecuted. Many species have been reduced by destruction of necessary environmental conditions; the *coup de grâce* seems to have been given by direct killing. Only concerted action by conservationists can save other species from the same fate.

27. RED-HEADED WOODPECKER

(MELANERPES ERYTHROCEPHALUS)

Range: From British Columbia and Hudson Valley to New Mexico and Florida. *Habitat:* In open woodlands, farm country, etc. *Identification:* Small size—about 9 inches—and large white wing patches; *entirely red head of adult. Breeding:* Four to six eggs in hole in dead tree or pole. *Food:* Fruits, nuts, insects. This species is one that has suffered by competition—for nesting sites—with the introduced European Starling. It is also one of the birds most frequently killed by automobiles.

28. BLUE-HEADED VIREO
(VIREO SOLITARIUS)

Range: Breeds from British Columbia, Mackenzie and Cape Breton Island to Guatemala and Georgia. Winters from Gulf states and South Carolina to Central America. *Habitat:* Woodlands, especially coniferous. *Identification:* Slate-blue head, ring around eye, wing-bars. Length, about 5½ inches. Vireos may be known from Warblers by their slow, deliberate, feeding habits. *Voice: Verily, verily,* suggestive of the Red-eye's, but stronger. Races of this bird are called Mountain, Plumbeous, Cassin's, and San Lucas Vireo.

29. TOWHEE

(PIPILO ERYTHROPHTHALMUS)

Range: Breeds from Saskatchewan and Maine to Alabama and Florida. Winters from Nebraska and New York to Texas and Florida. *Habitat:* Mostly on the ground in or near brush. *Identification:* The marked color-pattern, especially brown flanks. It often attracts attention to itself by its vigorous scratching in the dried leaves. The southern White-eyed race has a light iris. The Arctic Towhee has a white-spotted back. Length, about 8 inches. *Voice:* A clear, strong *see-towhee-ee-ee-ee;* and a ringing *cherink!*

30. PINE WARBLER

(DENDROICA PINUS)

Range: Breeds from Manitoba and New Brunswick to Texas and Florida. Winters from Illinois and Virginia to Mexico and Florida. *Habitat:* Pine woods. *Identification:* Large size, for a Warbler— length about 5½ inches—wing bars, white in tail. Bright yellow, with more or less distinct streaks on breast of male, fading into drabness in female and young. *Song:* A thin, pleasing trill. *Breeding:* Four to five eggs, in nest usually well up in a pine. *Food:* Largely insects. One of the first Warblers to arrive in spring.

31. BALD EAGLE
(HALIAEETUS LEUCOCEPHALUS)

Range: Breeds from Alaska and Ungava to Lower California and Florida. Exterminated over much of its range. *Habitat:* Near water, whence comes its principal food—fish. *Identification:* Large size—length about 3 feet, wing-spread up to about 7½ feet—coupled with *white head and tail,* makes adults unmistakable. Immature, generally dark all over. This bird, our National Emblem, is now protected by an act of Congress. Its feeding habits are usually harmless, and it is one of our most inspiring wild creatures. See Plate 11.

32. BLACK-BILLED CUCKOO
(COCCYZUS ERYTHROPTHALMUS)

Range: Breeds from Alberta and Prince Edward Island to Arkansas and Georgia. Winters from Colombia to Peru. *Habitat:* Much like Yellow-bill's. *Identification:* All black bill; lacks light area in wing, and heavy white areas in tail. Length, about 1 foot. *Voice:* "The *cow cow* notes are *connected* in the Black-billed, *separate* in the Yellow-billed" (Griscom). *Breeding:* Much like that of Yellow-bill. This bird, and the Yellow-bill, are supposed to be especially vociferous before rain. See Plate 2.

33. GOLDFINCH

(SPINUS TRISTIS)

Range: Breeds from British Columbia and Newfoundland to Lower California, Colorado and Georgia. Winters over most of its breeding range, and south to Mexico and the Gulf. *Habitat:* Fields that have brush, low trees, etc., as nesting places. *Identification:* "The only small yellow bird with black wings," (Peterson). The dull female characterized, of course, by thick bill. Length, about 5 inches. *Voice:* Among others, a sweet *per-chic-o-ree,* as it swoops upward in flight. Comes readily to sunflower heads at feeding stations.

34. WORM-EATING WARBLER
(HELMITHEROS VERMIVORUS)

Range: Breeds from Iowa and the Connecticut River Valley to Alabama and Georgia. Winters from Mexico to Panama, in Cuba and the Bahamas. *Habitat:* Woods, often when wet and low. *Identification:* The markedly striped head. Length, about 5½ inches.

Voice: A chipper, very like that of Chipping Sparrow—though one is not likely to find these birds in the same habitat. *Breeding:* Three to six eggs in ground nest. *Food:* As in most Warblers, principally insects.

35. YELLOW WARBLER

(DENDROICA AESTIVA)

John George Children, Secretary of the Royal Society of London, was the friend whose name Audubon endeavored to perpetuate in naming this bird. Unhappily for his design, however, it proved to be not a new species but merely the immature of the Yellow Warbler or, as it is called in New England, Summer Warbler. One of the most brilliant of its glowing family, it is also one of the commonest.

36. COOPER'S HAWK

(ACCIPITER COOPERI)

Range: Breeds from British Columbia and Prince Edward Island to northern Mexico. Winters from British Columbia and southern Maine to Mexico. *Habitat:* Woods. *Identification: Short, rounded* wings, *long, rounded* tail. Length, about 17 inches. Not commonly given to soaring, and often overlooked because of its arboreal habits. *Food:* Birds, mammals, reptiles, batrachians, insects. The depredations of this bird often draw ire upon the head of other Hawks, most of which are allies of man and deserving of complete protection.

37. FLICKER

(COLAPTES AURATUS)

Range: Breeds from Canada (east of the Rockies) and north to the limit of trees, and throughout the northern and central U. S. south to Texas and Florida. *Habitat:* Common nearly everywhere there are places in which to nest. *Identification:* A large brown Wood-pecker with *white rump* and *yellow wing linings.* Length, about 12½ inches. *Voice: Flicker,* as though said with a cleft palate; *kuck-kuck-kuck,* etc. *Breeding:* In tree holes; will use nest boxes. *Food:* Borers and other insects—particularly ants.

38. KENTUCKY WARBLER

(OPORORNIS FORMOSUS)

Range: Breeds from Nebraska and Hudson Valley to Texas and Georgia. Winters from Mexico to Colombia. *Habitat:* In woods with heavy cover, and brush tangles, especially near water. *Identification:* The facial pattern, particularly the half-mask below eye, along with olive back and yellow underparts. Length, about 5½ inches. *Voice:* A ringing *wheedle,* much like that of Carolina Wren. *Breeding:* Four to five eggs in nest on the ground, or near it. *Food:* Mostly insects.

39. TUFTED TITMOUSE

(BAEOLOPHUS BICOLOR)

Range: Breeds from Nebraska and New Jersey to Texas, the Gulf coast and Florida. *Habitat:* In woods where there are nesting sites. *Identification:* Small size—length about 6 inches—gray coloration, and *crest. Song:* A loud, clear *péto, péto, péto. Breeding:* Four to eight eggs, in natural holes in trees, or in old nesting places of Woodpeckers. *Food:* Mainly insects, seeds, etc.

40. AMERICAN REDSTART
(SETOPHAGA RUTICILLA)

Range: Breeds from British Columbia, Mackenzie and Newfoundland to Oregon, Arkansas and Georgia. Winters in the West Indies and from Mexico to Guiana. *Habitat:* Woods, swamps, orchards, etc. *Identification:* Small size—length about 5¼ inches—coupled with striking pattern; habit of fanning tail. *Voice:* A thin, clear *swee-swee-swee-swee-swéechee,* sometimes difficult to distinguish from song of Yellow Warbler and Chestnut-side. *Breeding:* Three to five eggs in one of the most exquisite nests built by any Warbler.

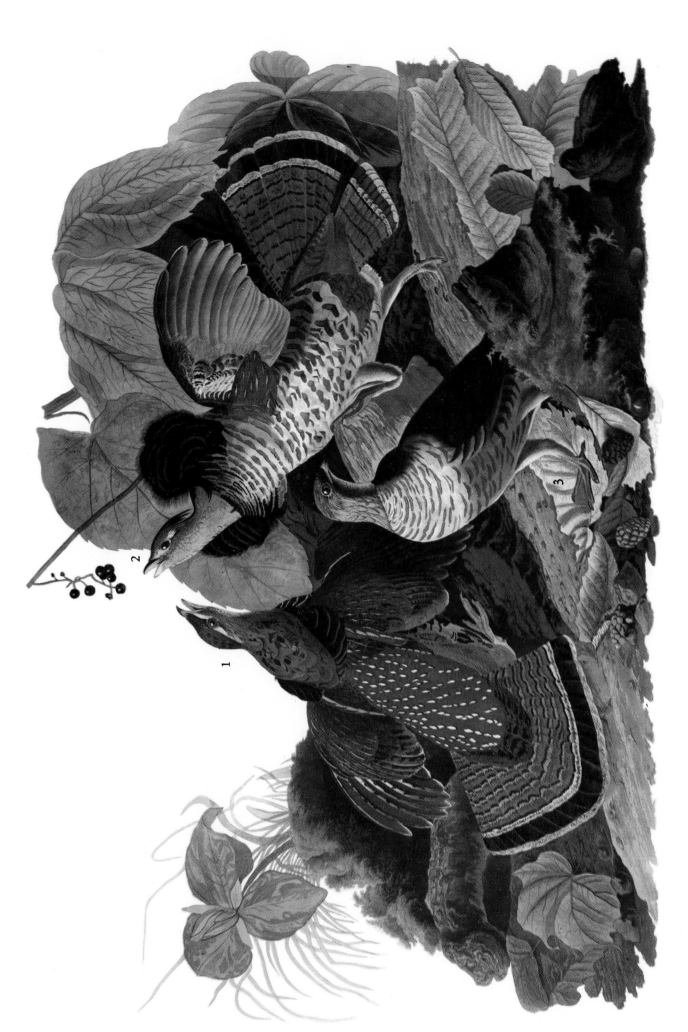

41. RUFFED GROUSE
(BONASA UMBELLUS)

Range: From Alaska and Nova Scotia to Colorado and Alabama. *Habitat:* Woodlands, coniferous or mixed, and most often near clearings, trails and other edges. *Identification:* A short-tailed, hen-like, brown bird that flies up with an explosive sound. Most often detected by its wing-drumming, which sounds like a distant gasoline motor. *Breeding:* Eight to fourteen eggs on the ground. *Food:* Largely vegetable matter. Populations of this bird are subject to sharp fluctuations whose cause has not been determined.

42. ORCHARD ORIOLE

(ICTERUS SPURIUS)

Range: Breeds from North Dakota and Massachusetts to Mexico. Winters from Mexico to Colombia. *Habitat:* Orchards and other cultivated lands, shade trees. *Identification:* Size—about 7¼ inches long; chestnut and black plumage in adult male. Second year male like female "but usually with a black throat." (Roberts). Female smaller than Baltimore, and duller. *Voice:* A beautiful deep, rich warble. *Breeding:* Four to six eggs, usually 10-40 feet up, in "a deep pouch, neatly woven of *green* grass." (Roberts).

43. CEDAR WAXWING

(BOMBYCILLA CEDRORUM)

Range: Breeds from British Columbia and Cape Breton Island to California and Georgia. Winters throughout most of the United States and to Panama. *Habitat:* More or less open country, farms, etc. *Identification:* Dove-color, yellow-tipped tail, *crest,* size—about 7¼ inches; Bohemian Waxwing, Plate 363, has reddish under-tail coverts and a white wing-bar. *Voice:* A weak *tsip. Breeding:* Three to five eggs, 5-45 feet up, often later than other birds. *Food:* Largely vegetable matter.

44. SUMMER TANAGER
(PIRANGA RUBRA)

Range: Breeds from Nebraska and Delaware to Mexico and Florida. Also from Nevada south. Winters from Mexico to Peru. *Habitat:* In open woods. *Identification:* Male, *our only all-red bird without a crest*. Female, greenish above, yellow below, not so contrasty as in Scarlet Tanager. *No wing-bars.* Length, about 7½ inches. *Voice:* A warble, somewhat like the Scarlet Tanager's, but not so reedy. *Breeding:* Three or four eggs, "usually on a horizontal limb of a pine or oak." (Howell).

45. ALDER FLYCATCHER

(EMPIDONAX TRAILLI)

Range: Breeds from Alaska and Newfoundland to Lower California and Kentucky. Winters in Central and South America. The western race is known as the Little Flycatcher. *Habitat:* Alders and willows on brook and swamp edges. *Identification:* The birds of the genus *Empidonax* are our most difficult species to identify. The best clue to this bird is its note—a rather explosive *fle-bé-o*. Length, about 6 inches. The *brownest* of its group. *Breeding:* Two to four eggs in nest near ground; in swampy tangles.

46. BARRED OWL

(STRIX VARIA)

Range: Breeds from Wyoming and Saskatchewan and Newfoundland to Texas and Florida. *Habitat:* Deep woods, swamps—though sometimes even the vicinity of houses. *Identification:* Large size—length almost two feet—and *absence of "ear-tufts."* *Voice:* A series of loud, staccato hoots *ending in an emphasized hoo-aw.* *Breeding:* Two to three eggs in hollow tree, old Crow's nest, etc. *Food:* Rodent-competitors of man to such an extent that this Owl should be protected at all times.

47. RUBY-THROATED HUMMINGBIRD
(ARCHILOCHUS COLUBRIS)

Range: Breeds from Alberta, North Dakota and Cape Breton Island to Texas and Florida. Winters from Florida and Louisiana to Panama. *Habitat:* Swamps, woods, orchards. *Identification:* Over most of range can be confused only with sphinx or hawk moths, which feed in similar manner. *Breeding:* Two eggs in a tiny nest of plant down held together by spider web. *Food:* Nectar, spiders, etc. May be attracted to gardens by sugar-water in small test-tubes, decked with red ribbon.

48. CERULEAN WARBLER

(DENDROICA CERULEA)

Range: Breeds from Nebraska and New York to Texas and Georgia. Winters in Venezuela, Ecuador and Peru. *Habitat:* Open woodlands. *Identification:* Blue above, white below, *the male with a dark breast band.* Female and young lack breast band and are duller; have wing-bars. Length, about 4½ inches. This bird is most often discovered near the tops of tall trees. *Voice:* Several staccato buzzes, then a long buzz, suggesting song of Parula Warbler. The next plate shows a young bird.

49. CERULEAN WARBLER

(DENDROICA CERULEA)

Few birds have given more bird students stiff necks than this tiny inhabitant of the remote tree-tops. The presence of most birds is first detected by their notes, and he who would become an expert in field identification should learn as many songs as possible. The phono-graph records issued with Albert Brand's *Songs of Wild Birds* and *More Songs of Wild Birds*, make it possible for the beginner quickly and easily to acquaint himself with the notes of more than three score common species.

50. MAGNOLIA WARBLER

(DENDROICA MAGNOLIA)

Range: Breeds from Mackenzie and Newfoundland to Minnesota and Virginia. Winters from Mexico to Panama; rarely in Haiti and Porto Rico. *Habitat:* Primarily coniferous forests. *Identification: White patch in tail, combined with yellow rump.* Length, about 5 inches. *Breeding:* Three to six eggs "usually in small evergreens, 4 to 6 feet from the ground, but may be considerably higher" (Roberts). *Food:* Insects, spiders, etc. One of the most brilliant of our Warblers, and frequently common. See Plate 123.

51. RED-TAILED HAWK

(BUTEO BOREALIS)

Range: Breeds from Alaska and Newfoundland to Lower California and Florida. Winters from British Columbia and Maine to Guatemala and the Gulf. Races are known as Krider's and Harlan's Hawk. (See Plate 86.) *Habitat:* Most frequently seen *soaring* over open country. *Identification:* Broad wings and *short* tail which, in adult, is bright chestnut above; young lack red. *Light area on breast.* Length, about 22 inches. *Food:* Largely destructive mammals; because of this, valuable to man and should be protected.

52. CHUCK-WILL'S-WIDOW
(ANTROSTOMUS CAROLINENSIS)

Range: Breeds from Kansas and Maryland to Texas and the Gulf states. Winters from Florida to the Greater Antilles, Central America and Colombia. *Habitat:* Swampy woodland. *Identification:* Looks like a big Whip-poor-will. Length, about 11½ inches. *Voice:* Represented by name, "with a slight accent on the first syllable" (Howell). *Breeding:* Two eggs on the bare ground, or on leaves.

53. PAINTED BUNTING

(PASSERINA CIRIS)

Range: Breeds from Kansas, Mississippi and North Carolina to New Mexico and Florida. Winters from Florida and Mexico to Panama. *Habitat:* Brushy areas, both near swamps and on cultivated lands. *Identification:* The brilliant coloration of the male identifies it; the female·is a strong greenish hue and may be known from Vireos and Warblers by its thick bill. Length, about 5 inches. *Voice:* Compared by Wayne to that of Canada Warbler. *Food:* Largely weed seeds and insects.

54. BOBOLINK

(DOLICHONYX ORYZIVORUS)

Range: Breeds from British Columbia and Cape Breton Island to California and New Jersey. Winters in South America to Brazil, Bolivia, Peru, Argentina and Paraguay. *Habitat:* Grassy fields. *Identification:* The pattern of the breeding male is unmistakable; fall male and female, buff with marked streaking above. Length, about 7 inches. *Voice:* A lovely, banjo-like melody well suggested by Bryant's poem. *Breeding:* Four to seven eggs in nest in grass. *Food:* Largely insects, on its breeding grounds; weed seed and grain on migration.

55. CUVIER'S REGULUS

This plate shows another of Audubon's unknown birds. It is somewhat like the Ruby-crowned Kinglet. Named in honor of Baron Georges Cuvier, the eminent French anatomist, "the published plate may have been based to some extent on memory. No similar bird has ever been seen since." (A.O.U. *Check-List*.) Audubon's memory has been proven faulty on more than one point, but in this failing he is not unique. Naturalists—including amateurs—do well to take careful notes on the spot!

56. RED-SHOULDERED HAWK
(BUTEO LINEATUS)

Range: Breeds from Ontario and Prince Edward Island to Kansas, Tennessee, North Carolina and west to the edge of the Great Plains. Also in California (Red-bellied race) and Texas. Winters from Iowa and New Hampshire to Mexico and the Gulf coast. Also in Cali-fornia. *Habitat:* Most likely to be seen soaring over open country near woods. *Identification:* Length, about 20 inches. Proportionately longer tail than Red-tail. Apparent *translucent spot* near ends of wings, in flight. *Food:* Rodents, etc.

57. LOGGERHEAD SHRIKE
(LANIUS LUDOVICIANUS)

Range: Breeds throughout most of the United States and southern Canada to Mexico and Lower California. Winters in California, southwestern states, and Mississippi Valley to Mexico. Races include Migrant, White-rumped, and California Shrikes. *Habitat:* Largely telephone wires, vicinity of thorny shrubs. *Identification:* Gray, white and black coloration, *black mask;* lower mandible black. See Plate 192. *Food:* Largely insects, some birds and small mammals. Food habits considered beneficial.

58. HERMIT THRUSH

(HYLOCICHLA GUTTATA)

Range: Breeds from Alaska and Quebec to Lower California and Virginia. Winters south to Mexico and Guatemala and north to Massachusetts. Races include Alaska, Dwarf (See Plate 419), Monterey, Sierra, Mono, Audubon's and Eastern Hermit Thrushes.

Habitat: Coniferous forests. *Identification:* Robin shape, spotted breast, brown coloration identify it as Thrush, a markedly rufous tail as a Hermit. Length, about 7 inches. *Voice:* Flute-like and unimaginably lovely. *Breeding:* Three to four eggs, usually on ground.

59. CHESTNUT-SIDED WARBLER
(DENDROICA PENSYLVANICA)

Range: Breeds from Saskatchewan, Nebraska and Newfoundland to Tennessee and South Carolina. Winters from Guatemala to Panama. *Habitat:* Widely distributed where there are brushy thickets. *Identification:* Adults, yellow crown and chestnut sides; imma-ture, greenish-yellow above, white below, white eye-ring, wing-bars. Length, about 5 inches. *Voice:* Strong *swee-swee-swee-swéechu,* often so like song of Redstart and Yellow Warbler that discrimination is difficult. *Breeding:* Three to five eggs in cup, near ground.

60. CARBONATED WARBLER

This is, perhaps, the most famous of Audubon's *aves ignotae.* "Known only from Audubon's description and plate of two specimens obtained in May, 1811. As a number of his drawings of birds obtained about this time were later destroyed it is possible that the published plate may have been based to some extent upon memory." (A.O.U. *Check-List.*) It is incredible that he could have collected a bird that has escaped detection by ornithologists during the ensuing century.

61. GREAT HORNED OWL
(BUBO VIRGINIANUS)

Range: Breeds from Alaska and Ungava to Lower California and Florida. Many races have been named. *Habitat:* Undisturbed woods, especially near water. *Identification:* Large size—length about 22 inches—and *"ear tufts."* *Voice:* A deep, repeated *hoo-hoo-hoo,* lack-ing the terminal *aw* of the Barred Owl. *Breeding:* Two to three eggs in old Hawk or Crow nest in the late winter. *Food:* Rats, rabbits, skunks, Crows and other birds, insects, fish, etc. One of the most magnificent creatures of our forests!

62. PASSENGER PIGEON
(ECTOPISTES MIGRATORIUS)

Audubon gives a dramatic description of a flight of these birds he witnessed near Louisville in 1813. He estimated that one flock contained 1,115,136,000 birds, and that they must consume 8,712,000 bushels of food a day. The attention of business men was attracted to this great natural resource, and during the 19th Century thousands of barrels were shipped to market. The last known Passenger Pigeon died in 1914—in the Cincinnati Zoo. Biological and financial bankruptcy usually follow attempts to commercialize wild life.

63. WHITE-EYED VIREO
(VIREO GRISEUS)

Range: Breeds from Nebraska and Massachusetts to Mexico and Florida. Also in Bermuda. Winters from Texas and South Carolina to Honduras. *Habitat:* Areas of thick brush, especially in swampy places. *Identification:* Wing-bars, white throat and breast, *staring white eye.* Length, about 4¾ inches. *Voice:* An explosive sputtering, that in part might be rendered *"See me, you hick!"* Often mimics other birds. *Breeding:* Four eggs in cup-like nest, near ground. *Food:* Almost entirely insects.

64. SWAMP SPARROW

(MELOSPIZA GEORGIANA)

Range: Breeds from Mackenzie and Newfoundland to Missouri and New Jersey. Winters from Nebraska and New Jersey to the Gulf coast. *Habitat:* As name indicates. *Identification:* Reddish crown, general mahogany tone of wings and back. Young birds streaked, on crown and elsewhere, but markedly dark. Length, about 5½ inches. *Voice:* A clear, sweet *chee-chee-chee,* not so rapid as the Chipping Sparrow's note. *Breeding:* Four to six eggs, on or near ground. *Food:* Weed seeds, insects, etc.

65. YELLOW WARBLER

(DENDROICA AESTIVA)

This bird, named Rathbone's Warbler in honor of a Liverpool merchant, is actually an immature Yellow Warbler. (See Plates 35 and 95.) It is not strange that Audubon should have misnamed some of the birds he portrayed. He worked virtually without bird books and, over long periods, without adequate collections of study skins with which he could compare his specimens. The modern ornithologist, with fine prism binoculars and manuals, treads a broad highway in comparison with the tortuous path of his predecessors.

66. IVORY-BILLED WOODPECKER
(CAMPEPHILUS PRINCIPALIS)

Range: Now virtually extinct and the known remnants under protection by Audubon Association wardens. Formerly from Texas, Illinois and Indiana, south to the Gulf. *Habitat:* Virgin forests. *Identification:* Large size—about 20 inches long—crest, and white wing patches visible *as bird clings to tree. Voice: Kent*—"anyone can produce the sound very accurately by using the mouthpiece of a clarionet." (Allen and Kellogg, in an important paper in *The Auk,* journal of the American Ornithologists' Union, April, 1937.)

67. RED-WING

(AGELAIUS PHOENICEUS)

Range: Breeds from Alaska and Quebec to Mexico and Florida. Winters south to Mexico and north, occasionally, as far as Massachusetts. *Habitat:* Marshes and swamps. *Identification:* Buff-edged red "shoulder" patches of male; female, a heavily streaked brown bird. Length, about 9½ inches. *Voice:* A liquid *conk-a-reeee.* Reedy *checks. Breeding:* Three to six eggs in beautifully woven nest, usually low in grasses, cattails, button-bush, etc. *Food:* Insects, weed seeds, grain. A common, widely-distributed species. Many races described.

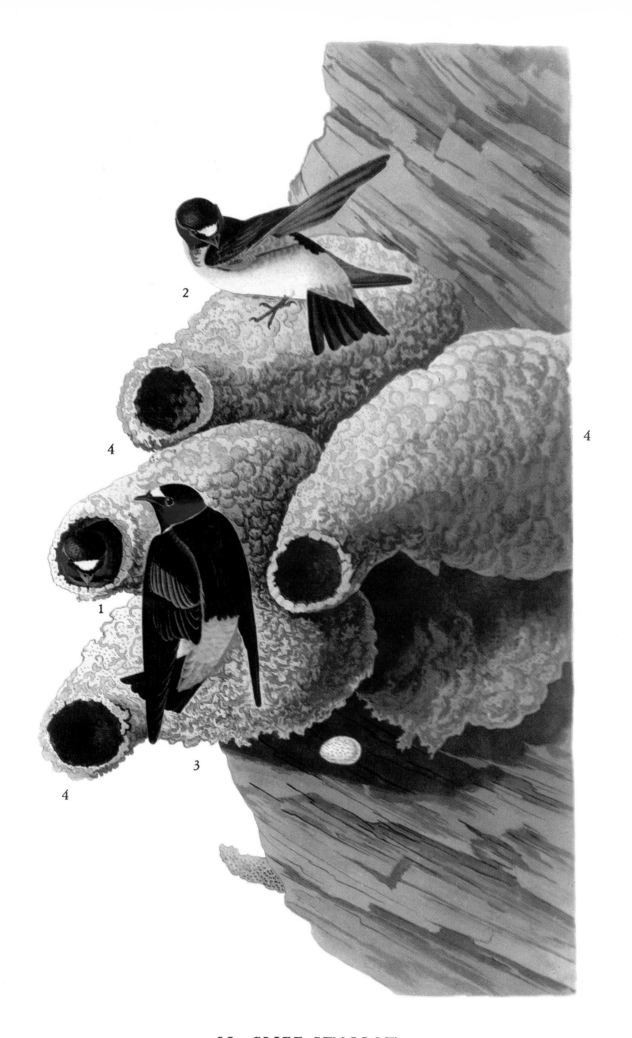

68. CLIFF SWALLOW

(PETROCHELIDON ALBIFRONS)

Range: Breeds from Alaska and Cape Breton Island to Guatemala. Winters in South America, but exact range is not known. *Habitat:* Vicinity of cliffs, barns, etc. Likely to be encountered hawking for insects over water. *Identification:* The light forehead, and patch at base of tail; characteristic Swallow shape, and flight. *Breeding:* Four to five eggs in beautiful bottle-shaped mud nest, in colonies on cliffs, or under eaves of barns, etc. *Food:* Virtually all insects; a most valuable bird.

69. BAY-BREASTED WARBLER

(DENDROICA CASTANEA)

Range: Breeds from Alberta and Newfoundland to Manitoba, the Adirondacks and Maine. Winters in Panama and Colombia. *Habitat:* Forests, especially coniferous. *Identification:* In spring, the bay-colored breast, though this may be obscure in female. In fall (See Plate 88) greenish above "dingy buffy-yellow below . . . under tail-coverts . . . yellow" (Peterson). In this plumage, one of the most difficult Warblers to identify. Length, about 5½ inches. *Breeding:* Four to five eggs, in nest in conifer, often in damp woods.

70. HENSLOW'S SPARROW

(PASSERHERBULUS HENSLOWI)

Range: Breeds from New York and New Hampshire to Virginia, and from South Dakota and Ontario to Texas and Ohio. Winters from Texas to the southeastern states and Florida. *Habitat:* Usually wet, grassy meadows. *Identification:* Small size—about 5 inches long —short tail, *streaked breast,* greenish hind-neck. *Voice:* The best field mark. A weak but definite *tee-sick* that always suggests, to me, the noise made by a tiny focal-plane shutter. Often sings throughout the night.

71. RED-SHOULDERED HAWK
(BUTEO LINEATUS)

The members of this genus—the true Buzzards, not to be confused with Vultures, known in the South as Buzzards—are a pitiful example of the innocent suffering for the sins of the guilty. Their feeding habits are almost entirely beneficial to man since their diet is largely composed of destructive rodents. Yet they are shot for the offenses of their poultry-killing relatives, and their beautiful soaring flight has become an uncommon spectacle in many parts of the United States. See Plate 56.

72. SWALLOW-TAILED KITE
(ELANOIDES FORFICATUS)

Range: Breeds from Minnesota and North Carolina to Mexico and Florida. Winters south of the United States. *Habitat:* "a semiprairie country, or a region of open pine glades dotted with small cypress swamps" (Howell). *Identification:* Airy flight, large size—length,

about 2 feet—and long, forked tail. *Breeding:* Two to three eggs, high in pine or cypress. *Food:* Snakes, lizards, frogs, insects, usually taken on wing. This bird, one of the most exquisite creatures alive, is threatened with extermination through wanton shooting.

73. WOOD THRUSH

(HYLOCICHLA MUSTELINA)

Range: Breeds from South Dakota and New Hampshire to Texas and Florida. Winters from Mexico to Panama. *Habitat:* Gardens, parks, woodlands, thickets near swamps. *Identification:* Robin shape; heavily spotted breast; brown *of head and neck* conspicuously brighter than that on rest of back. Length, about 8 inches. *Voice:* An indescribably lovely, liquid fluting. *Breeding:* Three to five eggs in bulky nest, 5 to 20 feet up. *Food:* Berries, fruits, insects, snails, worms, salamanders, etc. A familiar of suburban door-yards.

74. INDIGO BUNTING

(PASSERINA CYANEA)

Range: Breeds from North Dakota and New Brunswick to Texas and Georgia. Winters from Mexico to Panama, and in Cuba. *Habitat:* Brushy country, abandoned pastures, roadsides. *Identification:* Breeding male our only small bird—length, about 5½ inches—that is *blue all over.* Female, thick-billed, brown, with some bluish wash. *Voice:* A sweet, delicate *tsing-tsing-tsing, chipper-ipper-eee.* Likely to be recognized because bird sings in heat of day, and late summer, when most other bird-voices are still.

75. PIGEON HAWK

(FALCO COLUMBARIUS)

Range: Breeds from Alaska and Newfoundland to California and Maine. Winters from British Columbia and the Gulf States to South America, and in the West Indies. *Habitat:* We are likely to see it about the edges of copses, and in late summer it is sometimes a com- mon migrant along the barrier beaches. *Identification:* Small size— length about 11 inches—long tail, and *pointed, falconiform wings.* *Food:* Largely birds and insects. This species rarely conflicts with man and should be unmolested. See Plate 92.

76. BOB-WHITE
(COLINUS VIRGINIANUS)

Range: From South Dakota and Maine to Mexico and Florida. *Habitat:* Fields, especially those broken by brush-piles and heavy weed patches; farms. *Identification:* Small size—length, about 10 inches—more brownish than Hungarian Partridge. *Voice:* A sweet, ringing *Bob-white, ah, bob-white. Breeding:* Ten to twenty eggs, commonly in thick grass. *Food:* Insects and weed seeds. Audubon's plate shows Quail that are vulnerable to predation because of poor cover; better cover would have protected them.

77. BELTED KINGFISHER

(MEGACERYLE ALCYON)

Range: Breeds from Alaska and Labrador to California and the southern border of the United States. Winters from British Columbia and Virginia to South America. *Habitat:* Water-courses and lakes with steep banks. *Identification:* Size—about 13 inches long—crest, and aquatic habit. *Voice:* A rattle, as of a New Year's Eve noise-maker. *Breeding:* Seven to ten eggs, in hole in bank. *Food:* Small fish, crustaceans, etc. A large proportion of this species' food consists of enemies of trout.

78. CAROLINA WREN

(THRYOTHORUS LUDOVICIANUS)

Range: From Nebraska and Connecticut to Mexico and Florida. *Habitat:* Thickets, farms, etc. *Identification:* Reddish-brown upper parts, heavy white line over eye. Length, about 5½ inches. *Voice:* Varied; a frequently heard phrase has been written *teakettle, tea-* *kettle, teakettle,* though it is far more musical than the words suggest. *Breeding:* Four to six eggs, on the ground, in hollow logs, bird boxes, etc. *Food:* Insects, spiders, lizards. This bird periodically spreads north of its usual range until cut back by hard winters.

79. KINGBIRD

(TYRANNUS TYRANNUS)

Range: Breeds from British Columbia and Nova Scotia to New Mexico and Florida. Winters from Mexico to Peru and Bolivia. *Habitat:* Woods, orchards, thickets, often close to civilization. *Identification:* No wing-bars; white tip on tail; drab gray above, white below. Length, about 8¾ inches. *Voice:* A shrill *klick-ik-ik-ik-iker*. *Breeding:* Three to five eggs in high bush, tree, etc. *Food:* Mostly insects, taken on the wing. This bird is well named; it fearlessly guards the vicinity of its nest, even against Hawks and Crows.

80. AMERICAN PIPIT
(ANTHUS SPINOLETTA)

The omission of the white outer tail feathers from this bird, the best field-mark of the Pipit (See Plate 10), must have confused more than one student who relied solely on Audubon's plates as a guide to identification. The American Woodsman's effort to portray our birds in as lifelike a guise as possible was occasionally defeated by his colorists.

81. OSPREY

(PANDION HALIAËTUS)

Range: Breeds from Alaska and Labrador to Lower California and Florida. Winters from Lower California and Florida to the West Indies and Central America. Races occur in the Bahamas, Europe, Asia, Australia, etc. *Habitat:* Vicinity of lakes, rivers, bays. *Identification:* Large wing-spread—about 6½ feet—dark back, light underparts, dark patch at bend of underwing, diving for fish. *Voice:* A high whistle as though from escaping steam. *Breeding:* Two to four eggs in large nest. *Food:* Fish, often valueless kinds.

82. WHIP-POOR-WILL

(ANTROSTOMUS VOCIFERUS)

Range: Breeds from North Dakota, Manitoba and Nova Scotia to Arizona and Georgia. Winters from South Carolina and the Gulf States to Central America. *Habitat:* Woods, thickets, etc. *Identification:* Much more likely to be heard than seen. Active in darkness or semi-darkness. Lacks white wing patches of Nighthawk. Length, about 10 inches. If flushed during day, often settles close by. *Voice:* Repeatedly whistled rendition of its name. *Breeding:* Two eggs, on bare ground or in dead leaves. *Food:* Insects, taken on wing.

83. HOUSE WREN

(TROGLODYTES AËDON)

Range: Breeds from British Columbia and New Brunswick to Lower California and South Carolina. Winters from California and the Gulf States to Mexico. *Habitat:* Widely distributed where nesting cavities are available, especially near human habitations. *Identifica-* *tion:* Length, about 4¾ inches. Lighter than Winter Wren, and has longer tail. *Voice:* Chattering trill. *Breeding:* Six to ten eggs, in almost any hollow object—especially bird boxes. *Food:* Insects, spiders, etc. See Plate 179.

84. BLUE-GRAY GNATCATCHER
(POLIOPTILA CAERULEA)

Range: Breeds from California, Nebraska and New Jersey to Lower California and Florida. Winters from southern California and South Carolina to Guatemala. *Habitat:* "oak hammocks, open pine lands, and small cypress swamps" (Howell). *Identification:* Length, about 4½ inches. Long, white-edged tail; eye-ring. Extremely active birds. *Voice:* "squeaky, high-pitched notes" (Howell). *Breeding:* Four to six eggs on a limb 4 to 80 feet high. *Food:* Various kinds of insects, spiders, etc. One race is known as the Western Gnatcatcher.

85. YELLOW-THROATED WARBLER

(DENDROICA DOMINICA)

Range: Breeds from Nebraska and New Jersey to Texas and Florida. Winters from Mexico and Florida to Costa Rica, and in the Bahamas and Greater Antilles. *Habitat:* Pine woods, river edges, etc. *Identification:* The face pattern, and bright yellow throat. Crawls around branches to feed. The Sycamore Warbler, the mid-west race of this bird, is *white* between the eye and the bill and carries the subspecific name *albilora*. Length, about 5¼ inches. *Voice:* A loud ringing song, that suggests the Indigo Bunting's.

86. HARLAN'S HAWK

(BUTEO BOREALIS)

Range: Breeds in northwestern British Columbia, southwestern Yukon, and adjoining parts of Alaska south at least to southern Alberta. In winter down the Mississippi Valley to the Gulf States. Casual in California. The A.O.U. *Check-List,* which treats this bird as a sub-species of the Red-tail, is followed. Several outstanding taxonomists, however, regard it as a distinct species. *Identification:* Shape and size as of a small Red-tail; extremely dark, with mottled tail. *Food:* Mostly rodents. See Plate 51.

87. FLORIDA JAY

(APHELOCOMA COERULESCENS)

Range: Peninsula of Florida. *Habitat:* The sand scrub. *Identification:* Marked color pattern, very long tail. Total length about 1 foot. *Voice:* "These Jays are not so continuously noisy as the Blue Jays, but at times they give vent to a series of loud, harsh calls, which somewhat resemble the *churr* notes of the Boat-tailed Grackle" (Howell). *Breeding:* Two to four eggs in nests that often form loose, small colonies. *Food:* Nuts, berries, insects, lizards, mollusks and crustaceans.

88. BAY-BREASTED WARBLER

(DENDROICA CASTANEA)

The immature bird of this species, and of the Black-poll Warbler (See Plate 133), are two of the very few North American birds whose identification is difficult. These include Flycatchers of the genus Empidonax, and a few immature and fall Warblers. As the student puzzles over them, he may comfort himself with the thought that they are exceptions. The young Black-poll is likely to be whiter below than the frequently buffy Bay-breast, especially, under the tail. See Plate 69.

89. NASHVILLE WARBLER

(VERMIVORA RUFICAPILLA)

Range: Breeds from British Columbia and Cape Breton Island to California and Pennsylvania. Winters from Mexico to Guatemala. *Habitat:* Forests, especially swampy ones. *Identification:* Face pattern—eye-ring—and yellow underparts. Length, about 4½ inches.

Voice: "*Che-seé, che-seé, che-seé,* followed by a rapid twitter decreasing in volume and intensity to the end" (Roberts). *Breeding:* Four to five eggs in well-hidden ground nest. The western race is known as the Calaveras Warbler.

90. BLACK AND WHITE WARBLER
(MNIOTILTA VARIA)

Range: Breeds from Mackenzie, South Dakota and New Brunswick to Texas and Georgia. Winters from Mexico to Ecuador, in Florida, and the West Indies. *Habitat:* Woodlands. *Identification:* Black and white streaking, *without cap* of Black-poll, feeds by creeping over bark. Length, about 5 inches. *Voice:* A thin *seezle-seezle-seezle* that may easily pass unnoticed. *Breeding:* Four to five eggs, in ground nest, especially well concealed. The name Black and White Creeper gives a good clue to this bird's identification.

91. BROAD-WINGED HAWK
(BUTEO PLATYPTERUS)

Range: Breeds from Alberta and Cape Breton Island to the Gulf coast and Texas, mainly east of the Mississippi. Winters from Florida and Mexico to Peru. Races are resident in the Lesser Antilles. *Habitat:* Woodlands. *Identification:* Small size—wing-spread about 3 feet. Broad wings and short tail, characteristic of the genus. Broad bars on tail of adult. *Breeding:* Two to three eggs, often in old Crow's nest. *Food:* Snakes, frogs, rodents, large insects. Beneficial in feeding habits; should be protected.

92. PIGEON HAWK

(FALCO COLUMBARIUS)

It may seem paradoxical that, although this is a bird-killing Hawk, conservationists strongly urge its protection. Its prey consists largely of song birds, and for many centuries nature has geared their reproduction rate high enough to absorb such losses as those by predation.

Many species achieve a 400% increase annually, and if there were not checks such birds as the Robin would overwhelm the earth. Furthermore, these Hawks are beautiful, interesting creatures that are much enjoyed by those who know them. See Plate 75.

93. SEASIDE SPARROW

(AMMOSPIZA MARITIMA)

Range: Breeds in the salt marsh from Massachusetts to Texas. Winters from Virginia to Texas. *Habitat:* Wetter portions of salt marsh. *Identification:* Length, about 6 inches. Gray underparts, white throat. Yellow before eye. *Voice:* A buzzy *ah-gee-e-e-e! Breeding:*

Three to five eggs in nest in coarse grass. *Food:* Insects and crustaceans. This attractive bird thrives only in wetter parts of the marsh, and its numbers have been greatly reduced by wide-spread drainage operations. Many races have been described. See Plate 355.

94. VESPER SPARROW

(POOECETES GRAMINEUS)

Range: Breeds from British Columbia and Cape Breton Island to New Mexico and North Carolina. Winters from the southern part of its breeding range south. *Habitat:* Fields, clearings, road-sides. *Identification:* A streaked, obvious Sparrow, *with white outer tail feathers.* Length, about 6 inches. *Voice:* Suggests that of Song Sparrow, but less impetuous, and sweeter. *Breeding:* Three to five eggs in ground nest. *Food:* Insects, weed seeds, waste grain. Each Sparrow carries virtually as definite a tag as the Vesper's.

95. YELLOW WARBLER

(DENDROICA AESTIVA)

Range: Breeds throughout North America from tree limit south to Mexico and South Carolina. Winters from Mexico south. *Habitat:* Brushy areas from Canadian wilderness to suburban gardens; in weed patches, and tree clumps. *Identification:* An all-yellow Warbler; male with reddish streaking below; streaks more obscure or wanting in female. Length, about 5 inches. *Voice: Swee-swee-sweeswee. Breeding:* Four to five eggs in well-upholstered nest near ground. *Food:* Mostly insects. See Plates 35 and 65.

96. COLLIE'S MAGPIE-JAY

(CALOCITTA COLLIEI)

Audubon's early resolve never to paint from stuffed specimens was not entirely adhered to, later in life, and the inclusion of this magnificent creature among his northwestern birds is one result of his weakened resolution. A native of Mexico, according to Ridgway, it was secured by Audubon from a friend; he ascribed it to the Columbia River region.

97. SCREECH OWL

(OTUS ASIO)

Range: From Alaska and New Brunswick to Mexico. *Habitat:* Almost anywhere—including cities—it can find trees with hollows, especially old orchards. *Identification:* Small size—length about 8½ inches—and "ear tufts." *Voice:* A quavering, sweet whistle that descends in pitch. Easily imitated, and the bird frequently responds. *Breeding:* Three to seven eggs in tree hollow or bird box. *Food:* Mice, insects, amphibians, small birds, etc. Its enemies include large owls—and tree surgeons!

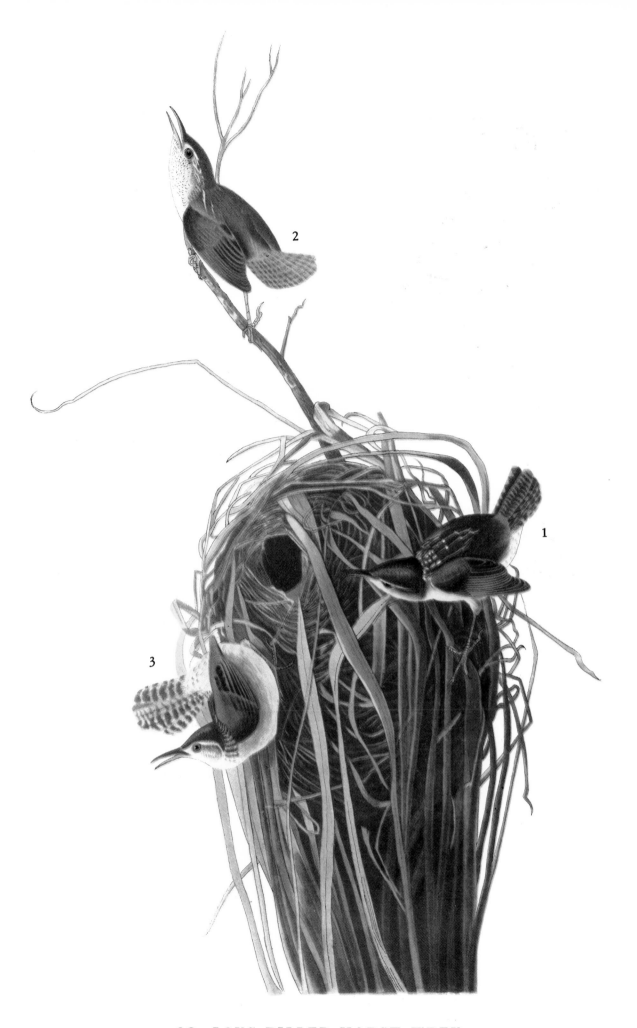

98. LONG-BILLED MARSH WREN

(TELMATODYTES PALUSTRIS)

Range: Breeds from British Columbia and Rhode Island to southern California, the Gulf coast and Florida. Winters from California and New Jersey to Mexico. *Habitat:* Marshes, especially in cattails and tules. *Identification:* Length, about 4½ inches. Conspicuous white line over eye, and prominent white markings on back. Short-billed rarely found in similar cover. *Voice:* A varied series of bubbling clicks. *Breeding:* Five to eight eggs, in spherical nest. *Races:* Worthington's, Marian's, Prairie, Tule Marsh Wrens, etc.

99. COWBIRD

(MOLOTHRUS ATER)

Range: Breeds from British Columbia, Mackenzie and New Brunswick to Mexico and Tennessee. Winters south to Mexico. *Habitat:* More or less ubiquitous—The Wandering Jew of North American birds. *Identification:* Walks. Length, about 7½ inches. Male, black with brown hood; female, dingy gray-brown. *Voice:* A thin *psee-eek,* etc. *Breeding:* Leaves eggs in nests of other birds. *Food:* Weed seeds, insects, etc. This parasite, in behavior the analogue of Old World Cuckoos, is one of our most interesting species.

100. TREE SWALLOW

(IRIDOPROCNE BICOLOR)

Range: Breeds from Alaska and Quebec to California and Virginia. Winters from California and New Jersey to Mexico, Honduras and Cuba. *Habitat:* Where water and nesting sites are combined. *Identification:* Length, about 5½ inches. Blue-green above, white below.

Voice: A sweet chirruping, higher pitched than Martin's. *Breeding:* Four to seven eggs in hollow trees, nest boxes, etc. *Food:* Insects, largely taken over water; fruits such as Virginia creeper and bayberry. An early spring, and late fall, migrant.

101. RAVEN

(CORVUS CORAX)

Range: Alaska and Greenland to Nicaragua and Georgia. Allied races are found in Europe and Asia. *Habitat:* Remote forests, sea-coasts, especially where there are cliffs. *Identification:* A large, black bird—spread over 4 feet—that soars with wings *flat,* whereas Crows use considerable dihedral. "Bearded" appearance of throat and breast when bird is at rest. *Voice:* A guttural croak. *Breeding:* Four to seven eggs in tree-tops or on rocky ledges. *Food:* Omnivorous. As Audubon pointed out, habits largely beneficial.

102. BLUE JAY

(CYANOCITTA CRISTATA)

Range: Breeds from Nebraska, Alberta and Newfoundland to Texas and Florida. Ranges farther south in winter. *Habitat:* Woodlands, farms, parks, etc. *Identification:* Length, about 1 foot. Blue and white coloration, *crest. Voice:* A loud scream, *jay-jay.* Song, rather bell-like, as though two pieces of crockery were knocking together. Mimics other birds. *Breeding:* Four to seven eggs in well-concealed nest at varying heights. *Food:* Insects, nuts, wild fruits, eggs, young birds, etc. One of our commonest, wisest, most beautiful birds!

103. CANADA WARBLER

(WILSONIA CANADENSIS)

Rare is the person who, knowing our spring Warblers, fails to capitulate to their bright beauty. It is unfortunate that their variety seems to overwhelm the neophyte in bird study. If one will, for a couple of hours, study color plates of the local warblers, one should not find difficulty in separating them in the field—though a glass is almost indispensable. Presence or absence of wing-bars, and the usually characteristic face pattern, should be especially noted. See Plate 5 for discussion of this species.

104. CHIPPING SPARROW

(SPIZELLA PASSERINA)

Range: Breeds from Yukon and Cape Breton Island to Mexico and Georgia. Winters from California and New Jersey south. *Habitat:* Especially about houses; in forest clearings, abandoned pastures, etc. *Identification:* Length, about 5½ inches; chestnut cap, light line over eye, dark line through it. *Voice:* A series of monotonous dry chips, given rapidly. *Breeding:* Three to five eggs in bush, tree, etc. nest usually lined with horsehair. *Food:* Insects, weed seeds. A species that, like the Martin, seems to choose the presence of man

105. RED-BREASTED NUTHATCH

(SITTA CANADENSIS)

Range: Breeds from the Yukon and Newfoundland to Minnesota and New York; south in the mountains to New Mexico and North Carolina. Winters from southern Canada south. *Habitat:* Northern —or high—forests. *Identification:* Small size—about 4½ inches long—reddish underparts, black line through eye. Feeds by creeping about branches. *Voice:* A high-pitched *yeh-yeh. Breeding:* Four to seven eggs in hollow in tree. *Food:* Largely insects. The Nuthatches spend much of their lives hanging *upside* down as they feed.

106. BLACK VULTURE
(CORAGYPS ATRATUS)

Range: From Texas, Missouri and Maryland to Central America. *Habitat:* Usually seen soaring high in air. *Identification:* Length, about 25 inches. Naked black head. Soars, much as does Turkey Vulture, but has notably shorter tail, beyond which feet may some-

times be seen. Shows white patches underneath wings, near tips. *Breeding:* Two to three eggs, in hollow logs, caves, etc., or on ground under bushes. *Food:* Principally carrion, though it is said also to take young birds and eggs.

107. CANADA JAY

(PERISOREUS CANADENSIS)

Range: Breeds from Alaska, Mackenzie and Labrador to Arizona and New York. *Habitat:* Northern and high forests. *Identification:* A large, long-tailed gray and white bird. Length, about 11 inches. According to Peterson, suggests overgrown Chickadee. *Voice:* A wide variety of notes, some suggesting calls of Blue Jay. *Breeding:* Four to six eggs, usually rather low in an evergreen. *Food:* Omnivorous—almost anything edible it can get. The Whiskey Jack is famous because of its tameness. See Plate 419.

108. FOX SPARROW

(PASSERELLA ILIACA)

Range: Breeds from Alaska and Quebec to California and Newfoundland. Winters from California and the Potomac valley to Lower California and Florida. Sixteen races of this bird have been

tangles and thickets. *Identification:* Large size—about 7 inches long —reddish color, especially on tail. *Voice:* A beautifully rich, sweet song, often given on migration. *Breeding:* Three to five eggs in nest

109. SAVANNAH SPARROW

(PASSERCULUS SANDWICHENSIS)

Range: Breeds from Alaska and Labrador to California and Pennsylvania. Winters from British Columbia and New Jersey to Guatemala. Several races have been described, including Bryant's Sparrow. *Habitat:* Grasslands, lush meadows. *Identification:* Length, about 5½ inches. Breast streaked. *Forked tail. Flesh-colored legs.* Yellow before eye. *Voice:* A thin *tsip, tsip, sssssss-tsip* with the insect-like quality of the Grasshopper Sparrows. *Breeding:* Three to five eggs in grassy cup on ground. *Food:* Insects, weed seeds, etc.

110. HOODED WARBLER

(WILSONIA CITRINA)

Range: Breeds from Nebraska and the Connecticut Valley to Louisiana and Florida. Winters from Vera Cruz to Panama. *Habitat:* Swampy woods and thickets. *Identification:* Length, about 5½ inches. Black hood identifies male. Female lacks hood but dusky markings of head and face seem to suggest it. Very variable. Much like smaller Wilson's Warbler, but has yellow forehead. *Breeding:* Four to five eggs in nest, usually near ground. *Food:* Insects. Many of these caught on the wing, Flycatcher-fashion. See Plate 9.

111. PILEATED WOODPECKER
(CEOPHLOEUS PILEATUS)

Range: From British Columbia, Mackenzie and Nova Scotia to California and Florida. *Habitat:* Forests; apparently becoming adapted to civilization and recently bred in Westchester County, New York. *Identification:* Length, about 17 inches. Flaming red crest. Large white wing patches *in flight only*. Rare Ivory-bill shows these when at rest. *Voice:* Like a Flicker's call, but deeper and slower. *Breeding:* Three to five eggs in cavity in tree or stub. *Food:* Ants, destructive borers. May often be detected by chiseled "workings."

112. DOWNY WOODPECKER

(DRYOBATES PUBESCENS)

Range: Alaska and Ungava to California and Florida. Races are known as Batchelder's, Gairdner's, and the Willow Woodpeckers. *Habitat:* Woodlands, often coming into suburbs and city parks. *Identification:* Small size—length about 6 inches—black and white coloration. Has black notches in white outer tail feathers, which larger and similar Hairy lacks, and a *much smaller bill. Voice:* A rapid, high-pitched *king-kink-kink,* etc. *Breeding:* Four to six eggs in hole. *Food:* Largely insects. Suet at feeding stations.

113. BLUEBIRD

(SIALIA SIALIS)

Range: Breeds from Montana and Newfoundland to Texas and Florida. The Azure race from Arizona to Mexico. Winters south of the middle states and Ohio valley. *Habitat:* Generally distributed where nesting holes are available. *Identification:* Length, about 6½ inches. Blue above, reddish below; female duller than male. *Voice:* A lovely, gentle warble; fall note a soft *chúr-ree. Breeding:* Four to six eggs in hollow trees, bird boxes, etc. *Food:* Insects, berries, etc. Nest boxes near ground are less attractive to House Sparrows.

114. WHITE-CROWNED SPARROW
(ZONOTRICHIA LEUCOPHRYS)

Range: Breeds from Alaska and Greenland to California (in mountains) and Quebec. Winters from California and the Ohio valley to Mexico. *Habitat:* On migration, and in winter, usually in weedy or brushy areas. *Identification:* Length, about 6½ inches. Large, square head; black and white striped crown. Black in front of eye, where Gambel's Sparrow is white or gray. *Voice:* Begins somewhat like White-throat's, ends in buzz that suggests song of Black-throated Green Warbler. Races: Gambel's, Puget Sound, Nuttall's.

115. WOOD PEWEE
(MYOCHANES VIRENS)

Range: Breeds from Nebraska, Manitoba and Prince Edward Island to Texas and Florida. Winters from Nicaragua to Peru. *Habitat:* Woodlands. *Identification:* Length, about 6½ inches. Fly-catching habits. Wing-bars. Does not often wag tail. Dark sides. *Voice:* A sweet, mournful *pee-a-wee,* the third syllable usually rising. *Breeding:* Three to four eggs, often on dead branch, 10 to 50 feet high. *Food:* Mostly insects. Often sings in heat of day when other woodland birds are still.

116. BROWN THRASHER

(TOXOSTOMA RUFUM)

Range: Breeds from Montana, Alberta and Quebec to the Gulf. Winters from Missouri and North Carolina to Texas and Florida. Occasionally as far north as New York, etc. *Habitat:* Brushy areas, including door-yards. *Identification:* Large size—nearly a foot long —bright brown coloration; *streaked*—not spotted—below; *long tail.* *Voice:* A rich outpouring of mimicry and originality, *usually in couplets as though each phrase were sung with exhaled and inhaled breath. Breeding:* Three to six eggs in thicket, fairly high.

117. MISSISSIPPI KITE

(ICTINIA MISISIPPIENSIS)

Range: Breeds from Kansas and South Carolina to Texas and Florida. Winters in Florida and Texas, south to Guatemala. *Habitat:* Woodlands, often near rivers and swamps. *Identification:* Length, about 15 inches; spread, about 3 feet. Falcon-shaped wings; long, *black,* slightly forked tail; light head. *Breeding:* Two eggs, in high, often Crow-like, nests. *Food:* Insects, snakes, frogs. This beautiful and useful bird has been exterminated over most of its range; vigorous protection is needed if it is to survive.

118. WARBLING VIREO
(VIREO GILVUS)

Range: Breeds from British Columbia and Nova Scotia to Lower California and North Carolina. Winters south to Guatemala. *Habitat:* Village streets, open woodlands. *Identification:* Length, about 5½ inches. Absence of wing-bars. Little or no yellow below. Light in front of eye. Face pattern obscure. A bird of the tree-tops. *Voice:* A headlong, throaty warble, much more complicated and sustained than the notes of our other Vireos. *Breeding:* Three to four eggs in nest in much the same site as the Baltimore Oriole's.

119. YELLOW-THROATED VIREO

(VIREO FLAVIFRONS)

Range: Breeds from Saskatchewan and Quebec to Texas and Flori-da. Winters from Mexico to Venezuela. *Habitat:* Woodlands, parks, towns. *Identification: Wing-bars,* bright yellow underparts, yellow about eye. Vireos may be separated from Warblers, which in some cases they resemble, by heavier bills and more deliberate feeding habits. Length, about 5½ inches. *Voice: Verily, verily,* slowly ren-dered; much like Red-eye's song, but with a *hoarse,* throaty quality —as though the bird had a slight cold. *Food:* Large insects.

120. PHOEBE

(SAYORNIS PHOEBE)

Range: Breeds from Mackenzie and Prince Edward Island to New Mexico and Georgia. Winters in the United States, chiefly south of latitude 37°, south to Mexico. *Habitat:* Vicinity of buildings, bridges, cliffs, near water. *Identification: Habit of wagging tail.* Absence of wing-bars. Dull underparts. Feeds by hawking for insects. Length, about 6½ inches. *Voice:* A soft, reedy *phé-be* often monotonously repeated. *Breeding:* Three to six eggs in nest of reinforced mud, under bridge, inside barn, etc. *Food:* Mostly insects.

121. SNOWY OWL
(NYCTEA NYCTEA)

Range: Breeds from the Bering Sea and northern Greenland to Keewatin and Ungava; also in northern Europe and Asia. Winters from the Arctic coast to southern prairie provinces. Periodically invades United States in some numbers. *Habitat:* When in United States, in open country, such as prairies, salt marshes, beaches. *Identification:* Large size—length about 2 feet; absence of "ear-tufts"; white or nearly so. *Food:* Injurious rodents, birds, fish. Winter bird students regard this beautiful bird as an especial "prize."

122. BLUE GROSBEAK

(GUIRACA CAERULEA)

Range: Breeds from the Sacramento valley and Maryland to Mexico and Florida. Winters south of the United States. *Habitat:* Edges of woods, brushy abandoned pastures, etc. *Identification:* Large size—length about 7 inches—heavy bill. Male blue above *and below,* with brownish wing-bars. Female a large, heavy-beaked brown bird, with noticeable wing-bars. *Voice:* "a rather weak but melodious warble, somewhat like the song of the Purple Finch, but less vigorous" (Howell). *Breeding:* Three to four eggs, in thickets, low trees.

123. MAGNOLIA WARBLER

(DENDROICA MAGNOLIA)

Man's chief competitors in the struggle for existence in the Temperate Zone include insects and rodents; both annually cost Americans hundreds of millions of dollars. In the inevitable warfare against these pests, birds are extremely helpful allies. Hawks and Owls destroy countless numbers of rats and mice annually, and computation of the quantities of insects eaten by birds would stagger even those accustomed to thinking in terms of light years. Warblers comprise some of the most effective insect destroyers. See Plate 50.

124. WILSON'S WARBLER
(WILSONIA PUSILLA)

Range: Breeds from Alaska and Newfoundland to California and Maine. Winters in Mexico, Central America and Panama. *Habitat:* Brushy, swampy areas, woodlands. *Identification:* Small size— about 4½ inches long; yellow coloration and black cap mark male.

Female may lack this; small size and marked activity diagnostic. *Breeding:* Four to five eggs in ground nest, usually in swamp. Races: Pileolated and Golden Pileolated Warblers. *Food:* Insects, many taken on the wing, Flycatcher-fashion.

125. BROWN-HEADED NUTHATCH

(SITTA PUSILLA)

Range: From Arkansas and Delaware to Texas and Florida. *Habitat:* Southern pine barrens. *Identification:* Small size—about 4 inches; Nuthatch habit of feeding by creeping over bark and hanging head-down; *brown* cap, somewhat more grayish in female; white spot on back of neck. *Voice:* Staccato *ya-ya-ya,* frequently uttered. *Breeding:* Five to six eggs in a hole in tree or telephone pole. *Food:* Insects, their eggs, pine seeds. Florida race the Gray-headed Nuthatch.

126. BALD EAGLE

(HALIAEETUS LEUCOCEPHALUS)

The Eagles, because of their size and impressiveness, have pro-
foundly stirred the imagination of man. They have not always
profited by human interest, however, since they have often—without
foundation—been accused of divers offenses. One of these is baby-
stealing, whose legend persists although *there has never been a sub-
stantiated case*. We are finally beginning to appreciate Eagles for
what they are—magnificent creatures that unfailingly inspire pleas-
ure and wonder in the human observer. See Plates 11, 31.

127. ROSE-BREASTED GROSBEAK
(HEDYMELES LUDOVICIANUS)

Range: Breeds from Mackenzie and Cape Breton Island to Kansas and Georgia. Winters from Mexico to Ecuador. *Habitat:* Woodlands, brush patches, orchards, gardens. *Identification:* Flashing black and white pattern of male, with red breast patch; female, brown and heavily streaked. Heavy bills. Length, about 7½ inches. *Voice:* A sweet, sustained warble that suggests Robin's song but is more drawn-out and clearer in tone. *Breeding:* Three to four eggs in often flimsy nest. *Food:* Wild fruits, weed seeds, insects.

128. CATBIRD

(DUMETELLA CAROLINENSIS)

Range: Breeds from British Columbia and Nova Scotia to New Mexico and Florida; resident in Bermuda. Winters from the southern states through the West Indies, and through Mexico to Panama. *Habitat:* Brushy areas, including parks and gardens. *Identification:* Length, about 9 inches. A slate-gray bird with chestnut patch under base of its long tail. *Voice:* A mewing call that has given it its name. A rich, varied and beautiful song, including much mimicry. Often sings at night as does the closely related Mockingbird.

129. CRESTED FLYCATCHER
(MYIARCHUS CRINITUS)

Range: Breeds from Manitoba and New Brunswick to Texas and Florida. Winters in Florida and from Mexico to Colombia. *Habitat:* Woodlands, cultivated lands. *Identification:* Large size—length, 8½ inches. Brown above, gray throat, sulphur-yellow belly. Not so colorful as Audubon's plate. *Voice:* A ringing *scaipe! Breeding:* In hollow tree, nesting box, etc. Habitually weaves discarded snakeskin into nest. *Food:* Mostly insects. One of the hole-nesting species that have suffered through the development of tree surgery.

130. GRASSHOPPER SPARROW

(AMMODRAMUS SAVANNARUM)

Range: Breeds from British Columbia and New Hampshire to southern California, Texas and Florida. Winters from California and North Carolina to Central America. *Habitat:* Grassland. *Identification:* A small—length about 5 inches—Sparrow with short, pointed tail and *unstreaked* breast. Somewhat similar Henslow Sparrow has breast streaked. *Voice:* An insect-like *z-z-z-z-z,* easil overlooked until it is known, when the bird will often be foun surprisingly common. *Breeding:* Four to five eggs, in nest in grass

131. ROBIN

(TURDUS MIGRATORIUS)

Range: Breeds from Alaska and Newfoundland to Mexico and Georgia. Winters from British Columbia and Massachusetts to Central America. *Habitat:* Ubiquitous. *Identification:* About 10 inches long. Brown back, reddish-brown below, white in outer tail feathers. Western Robin lacks this. Young paler below, and spotted. *Voice:* Song a repeated *cheerily, cheerily.* Many other notes. *Breeding:* Three to five eggs in reinforced mud nest. Several broods yearly. *Food:* Insects, fruits, worms.

132. ARCTIC THREE-TOED WOODPECKER

(PICOIDES ARCTICUS)

Range: From Alaska and Quebec to California and Maine. Casual farther south in winter. *Habitat:* Northern coniferous forests. *Identification:* Length, about 10 inches. Black back, *not* crossed by transverse white bands as in American Three-toed Woodpecker. Yellow on head of male. Presence may be surmised by the barkless trees it peels in its search for food. *Breeding:* Four eggs in hole in tree. *Food:* Borers and other insects, berries, etc. One of the most relished "finds" of winter bird students.

133. BLACK-POLL WARBLER
(DENDROICA STRIATA)

Range: Breeds from Alaska and Newfoundland to British Columbia and New Hampshire. Winters from Guiana to Brazil; migrates through the Bahamas and West Indies. *Habitat:* Northern forests, especially coniferous. *Identification:* Length, about 5½ inches. Black and streaked, with solid black crown, though this may be ill-defined in female. Young much like young Bay-breasted Warblers (*q. v.*), but yellower below and without the buffy wash they often show. *Voice: Tzee-tzee,* likely to be overlooked until one is familiar with it.

134. BLACKBURNIAN WARBLER

(DENDROICA FUSCA)

A pair of field glasses is one of the most useful tools of the bird student, and the better the glass the easier will be identification of difficult forms. A prism binocular of 7x, 8x or 9x power is most satisfactory for all-round use; good illumination, for early mornings and dull days, is important. American prism binoculars are now as good as those made in Europe. See Plate 135, for this Warbler.

135. BLACKBURNIAN WARBLER

(DENDROICA FUSCA)

Range: Breeds from Manitoba and Cape Breton Island to Minnesota and Massachusetts; in the Alleghenies to South Carolina. Winters from Venezuela and Colombia to Peru. *Habitat:* Coniferous forests. *Identification:* Length, about 5 inches. Intense orange-red on throat and breast identifies male; female similar but not so bright; young birds lack the bright colors but have the same color-pattern. *Voice:* A buzzy *zee-zee-zee*, etc. *Breeding:* Three to four eggs, in high nest, usually in conifer. See Plate 134.

136. MEADOWLARK

(STURNELLA MAGNA)

Range: Breeds from Minnesota, Nebraska and New Brunswick to Arizona and Florida. Winters from the Great Lakes and Maine, south. *Habitat:* Grassy fields. *Identification:* Large size—length, about 9 inches; white outer tail feathers, very obvious in flight; yellow of underparts not extending to face as in Western Meadowlark; black "V" on breast. Volplanes between periods of wing movement. *Voice:* A thin, clear, ringing whistle. A clattering chatter. *Breeding:* Four to six eggs, in grassy nest on ground.

137. YELLOW-BREASTED CHAT
(ICTERIA VIRENS)

Range: Breeds from British Columbia and New York to Mexico and Florida. Winters in Mexico and Central America. *Habitat:* Thickets, tangles, brushy swamps. *Identification:* Length, about 7 inches—the largest of our Wood Warblers. Characteristic facial pattern—white about eye, black before and under it. More often heard than seen. *Voice:* A complex and varied racket—clucks, whistles, cackles, often given as a flight song *Breeding:* Three to five eggs in nest near ground. Western race: Long-tailed Chat.

138. CONNECTICUT WARBLER

(OPORORNIS AGILIS)

Range: Breeds from Alberta and Manitoba to Minnesota and Michigan. Winters in northern South America. Rare in spring east of Alleghenies, common in Mississippi Valley; in fall, rare in latter, but common east of Alleghenies. *Habitat:* Bogs, clearings. *Identifi-* *cation:* Length, about 5½ inches. Male, gray hood (including throat). Female and young, no wing-bars. *White eye-ring. Walks,* rather than hops. *Voice:* "*Fru-chapple, fru-chapple, fru-chapple, whoit*" (Seton). In most places, rare on migration.

139. FIELD SPARROW

(SPIZELLA PUSILLA)

Range: Breeds from Montana and Magdalen Islands to Nebraska and Florida. Winters south to Mexico and Gulf coast. North to Missouri and New Jersey. *Habitat:* As name indicates. *Identification:* Length, about 5½ inches. Reddish cap, not so definite as in Chip-ping Sparrow, and *pink* bill. *Voice:* A lovely, clear piping, given in a series of ascending tones. Tempo rapid. Often sings at night. *Breeding:* Three to four eggs in nest on or near ground. *Food:* Insects, weed seeds, etc.

140. PINE WARBLER

(DENDROICA PINUS)

One may state, as a general proposition, that the richer the land occupied, the heavier will be the wild-life population. This follows naturally from the fact that plants flourish on rich land, and that they are the basic food on which all animals, directly or indirectly, depend. Animal populations tend, however, to fill all available habitats; thus—except for cyclic species—they maintain approximately stable numbers. This Warbler thrives in the vegetation of poor soil, and is common in coastal pine barrens. See Plate 30.

141. GOSHAWK

(ASTUR ATRICAPILLUS)

Range: Breeds from Alaska and Ungava to Mexico and Maryland. Winters through much of the breeding range, to Mexico and Virginia. Periodically moves southward in considerable numbers. *Habitat:* Woodlands. *Identification:* Large size—length about 2 feet— and typical accipitrine shape: *short, rounded wings, long tail*. The gray adult, finely streaked below, with dark cap, is easily recognized. Immature birds have prominent white line over eye. This, and size, identify them. For Cooper's Hawk (Number 3) see Plate 36.

142. SPARROW HAWK

(FALCO SPARVERIUS)

Range: Breeds from the Upper Yukon and Newfoundland to Mexico and Florida. Winters from British Columbia and Massachusetts to Panama. *Habitat:* Of general distribution. Most often seen perched on exposed stub, or telephone pole. *Identification:* Long pointed wings and long tail, typical of Falcons. Bright reddish brown on upper parts. *Hovers,* while searching for prey. When it perches, *flicks tail.* Length, about 10 inches. *Voice:* A not unmusical *killy-killy-killy. Food:* Insects, rodents, etc. Should be protected.

143. OVEN-BIRD

(SEIURUS AUROCAPILLUS)

Range: Breeds from Mackenzie and Newfoundland to Alabama and Georgia. Winters from Mexico and Florida to Colombia. *Habitat:* Woodlands. *Identification:* The *yellowish crown-stripe,* responsible for the name used by Audubon—Golden-crowned Thrush. Suggests a small Thrush—length, about 6 inches—but is striped rather than spotted on underparts. *Walks. Voice:* Note most often heard a ringing *teacher,* TEACHER, TEACHER, *TEACHER. Breeding:* Five to six eggs in ground nest, shaped like Dutch oven.

144. ACADIAN FLYCATCHER
(EMPIDONAX VIRESCENS)

Range: Breeds from Nebraska and Massachusetts to Texas and Florida. Migrates through Central America. Winters in Colombia and Ecuador. *Habitat:* Swampy woods. *Identification:* One of the few North American birds whose determination in the field is problematical. Lack of yellow throat distinguishes it from the Yellow-belly; not so brown as the Alder. Larger than the Least. Most reliable character the note. Length, about 6 inches. *Voice:* A strong, staccato *eeep!*

145. YELLOW PALM WARBLER

(DENDROICA PALMARUM)

Range: Breeds from Ontario and Newfoundland to Maine and Nova Scotia. Winters from Louisiana to Florida. *Habitat:* Swamps, brushy areas, abandoned pastures. *Identification:* Length, about 5 inches. Reddish crown. *Bright* yellow below—Western Palm Warbler duller. *Wags tail. Breeding:* Four to five eggs, in nest on or near ground, often in wet places. *Food:* Mostly insects, some seeds.

146. FISH CROW

(CORVUS OSSIFRAGUS)

Range: Atlantic and Gulf coasts from Massachusetts to Texas. *Habitat:* Usually near water, swamps, rivers, etc. *Identification:* Appears identical with Eastern, or Common, Crow, but is smaller; separation on this basis is unreliable unless birds are together and, thus, can be compared. The note of the Fish Crow is more guttural and croaking than that of its more widely spread congener, but the young of the latter often sound like Fish Crows. *Food:* Carrion, wild fruits, young birds and eggs.

147. NIGHTHAWK
(CHORDEILES MINOR)

Range: Breeds from Yukon and Newfoundland to Mexico and Florida. Winters in South America. *Habitat:* Open country, cities. *Identification:* Length, about 9 inches. Long tail and wings, the latter with white bands—that appear transparent—near their tips.

Perches in prominent places, as along exposed limbs, relying on its protective coloration for concealment. More active in daylight than Whip-poor-will. Not a Hawk! *Voice:* A resonant *peent. Breeding:* Two eggs on bare ground, rocks, gravelled roofs, etc.

148. BLACK-THROATED BLUE WARBLER
(DENDROICA CAERULESCENS)

In the 1920's one of our foremost experts on field identification published a book on the birds of his region and categorically listed a number of species as impossible of determination in the field. Subsequently, ways of identifying these birds have been found—many by the same author—and now few American birds need escape the careful observer. The use of this book, and those listed in the Introduction, will solve virtually all identification problems. Plate 155 discusses this Warbler.

149. SHARP-TAILED SPARROW

(AMMOSPIZA CAUDACUTA)

Range: Breeds from Quebec to Virginia, in salt marshes; from Great Slave Lake and Alberta to Minnesota and South Dakota (Nelson's race) in fresh marshes. Winters from New Jersey to Texas. *Identification:* Marsh habitat. Short, pointed tail. Strong buffy face patch and relatively strong streaking in eastern race. Acadian race, paler, grayer on back. Nelson's race, buffier on breast, streakings very dim. *Voice:* A buzzy *tea-kettle-de-eee. Breeding:* Three to six eggs in well-hidden grassy nest, on ground. *Food:* Insects, crustaceans.

150. RED-EYED VIREO

(VIREO OLIVACEUS)

Range: Breeds from British Columbia and Cape Breton Island to Mexico and Florida. Winters in South America. *Habitat:* Woodlands, orchards, etc. *Identification:* Length, about 6 inches. Olive above, white below, crown gray; *broad white line over eye,* dark line through it. The most sharply marked of its genus. *Voice: Verily . . . verily . . . verily,* deliberately repeated, even through middle of day and hot summer months, when most other birds are still. *Breeding:* Three to four eggs, commonly in low nest.

151. TURKEY VULTURE

(CATHARTES AURA)

Range: Breeds from British Columbia and Connecticut to Lower California and Florida. Winters throughout most of its regular range on the Atlantic slope, but not north of the Ohio valley, Nebraska and California. *Habitat:* Usually seen soaring, or at carrion, as on garbage dumps. *Identification:* Reddish, naked head. Wingspread, about 6 feet. Soars, often without apparent wing motion, with wings well above horizontal. Marsh Hawk also does this, but usually flies low. Distinguished from Black Vulture by *long tail*.

152. WHITE-BREASTED NUTHATCH

(SITTA CAROLINENSIS)

Range: Breeds from British Columbia and Quebec to Lower California and Florida. Races include: Florida, Rocky Mountain, Slender-billed Nuthatches. *Habitat:* Almost any place it can find food. *Identification:* Length, about 5½ inches. Feeds much in up-side-down position, as does Red-breast. Black cap; white underparts. *Voice:* A nasal *yank, yank. Breeding:* Six to nine eggs in tree hole or nesting box. *Food:* Insects, seeds, etc. A regular patron of winter feeding stations; especially fond of suet.

153. MYRTLE WARBLER

(DENDROICA CORONATA)

Range: Breeds from Alaska and Quebec to British Columbia and Massachusetts. Winters from Kansas and southern New England to Mexico. *Habitat:* Evergreen forests in breeding season. In winter, especially where there are bayberries. *Identification:* Length, about 5½ inches. Yellow patches on crown, rump, each side of breast. *Voice:* Its dry chip is much more easily recognized than those of most warblers. *Breeding:* Four to five eggs, usually in evergreens and not far from ground. *Food:* Insects, wild fruits and berries.

154. TENNESSEE WARBLER

(VERMIVORA PEREGRINA)

Range: Breeds from the Yukon Valley and Anticosti Island to British Columbia and Maine. Winters from Oaxaca to Colombia and Venezuela. *Habitat:* North woods, often in tamarack swamp. *Iden-* *tification:* Length, about 5 inches. Gray head, greenish back, white line over eye. Suggests Red-eyed Vireo in appearance, but is smaller, with slender bill. *Breeding:* Five to seven eggs, in deep ground nest.

155. BLACK-THROATED BLUE WARBLER

(DENDROICA CAERULESCENS)

Range: Breeds from Minnesota and Quebec to Georgia. (Southern Allegheny race known as Cairns's Warbler.) Winters from Key West to Colombia. *Habitat:* Woods of north—and of higher altitudes. *Identification:* Length, about 5 inches. Blue back, black throat of male. Female (see Plate 148) a nondescript brown bird that may be identified by the white notch in the wing—at the base of the flight feathers. *Voice:* Buzzing notes, sometimes rising, sometimes falling, in pitch.

156. CROW

(CORVUS BRACHYRHYNCHOS)

Range: Breeds from Alaska and Newfoundland to Lower California and Florida. Races include: Eastern, Southern, Florida, Western and Northwestern Crows. *Habitat:* Almost ubiquitous—from the wilderness to city parks. *Identification:* Length, about 19 inches.

All black. *Voice:* The most familiar note, *caw.* (See Fish Crow, Plate 146.) *Breeding:* Four to seven eggs, in nest that may be in marshes, high trees, etc. *Food:* Insects, mice, etc. Apparently has increased recently, in part because of killing of Hawks and Owls.

157. RUSTY BLACKBIRD

(EUPHAGUS CAROLINUS)

Range: Breeds from Alaska and Quebec to British Columbia and Nova Scotia. Winters mainly south of the Ohio and Delaware Valleys to the Gulf coast. *Habitat:* On migration, and in winter, very likely to be seen in swampy areas—and with other Blackbirds.

Identification: Length, about 9 inches. Spring male, black with greenish reflections. (Brewer's is purplish on head.) Female, brownish. Fall birds brownish and barred. They walk or hop. Grackles have long tails, Starlings much shorter ones.

158. CHIMNEY SWIFT

(CHAETURA PELAGICA)

Range: Breeds from Montana, Alberta and Newfoundland to Texas and Florida. Wintering range not known. *Habitat:* Woodlands, where there are hollow trees; more frequently vicinity of man's abodes. *Identification:* About 5 inches long. Two wings form long flickering *arc,* in middle of which *body appears tailless. Voice:* A rapidly repeated twittering. *Breeding:* Four to six eggs in twig and saliva nest in chimney, hollow tree, deserted house, etc. This bird more prone to feed very high in air than are Swallows.

159. CARDINAL

(RICHMONDENA CARDINALIS)

Range: From South Dakota and the Hudson Valley to Texas and Florida; Arizona, New Mexico, Sonora; Bermuda. Races include: Florida, Louisiana and Gray-tailed Cardinals. *Habitat:* Brushy areas, as old pastures, woodlands, gardens. *Identification:* About 8½ inches long. Male, mostly red *with prominent crest*. Female duller, but also crested. *Voice:* A variety of loud, clear whistles. *Breeding:* Three to five eggs in low nest in tangle, vines, etc. *Food:* Insects, weed seeds, etc. A frequenter of winter feeding stations.

160. BLACK-CAPPED CHICKADEE

(PENTHESTES ATRICAPILLUS)

Range: Alaska and Newfoundland to New Mexico and North Carolina. Races include: Long-tailed and Oregon Chickadees. *Habitat:* Woodlands. *Identification:* Not likely to be confused except with "brown-headed" Chickadees, which lack the black cap. Length, about 5 inches. *Voice:* A reedy *chick-a-dee-dee-dee*. A sweet, descending whistle *Pee-wee*. *Breeding:* Six to nine eggs in tree hollow, nest box, etc. *Food:* Insects, fruits, seeds. A common frequenter of winter feeding stations that can be taught to feed from one's hand.

161. AUDUBON'S CARACARA

(POLYBORUS CHERIWAY)

Range: Lower California, Arizona, Texas and Florida, south through Mexico and Central America. An allied race is found in South America. *Habitat:* Open country—prairies, mesquite, etc. *Identification:* Spread about 4 feet. Long legs. *Large white areas at* *ends of wings.* White on breast, and in tail. *Breeding:* Two to four eggs in large nest, in Florida in top of cabbage palmetto. *Food:* Carrion, snakes, lizards, prairie dogs, etc. One of Florida's most spectacular birds, protected by Audubon wardens.

162. ZENAIDA DOVE

(ZENAIDA ZENAIDA)

Range: Florida Keys (formerly), the Bahamas, Cuba, Isle of Pines, Haiti, Puerto Rico, Virgin Islands, etc. An allied race on the coast of Yucatan. *Identification:* Length, about 10 inches. A round-tailed Dove, with outer tail feathers and rear edge of wings white-tipped. Neck and breast warm brown. Common in the West Indies, not recorded in Florida since Audubon's time.

163. YELLOW PALM WARBLER

(DENDROICA PALMARUM)

The Wood Warblers, a group confined to the New World, include some of our most brilliant birds. Many of them, nesting from the northern tier of the United States well into Canada, flash by bird students during a few spring days; the fall migration finds them with generally dimmed plumage that is obscured by dense foliage. To find them in numbers, one should seek rich, swampy woods—or park oases in large cities. They are most easily discovered shortly after dawn. See Plate 145.

164. VEERY

(HYLOCICHLA FUSCESCENS)

Range: Breeds from British Columbia and Anticosti Island to New Mexico and Georgia. Winters in South America, to Brazil. The western race is known as the Willow Thrush. *Habitat:* Woodlands, particularly in damp valleys. *Identification:* Length, about 7½ inches. Upper parts *uniform reddish brown.* Wood Thrush has only head and neck reddish, Hermit has reddish tail. *Voice:* An exquisitely pure fluting that sounds as though it might be made by whirling a silver ball inside a silver bell.

165. BACHMAN'S SPARROW

(AIMOPHILA AESTIVALIS)

Range: Breeds from Iowa and Pennsylvania to Texas and Florida. Winters from North Carolina south. The Pine-woods Sparrow of Florida is a race. *Habitat:* Open woods, deciduous in Midwest, pineries in Florida. *Identification:* Length, about 6 inches. ". . . a brown-backed bird with a *clear dingy-buff* breast" (Peterson). This bird was named in honor of Audubon's friend, John Bachman.

166. ROUGH-LEGGED HAWK

(BUTEO LAGOPUS)

Range: Breeds from Alaska and Ungava to Alberta and Newfoundland. Winters from British Columbia and Ontario to California and North Carolina. *Habitat:* When with us, usually seen hunting over open country, as prairie or salt marsh. *Identification:* Wing-spread, 4 feet or more. Typical wide wings and short tail of Buteos. *White patch in tail, near rump,* not to be confused with Marsh Hawk's labeling mark, which is *on rump.* Frequently hovers over land as Kingfisher or Osprey does over water. See Plate 422.

167 . KEY WEST QUAIL-DOVE

(OREOPELEIA CHRYSIA)

Range: Key West (formerly), the Bahamas, Cuba, Isle of Pines, Haiti. *Habitat:* Wooded areas of the Florida Keys, in summer months. *Identification:* Slightly larger than Mourning Dove. Upperparts reddish brown, *belly white. Voice:* "It may be imitated by pronouncing the following syllables *whoe-whoe-oh-oh*" (Audubon). *Breeding:* Two eggs in nest on or near ground. *Food:* Fruits, berries, sea-grape. Formerly much more abundant on the Keys but reduced as a result of tree-cutting (Maynard).

168. FORK-TAILED FLYCATCHER
(MUSCIVORA TYRANNUS)

Range: Southern Mexico to northern Patagonia. An accidental visitor to the United States. *Identification:* About 14 inches long. *Heavy black cap, coming well over face.* The Scissor-tailed Flycatcher lacks this. (See Plate 359.) The discovery of three birds of this species in the United States—one near Philadelphia, two near Natchez—is evidence of Audubon's remarkable skill as a field observer. The A.O.U. *Check-List* gives only seven records of the bird. It is thought to arrive with tropical hurricanes.

169. MAYNARD'S CUCKOO

(COCCYZUS MINOR)

Range: Southern coast of Florida, West Indies, Central America. The occurrence of the Mangrove race, which is darker below, in Florida, is based only on Audubon's specimen. *Habitat:* Mangrove tangles. *Identification:* Length about 11½ inches. Much like Yellow-bill, including white in tail, but underparts "white, *washed with pinkish-buff, and cinnamon-buff*" (Howell). *Voice:* "wholly unlike those of the other American Cuckoos, being a sort of clucking note, low and guttural . . . suggesting the notes of a squirrel" (Howell).

170. GRAY KINGBIRD

(TYRANNUS DOMINICENSIS)

Range: Breeds from South Carolina to Florida and Jamaica. Winters in northern South America. *Habitat:* Coast and Keys. *Identification:* Length, about 8½ inches. Similar to Kingbird, but tail is forked instead of rounded, and carries no white at tip. *Extremely heavy* bill. *Voice:* "*se-chee-ry,* similar to those of the common Kingbird, but not so harsh" (Howell). *Breeding:* Two to three eggs, usually in mangroves, over water. *Food:* Largely insects. This bird should be looked for, in the North, after hurricanes.

171. BARN OWL
(TYTO ALBA)

Range: Breeds from California and Connecticut to Nicaragua. Races occur in South America, West Indies, Europe, Asia, etc. *Habitat:* Barns, steeples, caves, hollow trees; often in towns. *Identification:* Length, about 18 inches. Very light underneath—in England known as the White Owl—"monkey face," long legs. *Breeding:* Four to seven eggs, on bed of pellets. These are undigested fur, bones, etc., that the bird coughs up. In buildings, etc., as above. *Food:* Largely rats, mice, etc. A most valuable bird!

172. BLUE-HEADED QUAIL-DOVE
(STARNOENAS CYANOCEPHALA)

"Audubon's record of this Cuban species on the Florida Keys is regarded as unsatisfactory; and as it has never been confirmed the species is now transferred to the Hypothetical List." (A.O.U. *Check-List.*) Audubon's sight record of this bird at Key West, in 1832, is unsupported by a specimen. Its normal range is Cuba and the Isle of Pines.

173. BARN SWALLOW
(HIRUNDO ERYTHROGASTER)

Range: Breeds from Alaska and Quebec to California, Mexico and North Carolina. Winters from Mexico to northern Argentina and central Chile. *Habitat:* Regions in which cliffs are abundant; farming country. *Identification:* Length, about 7 inches. Blue above, rufous below. *Long forked tail. Voice:* A cheerful, pleasant chippering. *Breeding:* Four to six eggs in mud nest, reinforced with straw, grass, twigs, etc., under eaves in barn, cave, etc. Will sometimes use nesting shelf. *Food:* Mostly insects, often caught over water.

174. OLIVE-SIDED FLYCATCHER
(NUTTALLORNIS MESOLEUCUS)

Range: Breeds from Alaska and Cape Breton Island south in coniferous forests to Lower California, Texas and North Carolina. Winters in northern South America. *Habitat:* Northern forests. *Identification:* Length, about 7½ inches. Likely to perch at extreme top of isolated, high tree—the most conspicuous place in sight. Dark of sides separated by white on belly. *White tufts on flanks,* as Audubon clearly shows. *Breeding:* Three to five eggs in high nest, usually in conifer. *Food:* Mostly insects.

175. SHORT-BILLED MARSH WREN

(CISTOTHORUS STELLARIS)

Range: Breeds from Saskatchewan and Maine to Kansas and Delaware. Winters from Illinois and New Jersey to Texas and Florida. *Habitat:* Wet, grassy meadows—*not* cattails. *Identification:* Length, about 4¼ inches. Back obscurely marked with white, line over eye dingier than in Long-bill. Brownish under tail. *Voice:* "*chap-chap-chap, chap, chap, chap-chap-p-p-p-r-r-r*" (Seton). Not so vigorous as in Long-bill. *Breeding:* Five to eight eggs in ball-shaped nest near ground. *Food:* Mostly insects and spiders.

176. SPRUCE GROUSE
(CANACHITES CANADENSIS)

Range: Alaska and Labrador to Minnesota and New England. *Habitat:* Northern coniferous forests, particularly near swamps. *Identification:* About 15 inches long. Male slaty; female browner, but lacks band that marks end of Ruffed Grouse's tail. So tame has long been called "Fool Hen." *Breeding:* Eight to fifteen eggs in nest of grass or leaves, on ground. *Food:* Buds, pine needles, berries, etc.

177. WHITE-CROWNED PIGEON

(COLUMBA LEUCOCEPHALA)

Range: From southern Florida Keys, Bahamas, to Panama. *Habitat:* Forests, thickets. On Florida Keys only in summer. *Identification:* Length, about 13½ inches. Slate-blue, crown white or whitish. *Voice:* "croohoo, coo-coo-coo" (Audubon). *Breeding:* One to two eggs; nest in mangrove—sometimes over water—royal palm, etc. *Food:* Fruits, seeds, etc. The diminution in numbers of this bird apparently results from destruction of the woods in which it lives, and from killing for food.

178. ORANGE-CROWNED WARBLER
(VERMIVORA CELATA)

Range: Breeds from Alaska and Manitoba to Lower California. Winters from San Francisco and Massachusetts (casually) to Guatemala. Races: Lutescent and Dusky Warblers. *Habitat:* Brushy areas. *Identification:* Length, about 5 inches. A nondescript little bird, greenish above, weak yellow below. No wing-bars. Orange crown patch often difficult to see. *Breeding:* Four or five eggs in nest on or near ground, in underbrush, thickets, etc. One of the first Warblers to arrive in the spring; often lingers late in the fall.

179. HOUSE WREN

(TROGLODYTES AËDON)

No bird so readily accepts the invitation offered by our bird houses as does the House Wren, and few avian neighbors have so many human friends. Its drab coloration is more than offset by its perky tameness, its almost explosive vitality, and its ever-bubbling song. If a bird box is not available, it will lay claim to a clothespin bag on the line, the mail box, an old hat, or any other receptacle that will hold its nest. See Plate 83. Often expresses intolerance of its neighbors by puncturing their eggs.

180. PINE SISKIN
(SPINUS PINUS)

Range: Breeds from Alaska and Quebec to Mexico (through high mountains), Nebraska, Maine, and the mountains of North Carolina. Winters over most of the United States. *Habitat:* Forests of North, or of high altitudes. *Identification:* Length, about 5 inches.

A markedly streaked bird with yellow in the wings and at base of forked tail. *Voice:* Suggests that of Goldfinch. *Breeding:* Four eggs, in coniferous trees. *Food:* Seeds, buds, insects, at times garden plants. Food habits generally beneficial.

181. GOLDEN EAGLE
(AQUILA CHRYSAËTOS)

Range: Breeds from Alaska and Mackenzie to Lower California and Oklahoma; formerly to North Carolina. In winter, south casually to Texas and Florida. *Habitat:* Usually remote mountains. Can be seen in some National Parks. *Identification:* Wing-spread up to 7½ feet. Adults, all dark. Young birds, some white in wings, and in tail where it contrasts with black tip. *Breeding:* Two to three eggs, usually on cliffs. *Food:* Mammals, birds. Generally so rare as to be harmless to man's interests.

182. GROUND DOVE
(COLUMBIGALLINA PASSERINA)

Range: From California and South Carolina to Guatemala; Bahamas, Bermuda, South America, etc. *Habitat:* Usually seen on the ground in gardens, along beaches, on fields. *Identification:* Length, about 6½ inches. Underwings reddish. The males sometimes ap-

pear at distance as red as Cardinals. *Voice:* A soft coo, often from an elevated perch. *Breeding:* Two eggs, on ground, in bushes, etc. *Food:* Mostly weed seeds. A common bird in the southern states, in winter, and one of the tamest.

183. GOLDEN-CROWNED KINGLET

(REGULUS SATRAPA)

Range: Breeds from Alaska and Cape Breton Island to New Mexico, Minnesota and, in the mountains, North Carolina. Winters from British Columbia, Iowa and New Brunswick to Guatemala. *Habitat:* Northern coniferous forests. *Identification:* Small size—length about 4 inches. Wing-bars. *Striped* face. (Ruby-crown has eye-ring.) Crown patch cannot always be seen. *Voice:* A thin *eee-eee,* like highest possible violin note. *Food:* Insects. Likely to be found late in fall in flocks of Chickadees and Nuthatches.

184. BLACK-THROATED MANGO

(ANTHRACOTHORAX NIGRICOLLIS)

Audubon recorded this Hummingbird as having been taken at Key West, but his evidence has not been deemed sufficient to justify its inclusion in the A.O.U. *Check-List*. Its normal range is from Pana-ma through Colombia, Venezuela, British Guiana, Brazil, Paraguay, Bolivia, Peru and Ecuador (Ridgway). This colorful and enchanting family is restricted entirely to the New World.

185. BACHMAN'S WARBLER

(VERMIVORA BACHMANI)

Range: Breeds from Missouri and Alabama to South Carolina; probably, also, in Indiana and North Carolina. Winters in Cuba. *Habitat:* Low, wet woods. *Identification:* Length, about 4¼ inches. Male, black on crown; large patch on throat and breast. Female, lacks black; gray on crown. No wing-bars. *Voice:* "a short, buzzing trill . . . resembling the song of the Worm-eating Warbler, but with the quality of the Parula's song." (Howell.) *Food:* Probably insects. Named by Audubon for his friend, John Bachman.

186. PRAIRIE CHICKEN
(TYMPANUCHUS CUPIDO)

Range: Alberta, Manitoba and Indiana to New Mexico and Louisiana. Now exterminated over much of range. Eastern race—the Heath Hen—completely wiped out. *Habitat:* Prairies, woodlands, swamps. *Identification:* A Hen-like bird, about 12 inches long. The transverse barring underneath, and the dark tail, differentiate it from the Sharp-tailed Grouse, which is light beneath and has white in tail. *Voice:* A cackle; a tooting or booming "like a distant outboard motor." *Food:* Insects, weed seeds, waste grains.

187. BOAT-TAILED GRACKLE
(CASSIDIX MEXICANUS)

Range: Delaware to Florida Keys, Texas and Colombia. *Habitat:* The coast, swamps, pond-edges, etc. *Identification:* Large size of male—about 16 inches long—and his gargantuan tail. Females, length about 13 inches. Brown, lighter line over eye. *Breeding:*

Three or four eggs in marsh vegetation, often over water. In colonies. *Food:* Crustaceans, insects, mollusks, grain. One of the most aquatic of "land" birds. Western race the Great-tailed Grackle. Allied races are found in western Mexico.

188. TREE SPARROW
(SPIZELLA ARBOREA)

Range: Breeds from Alaska and Quebec to British Columbia and Newfoundland. Winters from Nebraska and the Maritime Provinces to New Mexico and Georgia (rarely). *Habitat:* Weed and brush patches. *Identification:* Length, about 6 inches. Chestnut cap. Breast clear gray except for *spot in center*—which Audubon seems to have omitted. Wing-bars. *Voice:* A lovely, clear simple melody that can scarcely be described. *Breeding:* Four to five eggs on or near ground, in northern forests or beyond their limits. *Food:* Weed seeds.

189. SNOW BUNTING

(PLECTROPHENAX NIVALIS)

Range: Breeds from at least 83° N. latitude to the northern parts of the mainland from Alaska and northern Quebec. Also in Old World Arctic and sub-Arctic. Winters from Unalaska and Quebec to the northern United States. Casually south. *Habitat:* When in the United States, on prairies, ploughed fields, beaches. *Identification:* Length, about 7 inches. A black or brown and *white* bird, that travels in flocks—often of considerable size. *Food:* In winter, largely weed seeds. Common on barrier beaches.

190. YELLOW-BELLIED SAPSUCKER
(SPHYRAPICUS VARIUS)

Range: Breeds from Alaska and Cape Breton Island to Arizona and North Carolina. Winters to Panama. The distinctive races of this bird are known as Red-naped and Red-breasted Sapsuckers. (See Plate 416.) *Habitat:* Wooded areas. *Identification:* Red-breasted has entire head, neck and chest red. Red-naped has black chest separating red throat and yellow belly. The Yellow-belly, as pictured. Length, about 8 inches. Drills sap-wells in living trees; these holes as regular as corn on cob.

191. WILLOW PTARMIGAN
(LAGOPUS LAGOPUS)

Range: Alaska and Greenland to British Columbia and Newfoundland. Winters as far south as Saskatchewan and Quebec. Rarely migrates to northern United States. *Habitat*: Brushy areas, tundra, etc. *Identification*: Length, about 15 inches. A brown, Chicken-like bird, with varying amounts of white in plumage. In winter largely white. *Breeding*: Seven to eleven eggs in ground nest. *Food*: Leaves, fruits, insects, buds, twigs. Races include Ungava, Allen's, Alaska and Alexander's Ptarmigan. Other races in Old World.

192. NORTHERN SHRIKE

(LANIUS BOREALIS)

Range: Breeds from Alaska and Ungava to British Columbia and Quebec. Winters south to California and Virginia. *Habitat:* When with us is usually seen perched on an exposed tree-top, telephone wire, fence, etc. *Identification:* A black and gray bird, with a white patch in wing. Black mask through eye. *Lower mandible horn-color.* (See Plate 57.) *Finely barred below.* Length, about 10 inches. *Food:* Birds, mice, insects, carrion. Impales prey on thorns presumably because its feet are too weak to hold food.

193. LINCOLN'S SPARROW

(MELOSPIZA LINCOLNI)

Range: Breeds from Alaska and Newfoundland to New Mexico (in the mountains) and Nova Scotia. Winters from California and Pennsylvania to Guatemala. Casual south of Washington, D. C., east of the Alleghanies. *Habitat:* Brushy fields, edges of clearings, etc.

Identification: Length, about 5¾ inches. Like a pale Song Sparrow, with lightly streaked breast, across which is *a broad buffy band.* *Breeding:* Four to five eggs, on ground in marshy area. *Food:* Insects, weed seeds, etc.

194. HUDSONIAN CHICKADEE
(PENTHESTES HUDSONICUS)

Range: Breeds from Alaska and Labrador to British Columbia and the Adirondacks. In winter to Illinois, Pennsylvania and Massachusetts. Races: Columbian and Acadian Chickadees. *Habitat:* Coniferous woodlands. *Identification:* Length, about 5½ inches. Resembles Black-capped Chickadee, but cap is brown instead of black; brownish on back and sides. *Voice: Chick-dee-dee,* where Black-cap often says *Chick-a-dee-dee-dee. Breeding:* Six to seven eggs, in hollow tree or stump. *Food:* Insects, seeds, etc. See Plate 160.

195. RUBY-CROWNED KINGLET

(CORTHYLIO CALENDULA)

Range: Breeds from Alaska and Quebec to Lower California and Nova Scotia. Winters from British Columbia and Virginia to Guatemala. *Habitat:* Northern forests. *Identification:* Small size—length about 4 inches. Male's scarlet crown often concealed. A dull green bird, lighter below, with *prominent wing-bars* and *eye-ring*. Golden-crown has *striped face. Voice:* A weak *tsip,* that one may easily overlook. A rich, ringing, warbling song. In fall, spring, and winter frequently associated with Chickadees, Nuthatches, etc.

196. GYRFALCON

(FALCO RUSTICOLUS)

In the Arctic wastes where this great Falcon makes its home (see Plate 366) it is supreme—at the top of its food chain. Lowly land plants, or marine diatoms, transmute inorganic into organic substances in a natural laboratory whose wonders have not yet been plumbed by science. The plants feed Ptarmigan or lemmings, and small fish which are eaten in turn by Murres and Puffins. Upon these creatures feeds the Gyrfalcon, perhaps the most superb predator in the bird world.

197. RED CROSSBILL

(LOXIA CURVIROSTRA)

Range: Breeds from Alaska and Quebec to Guatemala, and Georgia in high mountains. Winters to Nebraska, Texas, District of Columbia, and Central America. Races are found in Europe and Asia. *Habitat:* Northern forests. Occasionally comes to feeding stations in winter. *Identification: Crossed mandibles.* Male red, with dark wings and tail. Female, greenish, with dark wings and tail; streaked. Length, about 6 inches. No wing-bars. *Voice:* Song said to resemble Goldfinch's. *Food:* Cone seeds, insects, etc.

198. SWAINSON'S WARBLER

(LYMNOTHLYPIS SWAINSONI)

Range: Breeds from Oklahoma and Virginia to Louisiana and Florida. Winters in Jamaica and Yucatan. *Habitat:* Swampy river-bottoms and wet woods. *Identification:* Length, about 6 inches. Light stripe over eye; like Worm-eating Warbler except for lack of heavily streaked crown. *Voice:* "resembles that of the Louisiana Water-Thrush" (Howell). *Breeding:* Three to four eggs in rather low nest, usually in or near a growth of cane. *Food:* Probably mostly insects.

199. SAW-WHET OWL

(CRYPTOGLAUX ACADICA)

Range: Breeds from Alaska and Nova Scotia to Mexico, Nebraska and Maryland. Winters to southern California and Virginia. *Habitat:* Woodlands. In winter, likely to be found in pine or cedar grove. Sometimes appears in cities. *Identification:* Small size—about 8 inches long—and absence of "ear-tufts." *Streaked* "forehead," whereas that of Richardson's Owl is spotted. Facial disk more pronounced than in Pygmy Owl. Often so tame it may be caught in the hand. *Voice:* Like noise of sharpening saw. *Food:* Mostly mice.

200. HORNED LARK
(OTOCORIS ALPESTRIS)

Range: Breeds from Alaska and Hudson Strait to Mexico and Virginia. Winters to Sonora and Florida. Sixteen races are listed in the A.O.U. *Check-List.* Additional races are found in Mexico, Colombia, Asia and Europe. *Habitat:* Open country. Breeds on golf courses. In winter on roads, prairies, beaches. *Identification:* Length, about 7 inches. Walks. In winter, travels in flocks. Black moustache marks, and crescent on throat; above crescent, white or yellow. White outer tail feathers. An early breeder.

201. CANADA GOOSE
(BRANTA CANADENSIS)

Range: Breeds from Alaska and Baffin Island to California and Tennessee. Winters from south of the frost line to Mexico and Florida. Races include: Lesser Canada, White-cheeked, Hutchins's and Cackling Geese. *Habitat:* Lakes, sloughs, marshes—on migration, grain-fields. *Identification:* Long black neck, white face patch. Often flies in V's; so do Cormorants, but they stop flapping once in a while, to sail, and they lack the conspicuous white belly of "Honkers." *Voice:* A trumpeting *her-ronk*. See Plate 277.

202. RED-THROATED LOON
(GAVIA STELLATA)

Range: Breeds from Alaska and Greenland to British Columbia and Newfoundland. Also throughout Arctic Europe and Asia. Winters from the Aleutian Islands to Lower California, and from the Great Lakes and Gulf of St. Lawrence to Florida. In the Old World, to the Mediterranean and South China. *Habitat:* In winter, most often seen just off coast. *Identification:* Size of small Goose; spotted back; slender bill, *seemingly* somewhat upturned. Loons habitually "fold" necks, whereas Grebes carry them upright.

203. K I N G R A I L
(RALLUS ELEGANS)

Range: Breeds from Kansas, Nebraska and Massachusetts to Texas and Florida. Winters mainly in the southern part of its breeding range. An allied race occurs in Cuba. *Habitat:* Fresh-water marshes. *Identification:* Large size—length about 18 inches. Long, down-curved bill. Warm brown plumage; similar Clapper is grayish, and a salt-water bird. *Voice:* A deep, quick *bup-bup-bup-bup. Breeding:* Ten to fourteen eggs in grassy nest, often over water. *Food:* Seeds, small aquatic animals.

204. CLAPPER RAIL

(RALLUS LONGIROSTRIS)

Range: Breeds on coastal salt marshes from Connecticut to Texas. Winters from New York south. Five races occur in the United States, others in the West Indies and South America. *Habitat:* As above. *Identification:* Length, about 14 inches. (See Plate 203.)

Voice: A dry, reedy, rather slow *keck-keck-keck-keck;* especially noisy about sunrise. *Breeding:* Six to twelve eggs in grassy nest. *Food:* Insects, mollusks, crustaceans, weed seeds. Often flushed from ditch on marsh.

205. VIRGINIA RAIL
(RALLUS LIMICOLA)

Range: Breeds from British Columbia and New Brunswick to Mexico and North Carolina. Winters from Utah and North Carolina to Guatemala and Florida. *Identification:* A small brown Rail—length about 9 inches—with rather long, *reddish* bill. *Voice:* A reedy *kee-dick, kee-dick.* Grunts, calls in great variety. *Breeding:* Seven to twelve eggs in nest of grass and reeds, often above water. *Food:* Seeds, insects, mollusks, worms, snakes, fish, etc.

206. WOOD DUCK

(AIX SPONSA)

Range: Breeds locally in almost every one of the United States and southern Canadian provinces. Winters from British Columbia and Massachusetts to Mexico and Jamaica. *Habitat:* Wooded swamps where there are hollow trees. *Identification:* A small Duck—length about 18 inches—with *crest*, less noticeable in female than in male. Short neck and narrow white line on rear edge of wing, in flight. *Voice: Hoo-eek.* This bird has increased significantly since hunting of it was curtailed.

207. WHITE-BELLIED BOOBY

(SULA LEUCOGASTER)

Range: Breeds on the Bahamas, some of the West Indies, islands off Central and South America, and Ascension Island. Winters throughout its breeding range. Additional races occur in Australia and New Caledonia. *Habitat:* Keys and coasts. *Identification:* About 30 inches long, 4 feet spread. Plumage brown, except for *white belly*. Bill and feet yellow. This bird was breeding in the Dry Tortugas when Audubon visited them, but has long since moved elsewhere. It is now only a casual visitant to these islands.

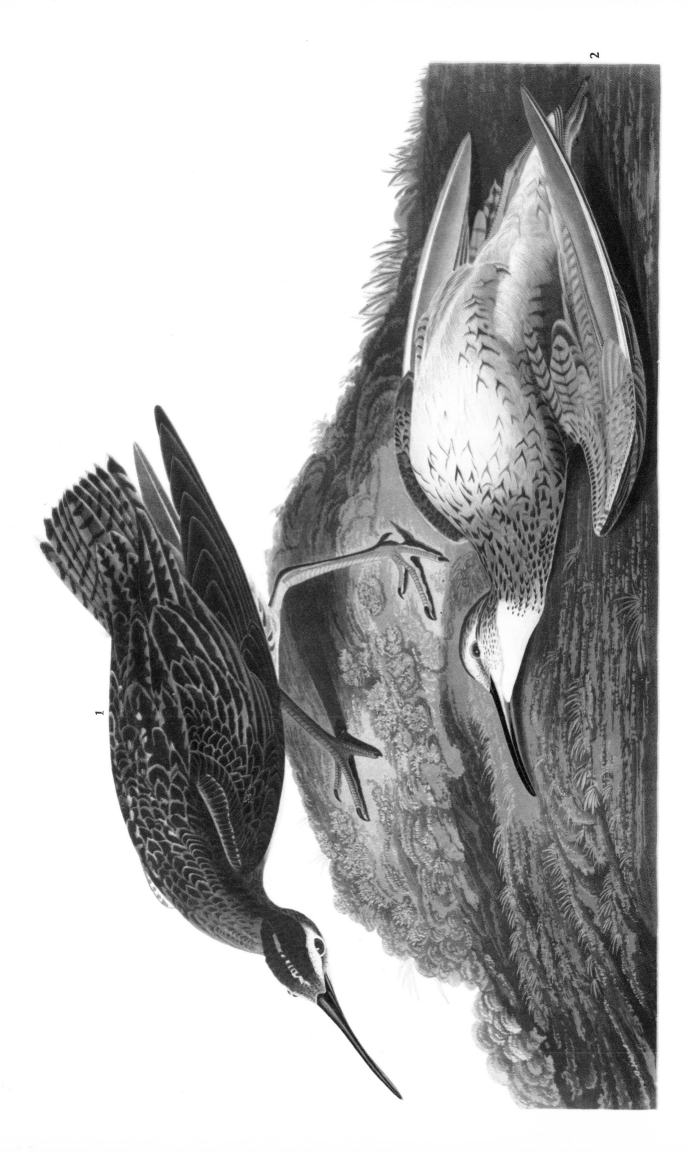

208. ESKIMO CURLEW
(PHAEOPUS BOREALIS)

Range: Formerly bred on the Barren Grounds of northern Mackenzie. Wintered in Argentina, Patagonia and Chile. *Identification:* Decurved bill. *Cinnamon wing linings. Primaries unbarred. So rare scrutinized. This erstwhile abundant bird was brought to the verge of extinction by market gunners and game hogs. While most shorebirds have increased under closed seasons, it is not certain enough

209. WILSON'S PLOVER

(PAGOLLA WILSONIA)

Range: Breeds from Virginia to the Bahamas and Texas. Winters from Florida to Texas, Brazil and the West Indies. Additional races are found in the West Indies, and from Lower California to Peru. *Habitat:* Beaches, tide-flats. *Identification:* Length about 7½ inches. Breast band. Darker and larger than Snowy Plover; bill blacker and *much heavier* than that of Semipalmated Plover. *Voice:* "a Tern-like quip" (Nichols). *Breeding:* Three to four eggs, in hollow in sand—no nest.

210. LEAST BITTERN
(IXOBRYCHUS EXILIS)

Range: Breeds from North Dakota and Quebec to the West Indies and Mexico; from Oregon to Guatemala. Winters from Georgia and Texas, and from southern California and Arizona to Guatemala. Other trees occur in South America. *Habitat:* Marshes. *Identifica-*

tion: Small size—length about 13 inches—large yellowish wing patch. *Voice:* Like a Mourning Dove imitating a Pied-billed Grebe. *Breeding:* Three to six eggs in marshes. *Food:* Small aquatic ani-

211. GREAT BLUE HERON

(ARDEA HERODIAS)

Range: Breeds from Alaska and Nova Scotia to Mexico, Bermuda. Winters from Alaska and New York south. Races include: Ward's, Treganza's, Northwest Coast and California Herons. *Habitat:* Ponds, marshes, tidal estuaries, river-banks. *Identification:* Large size—length about 4 feet, wing-spread about 6. Slate-gray coloration. Confused with Cranes, but these fly with neck outstretched, whereas Herons fly with neck folded. *Food:* Mice, fish, snakes, etc. Accused of decimating trout, actually it eats their enemies.

1

212. RING-BILLED GULL

(LARUS DELAWARENSIS)

Range: Breeds mainly on interior lakes—from Alaska and the Gulf of St. Lawrence to Colorado and New York. Winters from British Columbia and Maine to Cuba and Mexico. *Habitat:* A common winter Gull. *Identification:* Yellowish or greenish feet, shared with California and Short-billed Gulls. Short-bill has smaller bill; California is darker on back. Length, about 18 inches. In brown, immature plumage, a well-marked band near end of tail. *Food:* Insects mice, garbage.

213 . ATLANTIC PUFFIN
(FRATERCULA ARCTICA)

Range: Breeds from Greenland and Ungava to Maine; also from Norway and the British Isles to Portugal. Winters to New York, occasionally (Montauk Point), Morocco and the Azores. *Habitat:* Breeds on lonely coasts and islands. In winter, seen off-shore. *Iden-*

tification: Length, about a foot. Large, colorful bill, which has given it the name "Sea Parrot." Bumblebee-like flight. *Breeding:* One egg, under a rock or in burrow excavated by birds or rabbits. *Food:* Mostly fish.

214. RAZOR-BILLED AUK

(ALCA TORDA)

Range: Breeds from Greenland and Labrador to the Bay of Fundy; from Iceland to the British Isles and Norway. Winters from Labrador and Ontario to New York (Montauk Point), and from the British Isles to the Canaries. *Habitat:* Rocky shores. *Identification:*

Large black and white bill. On water, cocks up tail. Wren-fashion (Peterson). Length, about 17 inches. *Voice:* "hoarse guttural notes or low croaking sounds" (Bent). *Breeding:* One egg, under shelter of rock. *Food:* Shrimps, mollusks, fish.

215. NORTHERN PHALAROPE
(Lobipes lobatus)

Range: Breeds from Alaska and Greenland to the Aleutian Islands and Ungava; from Iceland to Siberia. Migrates to Patagonia, Africa and Asia. *Habitat:* Prairie sloughs, ocean. *Identification:* Length, about 7 inches. Thin bill, black legs, marked wing-stripe, habit of spinning about as it feeds—other Phalaropes do this—and the fact that it may be seen well at sea, as are other Phalaropes. *Breeding:* Four eggs in ground nest. Female, the brightly colored bird, takes the initiative in courtship; male incubates.

216. WOOD IBIS
(MYCTERIA AMERICANA)

Range: Gulf Coast from Texas to South Carolina; south to Argentina and Peru. *Habitat:* Swamps and marshes. *Identification:* Large white bird with black wing-tips; spread, about 5½ feet. Neck and legs outstretched in flight. Flaps and soars. Heavy decurved bill, and head, black. This bird is a Stork. *Breeding:* Two to three eggs, in nests that may be 100 feet high; in swamp. *Food:* Fish, alligators, rats, snakes, etc. May often be seen from one's car on the Tamiami Trail and other Florida highways.

217 · LOUISIANA HERON

(HYDRANASSA TRICOLOR)

Range: Breeds from North Carolina and Lower California to West Indies and Central America. Winters from Lower California and South Carolina south. Related races occur in South America and Trinidad. *Habitat:* Swamps and marshes. *Identification:* A small,

delicate Heron—length about 2 feet. Bluish neck and back, white belly. *Voice:* An explosive grunt, as of disgust. *Breeding:* Three to five eggs, in heronries, in low nests. *Food:* Fish, crustaceans, worms, insects. Another roadside bird, in the South.

218. ATLANTIC MURRE
(URIA AALGE)

Range: Breeds from Greenland and Labrador to Nova Scotia; winters south to Maine. California race breeds from St. Matthew Island to California; winters to southern California. *Habitat:* Rocky coasts; in winter, the sea. *Identification:* Length, about 16 inches. Coltern, much like Razor-bill's, but *slender bill. Voice:* "a hoarse ing guttural note" (Audubon). *Breeding:* One egg, on roc

219. BLACK GUILLEMOT
(CEPPHUS GRYLLE)

Range: Breeds from Siberia and the Arctic coasts to Maine; from Iceland to Scotland. Winters to Lake Ontario, Cape Cod; and northern France. Northern race is Mandt's Guillemot. *Habitat:* Rocky shores. *Identification:* Length, about 1 foot. In breeding plumage, like a White-winged Scoter—velvet black with white wing-patch, red bill and feet. In winter plumage, whitish but with white patches still notable in dark wings. *Breeding:* One to two eggs, in crevice in rocks. *Food:* Fish, mollusks, crustaceans.

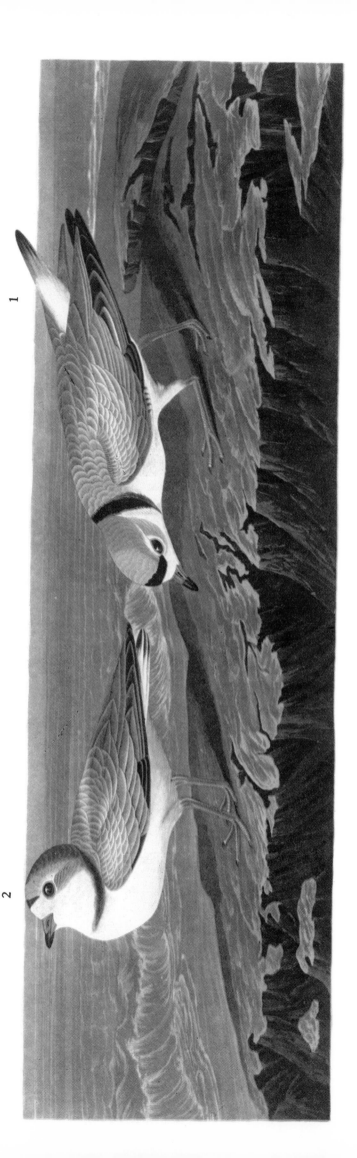

220. PIPING PLOVER
(CHARADRIUS MELODUS)

Range: Breeds locally from Alberta and Prince Edward Island to Nebraska and North Carolina. Winters on the coast from South Carolina to Texas. *Habitat:* Sandy beaches. *Identification:* Length, about 7 inches. Breast band often incomplete. Bill yellowish at base —Snowy Plover's bill black. Very light coloration. *Voice:* A sweet, melancholy *peép-lo. Breeding:* Four eggs, in hollow in sand. *Food:* Small crustaceans, fish, insects—especially tiger beetles. Since legal shooting of this bird has stopped, it has increased notably.

221. MALLARD
(ANAS PLATYRHYNCHOS)

Range: Breeds from Alaska and Nova Scotia to Lower California and Virginia; also in Europe and Asia. Winters from the Aleutians and Maryland to Panama, also to Africa, India, Burma, Borneo. *Habitat:* Marshes, ponds, rivers, swamps. *Identification:* Male— green head, white neck-band, white in tail. Female, white fringe around tail; lighter brown than black duck. *Breeding:* Eight to twelve eggs, in ground nest lined with down; often some distance from water. *Food:* Aquatic and marsh plants, mollusks, insects.

1

2

222. WHITE IBIS
(GUARA ALBA)

Range: Breeds from Lower California and South Carolina to Venezuela and Peru. Winters from Mexico and Florida southward. *Habitat:* Swamps, marshes, ponds. *Identification:* Length, about 2 feet. A white plumaged bird with black wingtips and bill. *Food:* Fishes, insects, crayfish, water moccasins, etc. The numbers of this bird were greatly reduced through human killing. Under protec-

and *feet. Breeding:* Four eggs, usually in low nest, in colony.

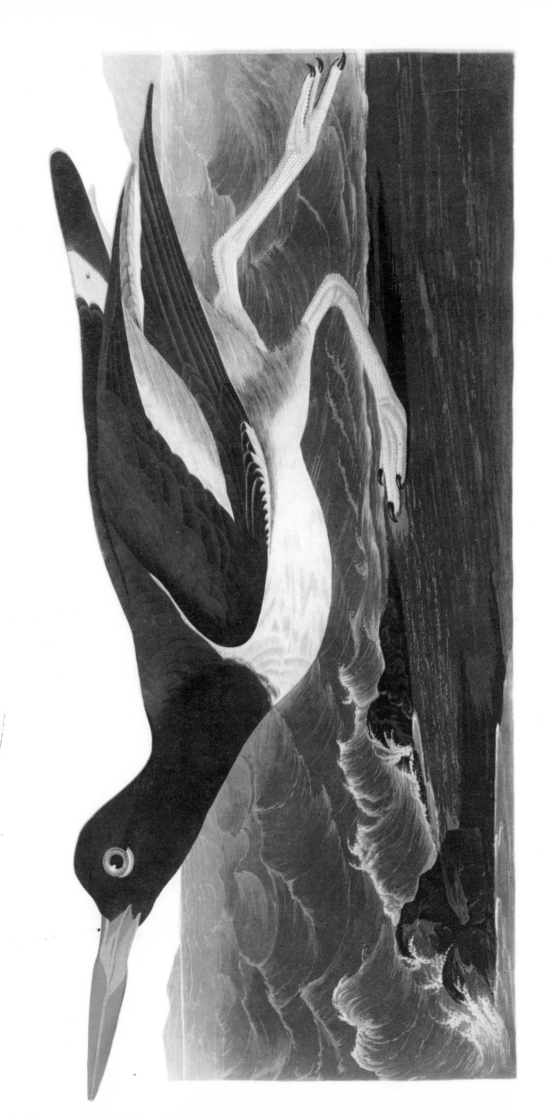

223. OYSTER-CATCHER
(HAEMATOPUS PALLIATUS)

Range: Breeds locally along the coast from Virginia and Lower California to Brazil. *Habitat:* Beaches and reefs. *Identification:* About 1½ feet long. Black hood, brown back, white belly. *Large red bill, pink legs.* Black Oyster-catcher (see Plate 427) has *black*

belly; found only in West. *Voice:* "*wheep, wheep, wheep, wheeop,* both vehement and penetrating" (Bent). *Breeding:* Two to three eggs, in hollows in sand. *Food:* Oysters, clams, echinoderms, crabs, worms, and other small animals of the littoral.

224. KITTIWAKE
(RISSA TRIDACTYLA)

Range: Breeds from Siberia and Baffin Island to Kamchatka and Gulf of St. Lawrence. Winters south to Lower California and New Jersey. *Habitat:* Rarely comes to land in winter—likely to be seen off-shore. *Identification:* Length, about 16 inches. *Black* legs and feet; solid black wing-tip, cut off perpendicular to the axis of the wing. *Voice:* "suggests its name" (Bent). *Breeding:* Two to three eggs on rocky islands and cliffs. *Food:* Fish, crustaceans, worms. One of the most pelagic of gulls.

225. KILLDEER
(OXYECHUS VOCIFERUS)

Range: Breeds from British Columbia and Quebec to Mexico. Winters from British Columbia and New York to Peru. Allied races are found in the West Indies and Peru. *Habitat:* Pastures, dumps, golf courses, mud-flats, etc. *Identification:* Length, about 10 inches. A brown bird with tawny rump and *two* breast bands. *Voice:* A thin whistled *kill-dee, kill-dee. Breeding:* Four eggs in ground nest that may or may not be lined. *Food:* A varied diet, including many destructive insects.

226. WHOOPING CRANE

(GRUS AMERICANA)

Range: Formerly bred from Mackenzie and Hudson Bay to Nebraska and Iowa; and in migration not uncommon from New England to Georgia. Wintered from the Gulf states to central Mexico. Now reduced to a few in a Texas refuge. *Habitat:* Marshes. *Identifica-*

tion: Great size: length, about 53 inches, spread about 7 feet. White with black wing-tips, small bill (Ibises have long curved bills), long legs (Snow Geese have short legs). Neck and legs extended in flight, as in all Cranes.

227. PINTAIL

(DAFILA ACUTA)

Range: Breeds from Alaska and James Bay to California and, rarely, Pennsylvania. Winters from British Columbia and New York to the West Indies and Panama; also in the Hawaiian Islands. Allied races occur in Europe, West Indies, Asia and North Africa. *Habitat:* Marshes, rivers, ponds, bays. *Identification:* Length, about 2 feet; *long, slender neck.* White line up side of neck in male; elongated middle tail feathers. Female a rather light gray Duck, with *white band at rear edge of wing.*

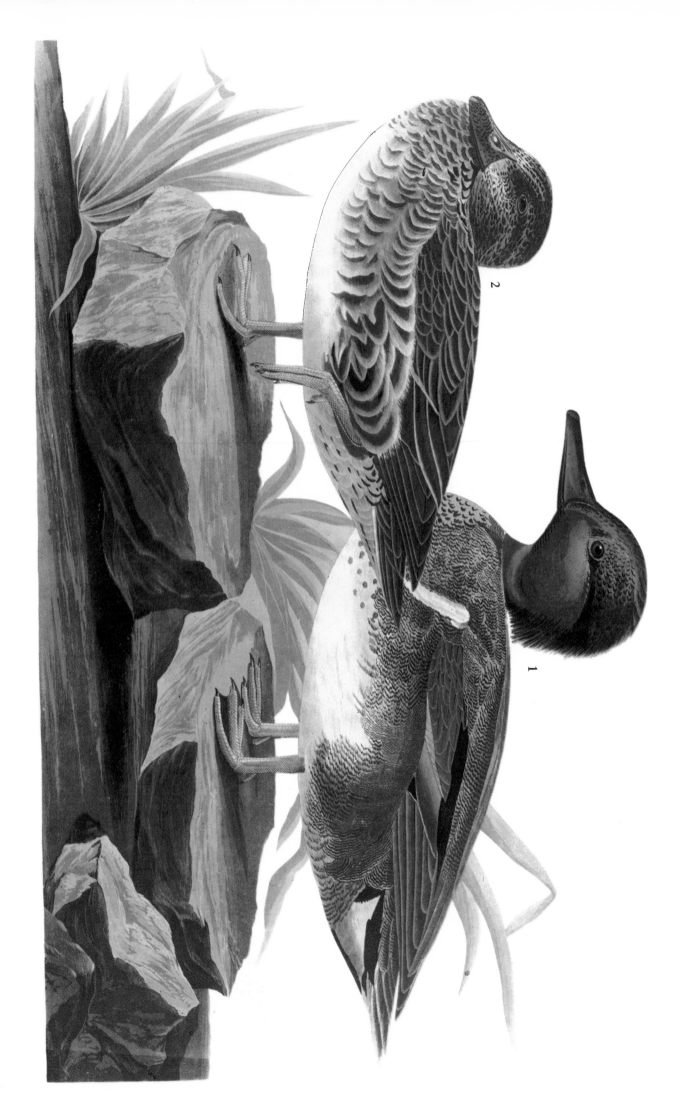

228. GREEN-WINGED TEAL

(NETTION CAROLINENSE)

Range: Breeds from Alaska and Ungava to California and Quebec. Winters from British Columbia and Chesapeake Bay to Honduras. *Habitat:* Marshes, rivers, lakes, etc. *Identification:* Small size—length about 14 inches. On water, male shows prominent white mark in front of wing; chestnut and green head. Female, in good light, shows glowing green wing-patch. *Voice:* A two-syllabled, clinking whistle in male; soft quack in female. *Breeding:* Six to twelve eggs in ground nest. One of the sportiest of our Ducks.

229. LESSER SCAUP DUCK
(NYROCA AFFINIS)

Range: Breeds from Alaska and Ontario to British Columbia. Winters from British Columbia and New Jersey to Panama. *Habitat:* Lakes, ponds, marshes. In winter, coastal waters. *Identification:* Length, about 16½ inches. Male, dark head, breast, and tail; whitish back and sides (at distance); *purple* head reflection at close range; wing-stripe short—actually shorter than in Audubon's picture. Female, brown with white patch at base of bill; same wing-stripe. More southern in range than Greater Scaup

230. SANDERLING
(CROCETHIA ALBA)

Range: Breeds on the Arctic islands, Southampton, north Greenland, Iceland, Spitzbergen, north Siberia. Winters from California and Virginia to Patagonia. Also to South Africa, Japan and various Pacific islands. *Habitat:* Principally at edge of surf, *where it follows*

waves up and down beach. Identification: Length, about 8 inches. *Marked wing-stripe.* Warm brownish coloration in spring; whitest of Sandpipers in fall and winter. *Black legs and bill. Voice:* "a soft *ket, ket, ket*" (Nichols). *Food* Crustaceans, insects, mollusks, etc.

231. LONG-BILLED CURLEW
(NUMENIUS AMERICANUS)

Range: Breeds in Utah, Idaho and Nevada. Winters from California and Arizona to Guatemala; formerly from South Carolina to Texas. *Habitat:* Prairies. *Identification:* The largest of our shorebirds—length, about 2 feet. Long, *decurved* bill. *Absence of dark* line through eye. Cinnamon under wings. *Breeding:* Four eggs in prairie grass. *Food:* Insects, crustaceans, berries. The Sickle-bill is one of the casualties of expanding civilization, through human encroachment on its prairie habitat.

232. HOODED MERGANSER
(LOPHODYTES CUCULLATUS)

Range: Breeds from British Columbia and New Brunswick to New Mexico and New York. Winters from southern Alaska and Massachusetts to Cuba and Mexico. *Habitat:* Smaller bodies of water. *Identification:* Small size—length about 17½ inches. Pointed Merganser bill. Relatively long neck. Male, white cockade, *edged with black.* Female, may be known from other Mergansers by *dark face and throat;* from female Wood Duck, by large white wing-patch. Mergansers fly with neck straight out and body-axis parallel to earth.

233. SORA
(PORZANA CAROLINA)

Range: Breeds from British Columbia and Nova Scotia to Lower California and Maryland. Winters from California and Florida to Venezuela and Peru. *Habitat:* Marshes. *Identification:* Length, about 9 inches. A gray-brown, Chicken-like bird, with *short yellow*

bill. Dark face. *Voice:* A loud, whistled *ker-wee*. *Breeding:* Six to eighteen eggs, often in cattails, over water. *Food:* Mollusks, insects, seeds, etc. Rails are more often seen than heard. A pistol fired into their breeding marsh will often evoke cries.

234. RING-NECKED DUCK
(NYROCA COLLARIS)

Range: Breeds from British Columbia and Ontario to Arizona. Winters from British Columbia and Chesapeake Bay to Guatemala. *Habitat:* Marshes, ponds, sloughs. *Identification:* Length, about 16½ inches. A small, dark-backed Scaup, with white of flanks cutting up in front of folded wing. Female, brown with *light face.* Both sexes with blue ring near tip of bill. Gray wing-stripe. *Breeding:* Six to twelve eggs in wet marsh, etc. *Food:* Pondweeds, crustaceans, mollusks, insects, etc.

235. SOOTY TERN

(STERNA FUSCATA)

Range: Breeds from the Bahamas and Dry Tortugas to Venezuela. Winters from Louisiana to the Falkland Islands. *Habitat:* Tropical and subtropical seas and beaches. *Identification:* Black above, white below, white forehead, white outer tail feathers. Somewhat like Black Skimmer's pattern, but that bird larger, with white rear edge of wing and enormous bill. Length, about 16 inches. *Breeding:* One egg, in hollow in sand. *Food:* Fish, picked up from surface. Most Terns dive for food.

236. BLACK-CROWNED NIGHT HERON
(NYCTICORAX NYCTICORAX)

Range: Breeds from Oregon and Quebec to Paraguay. Winters from California and New York southward. An allied race is found in the Eastern Hemisphere. *Habitat:* Marshes, swamps. Comes into cities, at times, to seek winter roosts. *Identification:* "a wide band of black supported by broad gray wings" (Bent). Bittern-like young, *lack* Bittern's black wing-tips. Length, about 25 inches. *Voice:* A guttural *quawk. Breeding:* Three to five eggs, in heronry. *Food:* Meadow mice, fish, snakes, crustaceans, etc.

237. HUDSONIAN CURLEW
(PHAEOPUS HUDSONICUS)

Range: Breeds from Alaska to Manitoba. Winters from Lower California to Honduras, from Ecuador to Chile, from British Guiana to the Amazon. *Habitat:* A regular visitant to coastal salt marshes. *Identification:* The common Curlew. Length, about 17 inches. *Long decurved bill.* Duck-like flocking. *Voice:* A series of mellow whistles, usually on one low pitch—*whoi-whoi-whoi-whoi*. *Food:* Crustaceans, insects, berries. Much of the feeding territory of this stirring bird has been destroyed by ditching.

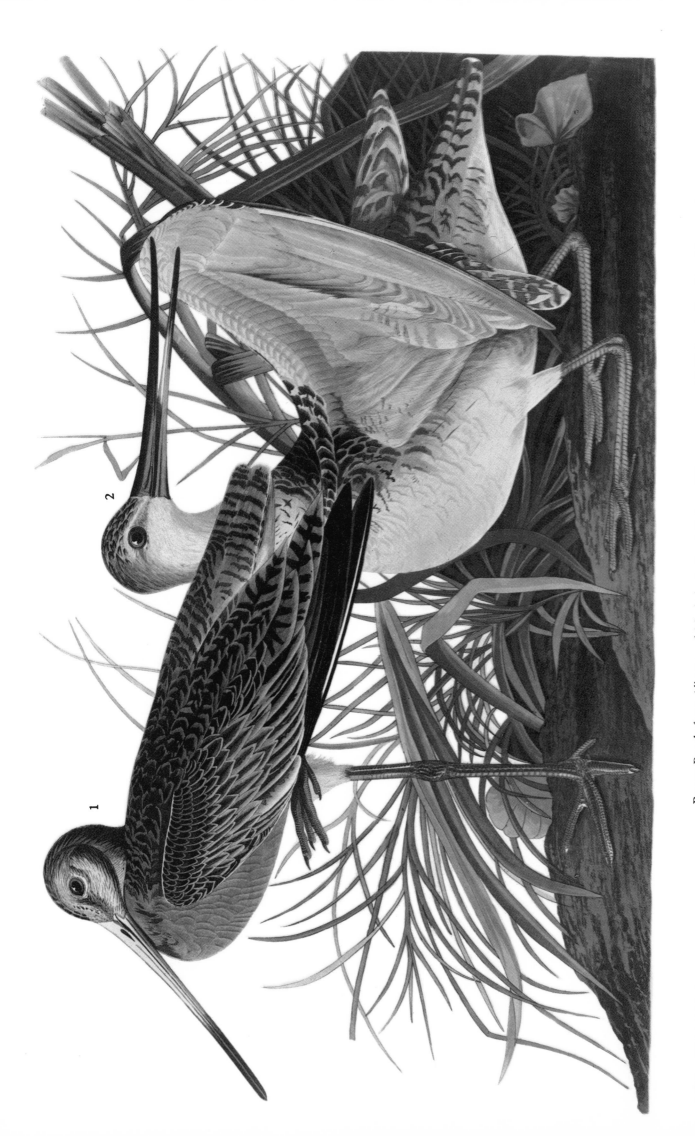

238. MARBLED GODWIT
(LIMOSA FEDOA)

Range: Breeds from Alberta and Manitoba to South Dakota. Winters from California and Georgia to Peru. *Habitat:* Prairies, mudflats. *Identification: Large size*—length, about 17 inches. *Long bill, slightly upturned.* A streaked buffy bird. *Voice:* "go-wit, go-wit, go-wit" (Roberts). *Breeding:* Three to four eggs in cup on prairie. Although this bird has suffered greatly from the white man's invasion of its prairie domain, the last few years have witnessed a slight increase. Abundant in West.

239. COOT

(FULICA AMERICANA)

Range: Breeds from British Columbia and New Brunswick to Mexico, New Jersey and, sporadically, Florida. Winters from Alaska and Massachusetts to the West Indies and Costa Rica. *Habitat:* Marshes, rivers, ponds. *Identification:* Length, about 14½ inches. A Chicken-like slate-gray bird with an *ivory-white bill.* When swimming, often jerks head back and forth as does a mechanical Duck. *Voice:* Almost infinite variety—cackles, groans, grunts, whistles, bleats—and in its incessant fighting splashes water noisily.

240. ROSEATE TERN

(STERNA DOUGALLI)

Range: Breeds locally from Nova Scotia to Venezuela and British Honduras; in Europe from 57° N. latitude to the Mediterranean, in Africa, Ceylon and China. Winters from Louisiana to Brazil. Allied races occur in Australia and the Indian Ocean. *Habitat:* Coast. *Iden-*tification: Very long outer tail feathers—reaching beyond wings when at rest. Pale back and wings. *Bill nearly or entirely black.* See other Terns. Rose flush on breast rarely visible. *Voice:* A strong *kak. Food:* Primarily fish.

241. GREAT BLACK-BACKED GULL
(LARUS MARINUS)

Range: Breeds from Labrador and Greenland to Maine; also the British Isles, Scandinavia and Russia. Winters from Greenland to the Great Lakes and Delaware Bay; and to the coast of Senegal. *Habitat:* Rocky coasts, lakes, ocean shores, rivers. *Identification:* Length, about 2½ feet. *Black* mantle. Brown immature may be known by large size and *heavy bill. Voice:* A deep *kah-h. Breeding:* Two to three eggs in ground nest of grass, rubbish, etc. *Food:* Eggs, young birds, carrion.

242. SNOWY EGRET
(EGRETTA THULA)

Range: Breeds from Long Island and Missouri to Texas; and from Utah and California to Lower California (Brewster's race). Winters from Florida and Mexico southward. In late summer may wander north of the Canadian border. *Habitat:* Swamps and marshes.

Identification: A *small* white Heron—length about 2 feet—with *black legs* and *yellow feet*. When feeding, will stir mud vigorously with foot. *Breeding:* In heronries. Three to four eggs, in flimsy nests, rather close to water. *Food:* Crustaceans, insects, frogs, etc.

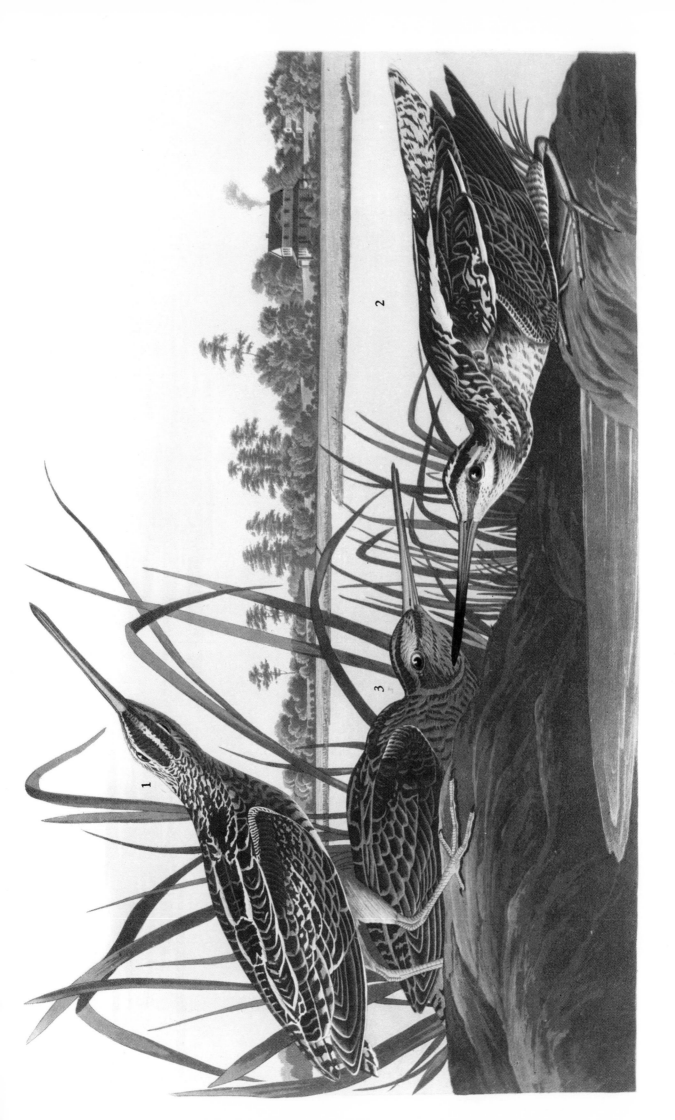

243. WILSON'S SNIPE
(CAPELLA DELICATA)

Range: Breeds from Alaska and Ungava to California and Pennsylvania. Winters from Alaska and Virginia to Brazil. *Habitat:* Marshes, bogs, wet meadows. *Identification:* Length, about 11 inches. Very long bill. As it rises, zigzags away, crying *scaipe*. Pointed wings.

Breeding: Four eggs in ground nest, in marsh or near it. *Food:* Worms, insects, etc. One of the two shore-birds remaining on the open list, this species has probably suffered far more from drainage than from shooting.

244. FLORIDA GALLINULE
(GALLINULA CHLOROPUS)

Range: Breeds from California and Vermont to Panama, the Galápagos Islands and Bermuda. Winters from California and South Carolina southward. *Habitat:* Marshes, swamps, heavily vegetated ponds. *Identification:* A gray, Chicken-like water bird with very long toes and a large red patch at the base of its *red, yellow-tipped bill.* Length, about 13 inches. *Voice:* Varied cackles. *Breeding:* Eight to twelve eggs in reedy nest in marsh grasses. *Food:* Snails, insects, worms, seeds, etc.

245. BRÜNNICH'S MURRE

(URIA LOMVIA)

Range: Breeds from Siberia and Greenland to the Aleutian and Magdalen Islands. Winters south to Japan and New York. Western race: Pallas's Murre. *Habitat:* Rocky coasts. In winter, off east coast of United States, and rarely in interior. *Identification:* Audubon shows it in winter plumage, as we are likely to see it. May be separated from Atlantic Murre by flesh-colored edge of lower mandible. Thinner bill than Razor-billed Auk. *Food:* Fish, crustaceans and mollusks.

2

1

1

246. AMERICAN EIDER
(SOMATERIA MOLLISSIMA)

Range: Breeds from Labrador and Greenland to Maine; also on Hudson Bay and James Bay. Winters from Greenland to Virginia (rarely). *Habitat:* Rocky off-shore islands. *Identification:* Large size—length, about 2 feet. Male, white on back, black underneath. Female, somewhat like Scoter, but more barred; has straighter bill profile than has female King Eider. *Breeding:* Four to six eggs on ground, usually sheltered by rock or stumps. *Food:* Mollusks, crustaceans, echinoderms, worms, etc.

247 . WHITE-WINGED SCOTER
(MELANITTA DEGLANDI)

Range: Breeds from Alaska and Ungava to Washington and the Gulf of St. Lawrence. Winters, on the coast from the Gulf of St. Lawrence to South Carolina, and from the Aleutian Islands to Lower California. Irregularly inland. *Habitat:* Coastal waters in winter. *Identification:* Length, about 22 inches. Male, black with large white wing-patch. Female, brown with wing-patch and two *light areas* on side of head. *Breeding:* Nine to fourteen eggs, near lakes and marshes. *Food:* Crustaceans, mollusks, etc.

248. PIED-BILLED GREBE
(PODILYMBUS PODICEPS)

Range: Breeds locally from British Columbia and Nova Scotia to Mexico. Winters from British Columbia and New York, southward. *Habitat:* Lakes, rivers, sloughs with weedy shores. *Identification:* Length about 13 inches. Horny bill. No white in wing. Compact neck erect, as do other Grebes. *Voice:* Loud, Cuckoo-like *cow-cow-cow-cow*. *Breeding:* Six to eight eggs on a weedy nest that is frequently floating. *Food:* Insects, crayfish, etc. Grebes are known as "Hell-divers from their ability to vanish underwater.

249. TUFTED PUFFIN
(LUNDA CIRRHATA)

Range: From Alaska to the Santa Barbara Islands; from Siberia to Japan. *Habitat:* Off-shore islands, and adjacent seas. *Identification:* Length, about 15 inches. Huge bill. Tufts in breeding plumage; these lacking, or nearly so, in winter plumage. *Breeding:* One egg in burrow, or under rock. In colonies, often of many hundred birds. *Food:* Fish, mollusks, echinoderms, algae, etc.

250. ARCTIC TERN
(STERNA PARADISAEA)

Range: Breeds from Alaska and Greenland to British Columbia and Massachusetts; and in the Arctic regions of Europe and Asia. Winters in the Antarctic Ocean, south to latitude 74°. *Habitat:* Coast, and islands. *Identification:* Long forked tail. Carmine feet and bill. Gray of underparts extends *almost* to black cap, leaving a noticeable white line. When perched with Common Terns, sits lower. Length, about 15 inches. Terns have thinner bills than Gulls, and habitually fly with bill pointed downward.

251. BROWN PELICAN

(PELECANUS OCCIDENTALIS)

Range: Breeds from California and North Carolina to Brazil. Winters from British Columbia and Florida southward. *Habitat:* Coastal waters. *Identification:* Brown coloration, pouch under bill. Sails between wing-beats. Spread, about 6½ feet. *Dives* for food. *Breeding:*

Colonial; three eggs in nest in bushes or on the ground. *Food:* Fish. "Of 3,428 specimens [of fish, in a Pelican colony] taken in Florida waters, only 27 individual fish were of a kind ever sold in markets for food" (Pearson).

252. DOUBLE-CRESTED CORMORANT
(PHALACROCORAX AURITUS)

Range: Breeds from Kodiak Island and Newfoundland to Lower California and the Isle of Pines. Winters on the Atlantic coast from Virginia south. Races: Florida, White-crested, and Farallon Cormorants. (See Plate 257.) *Habitat:* Lakes, interior swamps, bays, coastal islands. *Identification:* Length, under 3 feet. A long-necked brown bird with short tail. Flies in formation, but soars between flaps. On water, points bill upward. (See Plates 266 and 412.) *Breeding:* Two to seven eggs in colonies on ground or in trees.

253. POMARINE JAEGER
(STERCORARIUS POMARINUS)

Range: Breeds from Alaska to Greenland; also from Iceland along the Arctic coasts to Siberia. Winters off the coast of Virginia and in the Gulf of Mexico southward; in the Old World to South Africa and Australia. *Habitat:* Off-shore, especially on fishing banks. *Iden-tification:* A magnificent and agile flier likely to be seen harrying Terns. White area at base of flight feathers. Stubby, twisted central tail feathers showing beyond edge of tail. Length, about 22 inches. *Food:* Fish robbed from Terns, etc.

254. WILSON'S PHALAROPE
(STEGANOPUS TRICOLOR)

Range: Breeds from British Columbia and Manitoba to California and Indiana. Winters from central Chile, Argentina and Patagonia south to the Falkland Islands. *Habitat:* Prairie sloughs, mud flats. *Identification:* Like other Phalaropes, spins about in water as it feeds. *No wing-stripe.* Very thin bill. In full plumage, resembles Lesser Yellow-legs, but legs are darker. Often feeds, on land, with tail tilted high. Length, about 10 inches. *Breeding:* Four eggs, in grass nest on ground.

255. RED PHALAROPE
(PHALAROPUS FULICARIUS)

Range: Breeds from Alaska and Greenland to delta of the Yukon and Hudson Bay; also from Iceland to Siberia. Winters on the oceans off South America at least as far south as the Falkland and Juan Fernandez islands, and off Arabia and West Africa. *Habitat:* In southern latitudes it passes much time at sea. *Identification:* Length, about 8 inches. In breeding plumage, reddish underparts. Winter plumage, a pale bird with *wing-stripe*, and *yellowish* legs. Wilson's lacks wing-stripe; Northern has black legs.

256. REDDISH EGRET
(DICHROMANASSA RUFESCENS)

Range: Breeds from the Gulf coast of the United States to Guatemala; and (Dickey's Egret) in Lower California. Winters from southern Florida southward. *Habitat:* Swamps. *Identification:* A small Heron—length about 2½ feet. *Pink bill with black tip. White plumage, apparently a color phase. Breeding:* Three to four eggs in low nests in colonies. *Food:* Fish, frogs, tadpoles, etc. "Evidently the Reddish Egrets of the Florida coast were exterminated by plume hunters" (Bent).

257. DOUBLE-CRESTED CORMORANT

(PHALACROCORAX AURITUS)

One of the fundamental human impulses seems to be the blaming of someone else for one's own mistakes and failures. The Nazis blame the Jews; hunters blame Hawks; fishermen blame Cormorants—in the last case, because fish are not so abundant as they formerly were. Compared with the thousands of tons of fish taken by commercial fisheries, the small amounts eaten by birds are insignificant. A large proportion is fish inedible by human beings, and includes many enemies of commercial fishes.

258. HUDSONIAN GODWIT
(LIMOSA HAEMASTICA)

Range: Breeds from Alaska to Southampton Island. Winters in Chile, Argentina, Patagonia and the Falkland Islands. *Habitat:* Mud and tide flats in migration. *Identification:* Length, about 15 inches.

Godwit. Heavily banded tail indicates species. Old baymen know it as the "Ring-tailed Marlin." *Voice:* "a low sandpiper-like chattering" (Harrold). *Breeding:* Four eggs in mere suggestion of nest

259. HORNED GREBE
(COLYMBUS AURITUS)

Range: Breeds from near the Arctic coast to Maine and British Columbia; also in Iceland and northern Europe, and Siberia. Winters from Maine to Louisiana, and from Alaska to southern California. Interior records mostly from Great Lakes region. *Habitat:* Lakes, sloughs. In winter, ocean, just beyond surf. *Identification:* Length, about 13 inches. In breeding plumage, has red throat; in winter, much like Eared Grebe, but bill of latter appears slightly upturned. Difficult of discrimination in this plumage.

1

2

260. LEACH'S PETREL

(OCEANODROMA LEUCORHOA)

Range: North Atlantic from Greenland to the Equator; North Pacific from Alaska to Midway Island. Breeds from Greenland and Iceland to Maine and Ireland, and from the Aleutian to the Commander and Kurile islands. *Habitat:* Off-shore on ocean. Comes to

land to breed. *Identification:* Length, about 8 inches. *Forked tail.* Bounding flight, in which each downward wing-beat seems to whip the bird forward. Not so often seen near shore as Wilson's Petrel (q.v.) *Breeding:* In holes in ground

261. SANDHILL CRANE
(GRUS CANADENSIS)

Range: Breeds from Alaska and Baffin Island to California and in Michigan; also in Florida, Georgia, etc. Winters from California and Florida southward. *Races:* Little Brown and Florida Cranes. *Habitat:* Marshes, prairies, potholes in Florida. *Identification:*

Length, about 4 feet, spread about 7½ feet. Gray; short bill. Flies with neck and tail extended. *Voice:* A rolling, ringing *c-r-r-ruck*. The drainage that has lowered the water table of the Midwest has also destroyed the habitats of these magnificent birds.

262. YELLOW-BILLED TROPIC-BIRD
(PHAETHON LEPTURUS)

Range: Breeds in Bermuda, the West Indies and Bahamas. Winters from the Bahamas to Brazil and Ascension Island. *Habitat:* Tropical and sub-Tropical seas. *Identification:* Long, streaming tail feathers;

yellow bill; white back. Red-billed Tropic-bird has red bill and black barring on back. Length, about 31 inches. *Breeding:* One egg, in hole in rocks. Widely known as the Bosun-bird.

263. CURLEW SANDPIPER
(EROLIA TESTACEA)

Range: Breeds in Siberia. Winters from Africa to Australia; in migration occurs from Great Britain to China and the Philippines. Occasional in Alaska, Canada, and the northeastern states. *Habitat:* Mud-flats, pond edges, etc. *Identification:* In breeding plumage, somewhat like *small* Dowitcher, but with *decurved* bill. In winter plumage, like Red-backed Sandpiper—same size—except for *white rump* and less marked wing-stripe. "In the course of my extensive rambles . . . I have seen only three birds of this species" (Audubon).

264. FULMAR

Range: From northern Greenland to Cumberland Sound and Iceland; in the Bering Sea. Winters south to Georges Bank and Japan.

Herring Gull except for its *gliding Shearwater* flight; immature, like Sooty Shearwater, but paler. In flight, flaps and sails. *Breeding:*

265. BUFF-BREASTED SANDPIPER
(TRYNGITES SUBRUFICOLLIS)

Range: Breeds along the Arctic coast from Alaska to Mackenzie. Winters in Argentina and Uruguay; most abundant in migration in the Mississippi Valley and Canadian prairies. *Habitat:* Prairies, pastures, mud flats. *Identification:* Length, about 8 inches. A rather chunky bird, buffy below, with white-tipped tail. Suggests a small Upland Plover. *Food:* Insects. One of the rarest of the shore-birds in the Northeast; it is the discovery of such out-of-the-way birds as this that gives "birding" its zest.

266. EUROPEAN CORMORANT
(PHALACROCORAX CARBO)

Range: Breeds from Greenland and Cumberland Sound to the Magdalens; Iceland, British Isles, Russia. Winters from Greenland to New York; and the Canaries. *Habitat:* Coastal waters—rocky islands. *Identification:* Closely resembles Double-crested Cormorant (*q. v.*) but is larger. Length, about 3 feet. Has white throat-patch the Double-crest lacks. Immature, *white on belly to tail.* Winters farther north than Double-crest. *Breeding:* Four to five eggs in rubbishy nest on cliff.

267. LONG-TAILED JAEGER

(STERCORARIUS LONGICAUDUS)

Range: Breeds from Alaska and Greenland to northern Labrador; Arctic coasts of Europe and Asia. Winters to Gibraltar and Japan; in migration off the Atlantic coast and in Chile and Argentina. *Habi-* *tat:* Northern tundra and open sea. *Identification:* Length, nearly 2 feet. *Long, middle tail feathers.* See other species for comparison. *Breeding:* Two eggs in ground nest. Extremely rare.

268. AMERICAN WOODCOCK
(PHILOHELA MINOR)

Range: Breeds from Manitoba and Nova Scotia to Colorado, Louisiana and Florida. Winters from Missouri and New Jersey to Texas and Florida. *Habitat:* Wooded swamps, alder thickets. *Identification:* Length, about 11 inches. Extremely long bill, rounded wings.

Voice: A *peent,* much like that of Nighthawk. A richly sweet flight-song. Both nocturnal. *Breeding:* Three to five eggs in ground nest. *Food:* Mostly earthworms. A monograph of this species, by O. S. Pettingill, Jr., is published by the Boston Society of Natural History.

269. GREEN-SHANK

(GLOTTIS NEBULARIA)

"Audubon's record of this Old World species from Sand Key, six miles from Cape Sable, Florida . . . is regarded as unsatisfactory. There is no other evidence of its occurrence in North America, and it is now transferred to the Hypothetical List." (A.O.U. *Check-List*). The background will be recognized as representing St. Augustine, Florida.

270. WILSON'S PETREL
(OCEANITES OCEANICUS)

Range: All oceans except the Pacific north of the Equator, to Labrador and Great Britain, the Mediterranean and the Antarctic. Breeds on Mauritius, Kerguelen, South.Shetland, South Georgia and other islands. *Habitat:* In our latitudes marine, though often coming into river mouths. *Identification:* Fluttering flight, *yellow feet* that extend beyond tail. More likely to be seen inshore. *Breeding:* One egg, in rock crevice, hollow in ground, etc. The student may attract these birds by laying a slick of fish oil behind his boat.

271. MAN·O'·WAR·BIRD

(FREGATA MAGNIFICENS)

Range: Breeds in the West Indies, Bahamas, islands along the west coast of Mexico and Galàpagos archipelago. Winters in the breeding area and adjacent seas. Seen casually far northward. *Habitat:* Tropical seas. *Identification:* Aquatic environment, long forked tail, large size—spread 7 to 8 feet. *Breeding:* One egg in colonial nest on ground, in bushes, etc. *Food:* Fish, etc., picked off surface of sea. Gets much of its food by forcing other fish-eaters to give up their prey. An extraordinary aerialist.

272. PARASITIC JAEGER
(STERCORARIUS PARASITICUS)

Range: Breeds from Alaska and Greenland to the Aleutians and Labrador; also on the Arctic islands of Europe and Siberia, south to Scotland. Winters from California and Florida to the Straits of Magellan. *Habitat:* Arctic tundra, off our coasts in migration.

Identification: Length, about 17 inches, central feathers scarcely protruding beyond tail. See other Jaegers for comparison. This is the commonest of the group and the one most likely to be seen harrying Terns along our coast.

273. ROYAL TERN
(THALASSEUS MAXIMUS)

Range: Breeds from the West Indies to Texas and Virginia; Lower California and Mexico. Winters from Florida and California to Peru and Argentina. *Habitat:* Seas and shores. *Identification:* Length, about 20 inches. Deeply forked tail, so long that, when bird is at rest, it reaches to end of wing. Less dark in primaries than in Caspian Tern (Peterson). *Voice:* A sharp *kak. Breeding:* One to two eggs in hollow in sand. *Food:* Small fish, for which it dives. Sometimes seen in northern states after hurricanes.

274. WILLET

(CATOPTROPHORUS SEMIPALMATUS)

Range: Breeds locally on the coast from Nova Scotia to Texas, in the Bahamas and Greater Antilles; from Oregon and Manitoba to California and Colorado. Winters from California and North Carolina to South America. *Habitat:* Prairies inland, salt marsh, pastures, beaches on coast. *Identification:* Length, about 15 inches. Flashing wing pattern. More mottled below than Yellow-legs, with dark legs. *Voice:* Ringing *Pill-will-willet! Ka-a-a-ty, Kee-dik*—and many more notes! *Breeding:* Four eggs in grass nest on ground.

275. NODDY TERN
(ANOÜS STOLIDUS)

Range: From the Bahamas and Dry Tortugas to Venezuela; also on Tristan da Cunha, St. Helena and Ascension islands. *Habitat:* Tropical seas, shores. *Identification:* An entirely brown Tern except for lighter crown. Length, about 16 inches. Rounded tail.

Breeding: One egg on nest of cactus, bay-cedar, seaweed, etc. *Food:* Small fish. These birds were the subject of interesting studies by John B. Watson, the behaviorist, which made important contributions to our understanding of homing abilities in birds.

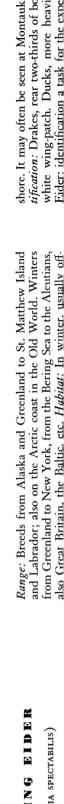

276. KING EIDER
(SOMATERIA SPECTABILIS)

Range: Breeds from Alaska and Greenland to St. Matthew Island and Labrador; also on the Arctic coast in the Old World. Winters from Greenland to New York, from the Bering Sea to the Aleutians, also Great Britain, the Baltic, etc. *Habitat:* In winter, usually off-shore. It may often be seen at Montauk Point and Cape Ann. *Identification:* Drakes, rear two-thirds of body mostly black, with large white wing-patch. Ducks, more heavily streaked than American Eider; identification a task for the expert.

277. HUTCHINS'S GOOSE

(BRANTA CANADENSIS)

This geographic race of the Canada Goose (see Plate 201) cannot be separated in the field by the inexperienced, though according to Dr. T. S. Roberts it has "slightly different, more cackling, higher-pitched notes." The numbers of Canada Geese breeding in the United States are but a fraction of those formerly found here. The vast drainage projects that honeycomb many parts of the country are largely the cause. These have destroyed wild life and, in many instances, the water supplies necessary to human beings.

278. WHITE-RUMPED SANDPIPER

(PISOBIA FUSCICOLLIS)

Range: Breeds from Alaska to Baffin Island. Winters from Paraguay to Patagonia and the Falkland Islands. In migration, most abundant in the Mississippi Valley. *Habitat:* On migration, shallow

than commoner Least and Semipalmated Sandpipers. *White rump* in flight. This character inexplicably not shown by Audubon; identification based on Ridgway. Those familiar with the bird can iden-

279. CABOT'S TERN
(THALASSEUS SANDVICENSIS)

Range: Breeds from Virginia to British Honduras, the Bahamas and West Indies. Winters from Florida to Brazil. *Habitat:* Sandy beaches, near-by waters. *Identification:* Length, about 15 inches. Rather large bill, with yellow tip. *Voice:* "Sharp, grating, and loud enough to be heard at the distance of half a mile" (Audubon). *Breeding:* One to two eggs, in hollow in sand. *Food:* Small fish.

280. BLACK TERN

(CHLIDONIAS NIGRA)

Range: Breeds from Alaska and Ontario to Missouri and Tennessee; also Ohio, Pennsylvania and New York. Winters from Surinam to Peru and Chile. Migrates mainly through the interior. *Habitat:* Prairie sloughs in breeding season; in fall, may be seen along coast.

Identification: Breeding adults, *black* underneath, with forked tail. Fall adults and immature, a spotty, pied appearance. Length, about 10 inches. *Voice:* Many calls, including a sharp *kek*. *Breeding:* Three eggs in grass or reed nest on edge of marsh.

281. GREAT WHITE HERON
(ARDEA OCCIDENTALIS)

Range: Florida Bay. *Habitat:* Mangrove keys, and shallow waters. *Identification:* Great size—length, about 4½ feet, spread 7 feet. Immaculate white with yellow-green bill and legs. Somewhat smaller American Egret, has legs *black*. *Breeding:* Three eggs on flat platform in mangroves. *Food:* Fishes, crustaceans, mollusks. The largest of our Herons. This bird was nearly wiped out by sponge-fishers who took its young for food. Under the protection of Audubon wardens it has shown a promising increase.

2

1

282. ICELAND GULL
(LARUS LEUCOPTERUS)

Range: Recorded in summer from Victoria Island to Greenland. Winters from Greenland to New Jersey and the Great Lakes; to France and the Baltic Sea. *Habitat:* Likely to be seen with Ring-billed or Herring Gulls. *Identification:* Rather small size—length, about 2 feet. Pale mantle *without black wing-tips.* Rather slight bill. *Food:* Garbage, fish, mollusks, etc. The dyed-in-the-wool bird student is afield throughout the year, and this rare bird is one of winter's principal attractions.

283. GREATER SHEARWATER
(PUFFINUS GRAVIS)

Range: Atlantic Ocean from Greenland and northern Europe to South Africa and southern South America. Breeds on Inaccessible Island, Tristan da Cunha. *Identification*: Dark above, light below, with dark cap extending just below eye. Glides on *set wings* along the crests of waves. Though there is some question as to the identity of this plate, Forbush considers it *P. gravis*, a determination I believe correct, because of the head and face pattern, and because of Audubon's Labrador records.

284. PURPLE SANDPIPER

(ARQUATELLA MARITIMA)

Range: Breeds from Melville Island and northern Greenland to Baffin Island and southern Greenland; also in Arctic Europe and Asia. Winters south to New Jersey and the Mediterranean. *Habitat:* In winter, on sea-sprayed rocks and, less often, beaches. *Identifica-*

tion: Length, about 9 inches. A chunky, dark gray bird with white belly. Usually seen when other Sandpipers have left our coast in fall. *Breeding:* Four eggs in ground nest. For third bird on plate, Wilson's Plover, see Plate 200 *A male bird, b*

285. SABINE'S GULL

(XEMA SABINI)

Range: Breeds from Alaska to Greenland, and in Arctic Europe and Asia. Winters on the coast of Peru. Casual on the Atlantic coast and in the interior. *Habitat:* Migrates well offshore though occasional individuals may be seen from the coast. *Identification:* Small size—length about 13 inches. *Slightly forked tail.* Mantle lighter than that of Laughing Gull; wing includes far more black than that of Bonaparte's Gull. For discussion of the Sanderling, on this plate, see Plate 230.

286. WHITE-FRONTED GOOSE

(ANSER ALBIFRONS)

Range: Breeds in Arctic America, Europe and Asia from the Yukon Valley to Bering Sea. Winters from British Columbia and Illinois to Mexico, in Japan, China and North Africa. *Habitat:* Lakes, marshy meadows, etc. *Identification:* A grayish brown Goose with gray-brown neck; belly lighter. Canada Goose and Brant have black necks, Blue Goose (see Plate 381) *whitish.* Small—length about 29 inches. *Voice:* "Its cries are said to be loud and harsh, sounding like the syllable *kah-lah-a-luck.*" (P———.)

287. IVORY GULL

(PAGOPHILA ALBA)

Range: Breeds in the high Arctic latitudes of both hemispheres. Winters in the Arctic regions, and casually south to Manitoba, Lake Ontario, Long Island, and France. *Habitat:* Icy seas. *Identification:* This bird is immaculate. Black legs and feet. Extremely rare in the United States and northern Europe.

and Iceland Gulls, spoken of as white-winged Gulls because they lack black wing-tips, actually are a pale gray on mantle. *Our only pure-white Gull.* The Glaucous Length, about 16 inches.

288. LESSER YELLOW-LEGS
(TOTANUS FLAVIPES)

Range: Breeds from Alaska and Ungava to British Columbia and Manitoba. Winters in Argentina, Chile and Patagonia and, casually, southern states. Rare in spring on the Atlantic coast. *Habitat:* Flats and tide-pools, especially grassy ones, on migration. *Identifica-*

tion: Length, about 10 inches. Gray back, largely white below. *Bright yellow legs.* Thin, straight bill. That of Greater Yellow-legs likely to be heavier and often slightly upturned. *Voice:* A clear, sweet whistled *wheu-wheu.*

289. SOLITARY SANDPIPER

(TRINGA SOLITARIA)

Range: Summers from Kotzebue Sound and Ungava to Washington, Colorado and Pennsylvania. Winters from Florida (casually) and Texas to Ecuador and Argentina. *Habitat:* Mud flats, woods, ponds. *Identification:* Length, about 8 inches. Absence of *wing-stripe.* Shares jerky wing movement and *weet-weet* call with Spotted Sandpiper, but that species has a prominent wing-stripe. *Breeding:* Four eggs in old nests of other birds—Robins, Waxwings, Jays, etc. *Food:* Insects, mollusks, spiders, crustaceans, frogs, etc.

290. RED-BACKED SANDPIPER
(PELIDNA ALPINA)

Range: Breeds in Siberia and from the mouth of the Yukon to Hudson Bay; migrates through the Great Lakes. Winters from British Columbia to Lower California and from New Jersey to Texas. Also Europe. *Habitat:* In migration, mud flats. *Identification:* Length, about 8½ inches. Chunky. In spring reddish back, black belly patch. In fall, gray with wing-stripe. *Long, down-curved bill. Food:*

2

1

291. HERRING GULL

(LARUS ARGENTATUS)

Range: Breeds from Siberia and Baffin Island to British Columbia and New York: Winters from Alaska and the Gulf of St. Lawrence to Yucatan, China and Japan. Races: Thayer's and Vega Gulls. Other races are found in Europe and Asia. *Habitat:* Our common "Sea Gull" in the East. *Identification:* Adults may be known from somewhat similar Ring-billed and California Gulls by pinkish legs; from Glaucous-winged, by black in wing-tips. Length, about 2 feet. *Food:* Garbage, mollusks, fish, etc. A useful scavenger in our harbors.

292. GREAT-CRESTED GREBE

(PODICEPS CRISTATUS)

With what American species Audubon confused this bird, it is difficult to surmise. He was thoroughly familiar with Holboell's Grebe. It has never been recorded in North America. Yet he says: "This beautiful species returns from its northern places of residence, and passes over the Western Country, about the beginning of September. A few remain on the lower parts of the Ohio, on the Mississippi, and the lakes in their neighborhood, but the greater number proceed towards the Mexican territories."

2

1

293. HORNED PUFFIN

(FRATERCULA CORNICULATA)

Range: Breeds on the Siberian coast, the Commander Islands, both sides of Bering Strait, Kotzebue Sound and St. Michael to Forrester Island, Alaska. Winters from the Aleutians and Commander Islands south to the Kurile Islands and from the Queen Charlotte Islands to California (where it has been taken once). It will be clear, from the range, that few Americans will need to concern themselves with the problem of identifying this bird. Audubon described it from one of Gould's skins, in London.

294. PECTORAL SANDPIPER
(PISOBIA MELANOTOS)

Range: Breeds from Siberia to Southampton Island. Winters from Peru and Bolivia to Patagonia. Rare migrant on the Pacific coast. *Habitat:* Shallow pools and tide flats, especially the grassy ones.

of breast well down over pectoral muscles. Length, about 8½ inches. *Voice:* A rolling, rather *loud, k-r-r-r. Breeding:* Four eggs in hollow on ground. *Food:* Insects, crustaceans, seeds, etc. One of the

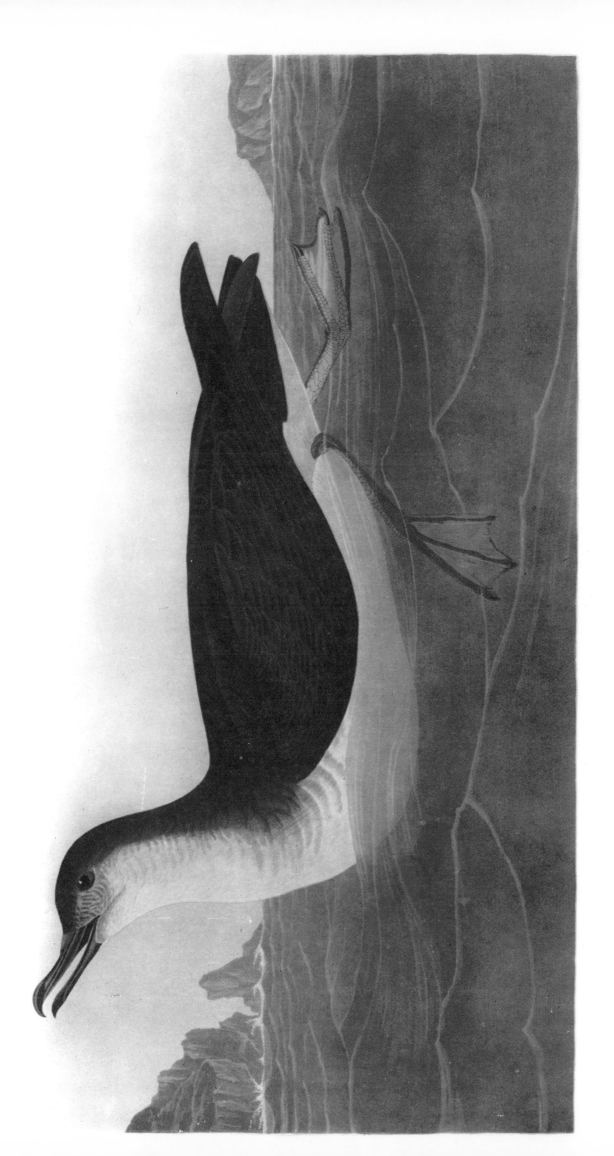

295. MANX SHEARWATER
(PUFFINUS PUFFINUS)

Range: Northeastern Atlantic Ocean from Norway and Great Britain to the Canaries. Accidental in northeastern United States. *Habitat:* Open seas. *Identification:* A small Shearwater, dark above and light below, of improbable occurrence off the United States. May be seen en route to Europe. Travellers will find that *Birds of the Ocean* by W. B. Alexander will while away many hours at sea.

296. BARNACLE GOOSE

(BRANTA LEUCOPSIS)

Range: Breeds in Greenland, Spitzbergen and northwestern Siberia. Winters south to the British Isles, rarely to the Azores and Italy. Casual in eastern North America. *Habitat:* Likely to be seen—if at all—

especially of the head. *Voice:* Notes of the flock have been compared to terriers' yelping. *Breeding:* Three to six eggs, in rock hollows and on ledges. *Food:* Apparently much the same as of our Snow

297. HARLEQUIN DUCK

(HISTRIONICUS HISTRIONICUS)

Range: Breeds from Iceland to Labrador, and from Alaska and Mackenzie to California. Winters south to Long Island (rarely) and to central California and Japan. *Habitat:* On breeding grounds, islands and mountain torrents. In winter, primarily coastal waters.

Identification: Brilliant male unmistakable. Female, two or three white spots on head. Might be confused with female Scoter, but is smaller—length, about 1½ feet. Though one has endured hours of cutting December winds, a glimpse of this bird seems rich reward.

298. HOLBOELL'S GREBE
(COLYMBUS GRISEGENA)

Range: Breeds from Siberia and northern Canada to Washington and Minnesota. Winters mainly on the coasts from Maine to North Carolina and British Columbia to California. *Habitat:* Marshes in summer; just offshore in winter. *Identification:* length, about 21 inches—smaller than Western Grebe and Loons, larger than Eared and Horned Grebes. Red neck, in breeding plumage. White wing patches. *Breeding:* Four to five eggs, in—frequently—floating nest. *Food:* Crustaceans, salamanders, insects, fish, etc.

299. AUDUBON'S SHEARWATER
(PUFFINUS LHERMINIERI)

Range: Warmer parts of western North Atlantic more or less regularly to Cuba, Gulf of Mexico, and casually to the coasts of Florida, South Carolina, Virginia and New Jersey. Breeds in Bermuda, the Bahamas, Lesser Antilles, etc. *Habitat:* Open sea. *Identification:* Very small—length about 1 foot. Same pattern as Greater Shearwater except for absence of white at base of tail. Often dives from surface. *Voice:* Said to resemble cat-call. *Breeding:* In colonies in rock crevices. One egg. *Food:* Fish, etc.

300. GOLDEN PLOVER
(PLUVIALIS DOMINICA)

Range: Breeds from Siberia and Baffin Island to Kotzebue Sound and Churchill. Winters from Brazil to Argentina, in the Hawaiian Islands, New Zealand, Australia, etc. *Habitat:* Upland fields, prairies —less often the coast and mud-flats. *Identification:* Large size—

length about 10½ inches. Mottled yellowish above, in breeding plumage, black below. In winter plumage a grayish, rather nondescript bird, resembling the Black-bellied Plover. Latter has white rump and tail, however, and a *black area on underside of wing*

301. CANVASBACK
(NYROCA VALISINERIA)

Range: Breeds from Alaska and Great Slave Lake to New Mexico and Wisconsin. Winters from British Columbia and Chesapeake Bay to Guatemala (rarely). *Habitat:* Marshes, lakes; in winter coastal bays. *Identification:* Profile, sloping in an almost straight line from top of the head to end of the bill, a good field mark even at long distances. Red head, black breast, nearly white back, mark male. Length, about 2 feet. *Breeding:* Seven to nine eggs in tule nest, over water, often of considerable depth.

302. BLACK DUCK
(ANAS RUBRIPES)

Range: Breeds from Ungava and Manitoba to North Carolina. Winters from New England to Louisiana. *Habitat:* Swamps, marshes, rivers, lakes, coastal bays. *Identification:* A dark brown Duck with *white wing linings.* Female Mallard, lighter brown, has white fringe around tail. *Voice:* Female, a loud, Mallard-like quack. Male, a grunting quack. *Breeding:* Six to twelve eggs in down-lined ground nest. *Food:* Insects, amphibians, crustaceans, mollusks. The most important Duck to the sportsman, in much of the East.

303. UPLAND PLOVER
(BARTRAMIA LONGICAUDA)

Range: Breeds from Alaska and Maine to Oregon and Virginia. Winters from southern Brazil to Argentina and Chile. *Habitat:* Prairies, upland fields. *Identification:* Length about 12 inches. *Short bill, long tail.* Rather nondescript markings, save for V-shaped spotting of breast and sides. *Voice:* "not unlike the rolling call of a tree toad" (Lynds Jones). *Breeding:* Four eggs, in grassy ground nest. *Food:* Largely insects. Dangerously reduced by shooting, it is increasing since it was placed on the protected list.

304 · RUDDY TURNSTONE
(ARENARIA INTERPRES)

Range: Breeds from Alaska to Baffin Island. Winters from California and North Carolina to Brazil and Chile. *Habitat:* Mud-flats, ocean beaches. *Identification:* Length about 8½ inches. In breeding plumage, reddish back and black underparts. In any plumage, the pied appearance that has given it the name "Calico Bird." *Food:* Insects, shore life, insect larvæ,

305. PURPLE GALLINULE

(IONORNIS MARTINICA)

Range: Breeds from Texas and South Carolina to Argentina. Winters from Texas and Florida southward. *Habitat:* Southern swamps. *Identification:* A brilliantly colored chicken-like bird, with *prominent blue patch on forehead.* Bright yellow legs and long toes.

Given to clambering among bushes. Should not be confused with commoner, gray, Florida Gallinule, which has a red forehead shield. *Voice:* Cackles—a noisy bird. *Breeding:* Five to eight eggs, in low grassy rushes in marshes. etc. *Food:* Insects, mollusks, seeds, etc.

306. COMMON LOON
(GAVIA IMMER)

Range: Breeds from Labrador and Illinois (formerly) to Pennsylvania (formerly); Lesser Loon from Wisconsin and California to Manitoba (probably). Winters from the Great Lakes and Maine to the Gulf coast, and from Alaska to California. Also European.

Habitat: Lakes, coastal waters. *Identification:* Large size—length nearly 3 feet. Dark back, light underparts. *Heavy bill.* In flight, rather slow wing-beat; flies much of time with *beak open.* *Voice:* One note like neighing of horses in sky. "Crazy laughter."

1

2

307. LITTLE BLUE HERON
(FLORIDA CAERULEA)

Range: Breeds from New Jersey and Arkansas to Central America. Winters from North Carolina and Texas southward. Wanders northward in late summer, sometimes beyond Canadian border. *Habitat:* Swamps, marshes and their environs. *Identification:* Small —length about 2 feet. Adults, deep blue with maroon neck and dark legs. In Little Green Heron, the chestnut extends down breast, and legs are orange-yellow. Immatures, white, with greenish yellow legs. Similarly small Snowy Egret has black legs and *thinner bill.*

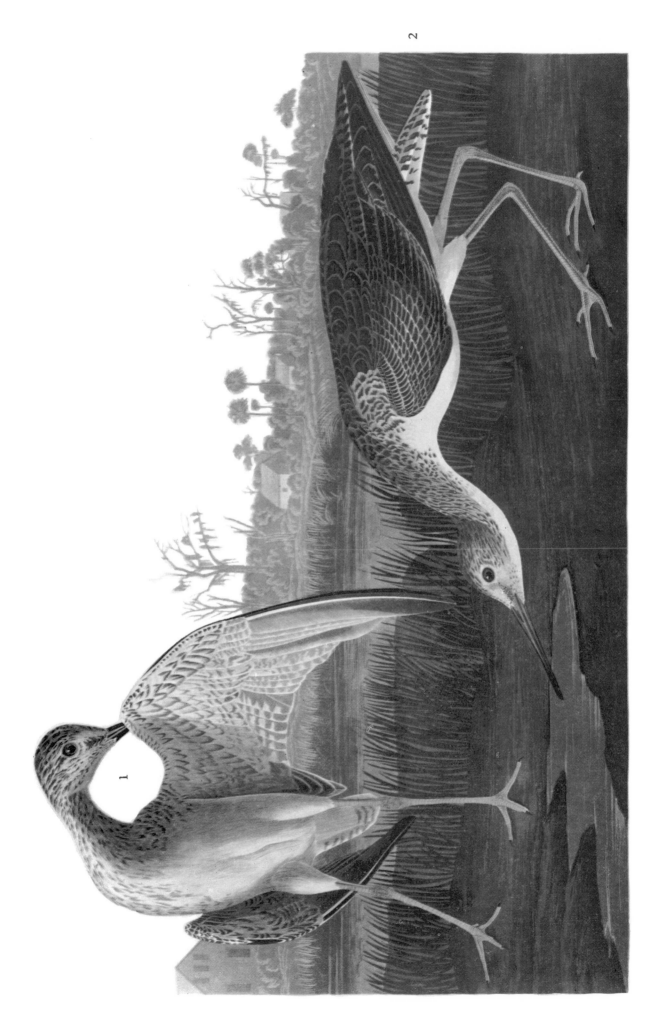

308 . GREATER YELLOW-LEGS
(TOTANUS MELANOLEUCUS)

Range: Breeds from Alaska and Labrador to British Columbia and Anticosti Island. Winters from California and South Carolina to Patagonia. *Habitat:* Mud-flats, marshes, shallow ponds, etc. *Identification:* Rather large—length about 14 inches—mottled gray above, white or nearly so below, with *long bright yellow* legs. Bill larger than that of similar Lesser Yellow-legs, and often *slightly upturned.* In flight, white tail shows like dragging petticoat. *Voice:* A clear, whistled *wheu,* given three or four times.

309. COMMON TERN

(STERNA HIRUNDO)

Range: Nearly cosmopolitan. Breeds from Great Slave Lake and Gulf of St. Lawrence to North Dakota and North Carolina. Also in Venezuela, West Indies, Gulf coast of the United States; Europe, Asia, North Africa, etc. Winters from Florida and Mexico to Straits of Magellan; in southern Asia and Africa. *Habitat:* Rivers, bays, lakes, etc. *Identification:* Length about 14 inches. Bill, black-tipped, red. *Flight-feathers with considerable dark near tips.* See also Forster's, Arctic, and Roseate Terns.

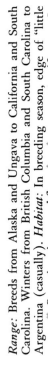

310. SPOTTED SANDPIPER

(ACTITIS MACULARIA)

Range: Breeds from Alaska and Ungava to California and South Carolina. Winters from British Columbia and South Carolina to Argentina (casually). *Habitat:* In breeding season, edge of "little breeding plumage, breast spotted like a Thrush's. Marked *wing-stripe.* In flight, rigidly curved wings travel through short arc. Teeters, as though body were fastened to legs with loose hinges.

2

311. WHITE PELICAN

(PELECANUS ERYTHRORHYNCHOS)

Range: Breeds from British Columbia, Great Slave Lake and Manitoba to California and Texas. Winters from California and Florida to Panama. *Habitat:* Lakes, rivers, the coast. *Identification:* Wingspread, 8 to 10 feet. White with black wing-tips and huge bill. Flaps and sails. *Food:* Fish—often those of no use for sport or food. These birds are massacred by some fishermen who completely disregard the right of bird students to enjoy one of the most impressive sights in the avian world.

312. OLD-SQUAW
(CLANGULA HYEMALIS)

Range: Breeds on the Arctic coasts of both hemispheres south to British Columbia, Churchill, Iceland, the Faroes, etc. Winters to California, the Great Lakes, and North Carolina. *Habitat:* Larger bodies of water, especially off the coast. *Identification:* Length, about 4½ feet. A heavily pied Duck in any plumage. Breeding male has long central tail feathers. Female with dark spot on white face. *Voice:* A clarinet-like trumpeting—often noisy and musical. In flocks these Ducks frequently wheel and twist as do shore birds.

313. BLUE-WINGED TEAL
(QUERQUEDULA DISCORS)

Range: Breeds from British Columbia and Maine to New Mexico and New Jersey. Winters from California and South Carolina to Brazil and Chile. *Habitat:* Swamps, marshes, ponds, etc. *Identification:* Small size—length about 15 inches. Male has large white crescent on face. Both sexes show extensive pale-blue patch on front of wing. Shoveller also has this but can be told by heavy bill. A "sporty" duck for the gunner, and a fine table bird. Unhappily rare in many regions.

314. LAUGHING GULL
(LARUS ATRICILLA)

Range: Breeds from Maine to Texas, California and Venezuela. Winters from South Carolina to Brazil and Chile. *Habitat:* Marshes, rivers, coasts, etc. *Identification:* In breeding plumage, *dark hood and mantle.* In winter, *dark mantle,* without hood. Length, about 16 inches. See Bonaparte's Gull. *Voice:* A high-pitched, cackling *ha-ha-ha-ha.* *Breeding:* Three eggs, in ground nest, on islands, marshes, etc. This bird has increased notably under warden protection; as I write I hear it from my New York apartment.

315. KNOT

(CALIDRIS CANUTUS)

Range: Breeds from Victoria Island to Greenland; migrates along both coasts and through Alberta. Winters from South Carolina and Florida to Patagonia. *Habitat:* Mud-flats, beaches, etc. *Identification:* In breeding plumage, *reddish underpart*; known from Dowitcher by much shorter bill. In winter plumage, nondescript pale gray. May be known by lack of contrast, indistinct wing-strip, and rather *stubby shape.* Length, about 10½ inches. *Voice:* A low-pitched reedy, guttural whistle. *Food:* Mollusks, crustaceans, etc.

316. WATER-TURKEY

(ANHINGA ANHINGA)

Range: Breeds from Arkansas and North Carolina to Argentina. Winters in nearly the same area, north to California and occasionally South Carolina. *Habitat:* Swamps, marshes. *Identification:* Length, about 3 feet. Like a Cormorant with extremely long, thin neck and fan-tail with *light tip*. Light areas in wings. May swim with only neck showing. *Breeding:* Three to five eggs in bulky nests, in or near swamps. *Food:* Fishes, insects, crustaceans, snakes, etc. Often soars for extended periods.

317. SURF SCOTER
(MELANITTA PERSPICILLATA)

Range: Breeds from Alaska and Greenland to Mackenzie and the Gulf of St. Lawrence. Winters from the Bay of Fundy to Florida and from the Aleutians to Lower California. Also on the Great Lakes and sparingly in the interior. *Habitat:* In winter most often seen on water just offshore, or flying *in long, low lines over sea.* *Identification:* Male, black except for markings that have given it the gunners' name of "Skunkhead." Female, brown with two white facial marks. These not shown by Audubon.

318. AVOCET
(RECURVIROSTRA AMERICANA)

Range: Breeds from Washington and Manitoba to California and Iowa. Winters from California and Texas to Guatemala. Rare east of Mississippi River. *Habitat:* Mud-flats, marshy meadows, shallow ponds, etc. *Identification:* Length, about 18 inches. Striking color pattern. Upturned bill. *Voice:* "A yelping scream—*wheat, wheat, wheat*" (Bent). *Breeding:* Three to four eggs, in ground nest. *Food:* Crustaceans, insects, seeds, etc. An extensive study of the closely related European Avocet was published in *Ardea* in 1926.

319. LEAST TERN
(STERNA ANTILLARUM)

Range: Breeds on the coast from Massachusetts to Texas, on islands in the river systems to South Dakota, Iowa and Nebraska, in the Bahamas and West Indies; on the Pacific coast from California to Mexico. Winters from Louisiana to Argentina and on the west coast of Africa. *Habitat:* Rivers, bays, coasts, etc. *Identification:* Small size—length, about 9 inches—white forehead, yellow bill, perhaps with black tip. *Voice:* A rasping *keé-deeck. Breeding:* Two to three eggs, in shell-lined hollow in sand.

320. LEAST SANDPIPER

(PISOBIA MINUTILLA)

Range: Breeds from Alaska and Labrador to the Yukon Valley and Nova Scotia. Winters from California and North Carolina to Patagonia. *Habitat:* Mud-flats, marshes, beaches, etc. *Identification:* Length, about 6 inches. Small size, slender bill, yellowish or greenish legs. *Voice:* Like that of Semipalmated Sandpiper (*q.v.*) but more wiry, and higher pitched. This bird is one of the "Peep," along with the Semipalmated, White-rumped and Baird's Sandpipers. The Western Sandpiper similar but with *longer bill, black legs.*

321. ROSEATE SPOONBILL
(AJAIA AJAJA)

Range: Breeds locally in Texas, Louisiana, and Florida, south to Argentina and Chile. *Identification:* Length, about 2½ feet. Can be confused only with much larger Flamingo—length about 4 feet—and with nothing if a reasonably good view is obtained. *Breeding:* Three to five eggs, usually in heronry with other birds. *Food:* Fishes, crustaceans, insects, water plants. This bird was nearly exterminated by the feather trade, but is notably increasing under Audubon Society guardianship. *Habitat:* Swamps and marshes.

322. REDHEAD

(NYROCA AMERICANA)

Range: Breeds from British Columbia and Manitoba to California and Michigan. Winters from British Columbia to Mexico and from Colorado, Illinois and the Chesapeake to the West Indies. *Habitat:* under 2 feet. Warm red-brown head and *gray back* of male. Canvas-back (q. v.) has white back and *sloping bill profile*. General dun color and gray wing-stripe in female. Rare European Widgeon

323. BLACK SKIMMER

(RYNCHOPS NIGRA)

Range: Breeds on coast from Long Island to Texas. Winters from the Gulf coast to South America. *Habitat:* Coastal beaches and waters. *Identification:* Large size—length, about 1½ feet, spread about 4 feet—shear-like red and black bill with elongated lower mandible, black and white coloration, habit of feeding by skimming surface of water with bill-tip submerged. *Voice:* A rather deep *bark*. *Breeding:* Four eggs, in hollow in sand. *Food:* Fish, crustaceans, etc. Often active by night as well as by day.

324. BONAPARTE'S GULL

(LARUS PHILADELPHIA)

Range: Breeds from Alaska and Mackenzie to British Columbia and Alberta. Winters from Alaska and Massachusetts to Yucatan. *Habitat:* Rivers, lakes, harbors, etc. *Identification:* Length, about 13½ inches. In breeding plumage, with black hood. Lacks this in winter, when has a dark spot to rear of eye. *Much white in forewing.* This area gray in similar Franklin's Gull which in winter has black mark *around* back of head. *Food:* Insects, fishes, crustaceans, etc. This bird's flight is Tern-like.

325. BUFFLEHEAD
(CHARITONETTA ALBEOLA)

Range: Breeds from British Columbia and James Bay to Montana. Winters from the Aleutian Islands and Maine to Texas. *Habitat:* Coastal bays, ponds, rivers, etc. *Identification:* Small—length about 14 inches. Male wears large white cockade *without* the black edging that characterizes the Hooded Mergansers. Female a chunky gray-brown duck with white face and wing patches. Excellent divers. *Breeding:* Six to twelve eggs in abandoned Flicker holes, etc. *Food:* Insects, fish, crustaceans, mollusks, plants, etc.

326. GANNET

(MORIS BASSANA)

Range: Breeds on Bird Rock, Bonaventure and Anticosti islands, on islets off Newfoundland, British Isles and Iceland. Winters from Virginia to Cuba and Vera Cruz, the Canaries and Azores. *Habitat:*

Spread about 6 feet. *Wedge-shaped* bills and *wings.* Adults, white with black wing-tips. Immature, brown or mottled. Swing over waves in circles, and plunge for food—often from considerable

327. SHOVELLER
(SPATULA CLYPEATA)

Range: Breeds from the Bering Sea and New York to California; also from the Arctic Circle to southern Europe and central Asia. Winters from British Columbia and South Carolina to Colombia and the Hawaiian Islands. Also to Africa, Australia, etc. *Habitat:* Marshes, swamps, ponds, etc. *Identification: The enormous bill.* Male, in flight, five contrasting areas of dark, light, dark, light, dark. Length about 19 inches. *Food:* Small aquatic animals, aquatic and marsh plants—these widely destroyed by drainage.

328. BLACK-NECKED STILT
(HIMANTOPUS MEXICANUS)

Range: Breeds from Oregon and Nebraska to Mexico, and from Florida and the Bahamas to Brazil and Peru. Winters from Lower California and Florida to Brazil, Peru, and the Galápagos. *Habitat:* size—length about 15½ inches—black and white coloration, extremely long pink legs. *Voice:* "a whistling cry" (Audubon). *Breeding:* Four eggs in sand hollow lined with shells, sticks, etc. *Food:*

329. YELLOW RAIL

(COTURNICOPS NOVEBORACENSIS)

Range: Breeds in North Dakota and California, and occurs in breeding season from Mackenzie and Ungava to Maine. Winters in the Gulf States and California. *Habitat:* Grassy marshes. *Identification:* Small size—length, about 7 inches. Yellow bill. A buffy, chicken-like bird. with white wing patch. *Voice:* "*kik-kik-kik-kik-kik queah*" (Ames). *Food:* Probably small animals, seeds, etc. This is one of the least known American birds, more often heard than seen. Unfortunately, few bird students are acquainted with its notes.

330. SEMIPALMATED PLOVER
(CHARADRIUS SEMIPALMATUS)

Range: Breeds from the Bering Sea and Greenland to British Columbia and Nova Scotia. Winters from California and South Carolina to Patagonia, Chile and the Galápagos. *Habitat:* Beaches, mudflats, etc. *Identification:* Length, about 7 inches. *Short* bill (Wilson's has long bill); single breast-band (Killdeer has two); dark back (Snowy and Piping Plovers are light). *Voice:* A plaintive chur-rée, not unlike Bluebird's fall note. *Breeding:* Four eggs, in sand hollow, lined or unlined. *Food:* Worms, mollusks, insects, crustaceans, etc.

1

2

331. AMERICAN MERGANSER
(MERGUS MERGANSER)

Range: Breeds from Alaska and Ungava to California and New York. Winters from the Aleutian Islands and Prince Edward Island to Mexico. *Habitat:* Primarily fresh water, whereas the Red-breasted Merganser is given to salt-water habitats as well. *Identification:* Length, about 2 feet. Male, *not crested.* Female, with clear, white chin and breast—not smudged, as in Red-breast. See other Mergansers, and Smew. *Breeding:* Six to seventeen eggs in hollow trees or on the ground. A common winter Duck.

1

2

332. LABRADOR DUCK

(CAMPTORHYNCHUS LABRADORIUS)

Range: Bred probably on the coast of the Ungava Peninsula. Wintered from Nova Scotia probably to Chesapeake Bay. Last record, 1878. The name of this bird must be entered in the dismal list of wild creatures....

Passenger Pigeon and Dodo. Many more are in current danger of joining this illustrious company of the dead, and can be saved only through vigorous, concerted efforts on the part of those who take

333. GREEN HERON
(BUTORIDES VIRESCENS)

Range: Breeds (or summers) from Oregon and Nova Scotia to Honduras. Winters from California and Florida south. Races include Anthony's and Frazar's Green Herons; related forms are found in the West Indies, Mexico, etc. *Habitat:* Generally distributed where there are swamps, brushy lake margins, etc. *Identification:* Length, about 1½ feet. Blue-green and chestnut; orange legs in spring, fading to yellow in summer. *Voice:* When flushed, rises with a guttural *skee-ow.*

334. BLACK-BELLIED PLOVER
(SQUATAROLA SQUATAROLA)

Range: Nearly cosmopolitan. Breeds on the Arctic coasts and islands of America, Europe and Asia. Winters from British Columbia and North Carolina to Peru and Chile; from the Mediterranean to South Africa; in India and Australia. Nesting: May and June; nest on the

low ponds, etc. *Identification:* In breeding plumage, striking coloration; known from Golden Plover by grayer back. In winter plumage, resembles Golden Plover but has *black patch* on underwings.

335. DOWITCHER
(LIMNODROMUS GRISEUS)

Range: Breeds from Alaska and Hudson Bay northward. Winters from California and Florida to Brazil and Peru. Includes Long-billed race. *Habitat:* Mud-flats, shallow ponds, etc. *Identification:* Large size—length, about 11½ inches—proportionately long bill, *white on rump, extending well up back.* In breeding plumage, reddish breast. *Voice:* A *wheu-wheu*, suggestive of the Lesser Yellowlegs but reedier and with a staccato termination to each syllable, that has a Junco-like definiteness. A common, easily identified bird.

336. YELLOW-CROWNED NIGHT HERON

(NYCTANASSA VIOLACEA)

Range: Breeds from Texas and Massachusetts (rarely) south to Brazil and Peru. Winters from Florida southward. *Habitat:* Marshes and swamps. *Identification:* Length, about 2 feet. Adult, a gray heron with *black head* and *light forehead.* Immature, very like Black-crowned Night Heron (*q. v.*) but in flight plainly shows feet beyond edge of tail, which Black-crown does not. *Breeding:* Three to four eggs in low nests, in heronries. *Food:* Land crabs, crayfish, fishes, snails, snakes, lizards, leeches. etc.

337. AMERICAN BITTERN
(BOTAURUS LENTIGINOSUS)

Range: Breeds from British Columbia and Ungava to California, New Jersey and less frequently the southern states. Winters from British Columbia and Virginia to Panama. *Habitat:* Marshes. *Identification:* A medium-sized Heron—length about 2½ feet. Streaked brown. When flying, plainly shows *black wing-tips. Voice:* A sound as though a stake were being driven into the ground. A booming *Dun-kee-doo,* by which name it goes in southern New Jersey. *Food:* Frogs, crustaceans, mice, etc.

338. BEMACULATED DUCK

This bird, later named Brewer's Duck by Audubon, was, as he suspected, a hybrid between the Mallard and the Gadwall. For some reason, Ducks are especially prone to hybridize, and many a bird that fell to the 12-gauge. Of course many sportsmen have never taken the trouble to learn identification of water-fowl, though it is not difficult, with the variety of popular bird guides currently

339. DOVEKIE

(ALLE ALLE)

Range: Breeds in Iceland, Greenland, Spitzbergen and Novaya Zemlya. Winters from Greenland to New York (Montauk Point) and from the North Sea to Madeira. *Habitat:* Wintry seas. *Identification:* Small size—length, about 8 inches—black and white coloration, small bill. *Breeding:* One egg, in cliff cavities. *Food:* Fishes, crustaceans, plankton, etc. Periodically this tiny Auk invades the land in considerable numbers that suggest the suicidal treks of lemmings. See *The Auk*, July, 1933, for a discussion of this.

340. STORM PETREL
(HYDROBATES PELAGICUS)

Range: Coasts of northern Europe, Labrador, Newfoundland, Nova Scotia and Maine, south along the coast of Africa to Zanzibar. Breeds mainly on islands in the northeastern Atlantic. *Habitat:* Open sea. *Identification:* Very small—length about 5 inches. Square tail, black feet. (See other Petrels.) Said to occur on the fishing banks, but is a bird most American amateurs will not encounter in a lifetime. *Breeding:* One egg in burrow, rock crevice, old building, etc. *Food:* Small marine animals, seaweed.

341. GREAT AUK
(PLAUTUS IMPENNIS)

Range: Now extinct. Last one killed in Iceland in 1844. Formerly bred on Funk Island, Newfoundland, the Faroes, Orkneys, etc. Wintered south to Massachusetts, and (casually) Florida; and Spain. This bird was the Arctic analogue of the Antarctic Penguins.

Had it survived into the Twentieth Century, protection might have saved it. Slaughtered, however, for food and feathers, it was wiped out before human beings had achieved the appreciation of birds that, today, makes their conservation possible.

2

1

342. AMERICAN GOLDEN-EYE
(GLAUCIONETTA CLANGULA)

Range: Breeds from Alaska and Labrador to British Columbia and the Adirondacks. Winters from Maine to South Carolina, from the Aleutians to Lower California, on the Great Lakes, in the Mississippi and Missouri valleys. *Habitat:* Widespread in winter from coast to inland lakes and waters. *Identification:* Male, white with dark head, back and tail. White spot in front of eye. Scaup somewhat similar at distance, on water, but with black breast. Similar Merganser long and slender. Golden-eye chunky.

343. RUDDY DUCK
(ERISMATURA JAMAICENSIS)

Identification: A *chunky* little bird, about 15 inches long. Small rounded wings beat very quickly. Male, reddish with white face and undertail. Female, gray-brown with *light face.* Likely to be tame —or stupid. Unhappily, they often amount to the same thing.

Range: Breeds from British Columbia and Manitoba to Lower California and Iowa. Winters from Chesapeake Bay to the West Indies, from British Columbia to Costa Rica, and from Arizona and Pennsylvania southward. *Habitat:* Marshes, ponds, in winter coastal bays.

344. STILT SANDPIPER
(MICROPALAMA HIMANTOPUS)

Range: Breeds from the Mackenzie to Hudson Bay. Winters in South America to Uruguay and Chile. *Habitat:* Pond edges, marshes, etc. *Identification:* Length, about 8 inches. In breeding plumage, Audubon. In winter plumage, resembles Lesser Yellow-legs, except for darker legs and *slight dip* at tip of bill. Its very long legs permit it to feed in deeper water than its fellows and it should be looked

345. BALDPATE

(MARECA AMERICANA)

Range: Breeds from Alaska and Manitoba to California and Indiana. Winters from Alaska and Chesapeake Bay to Panama. *Habitat:* A fresh-water marsh Duck, primarily. *Identification:* Length, about 20 inches. *Large white patch in fore edge of wing. Gray head contrasts with warm brown of flanks. Male has clear white pate.* On water, carries head and neck forward at Coot-like angle. *Voice:* Female, a soft quack. Male, a sweet, whistled *wheu-wheu,* very characteristic. *Food:* Largely pondweeds, etc.

346. PACIFIC LOON
(GAVIA ARCTICA)

Range: Breeds from Point Barrow and Southampton Island to the Alaska Peninsula and York Factory. Winters mainly on the Pacific coast from Alaska to Lower California. Other races occur in northern Europe and Asia. Audubon's plate probably from European birds (F. S. Hersey, *Auk,* 1917, p. 285). *Habitat:* In winter, mostly along the coast. *Identification:* Length, about 2 feet—smaller than Common Loon (Plate 306). Neck gray behind, throat and foreneck black. *Breeding:* Two eggs, in ground nest, very close to water,

1

2

347. SMEW

(MERGELLUS ALBELLUS)

"Audubon's sight record of this Old World species and several other alleged occurrences in America are regarded as unsatisfactory and the species is therefore transferred to the Hypothetical List." (A.O.U. *Check-List*.) The American relatives of this bird—the American Red-breasted and Hooded Mergansers—share certain characteristics that should be familiar to the student. They fly with bodies parallel to the earth, often in long lines, and appear extremely long-necked. Their thin, serrated bills appear un-Duck-like.

348. GADWALL
(CHAULELASMUS STREPERUS)

Range: Breeds from Little Slave Lake and Hudson Bay to California and Iowa; also in British Isles, Europe and Asia. Winters from British Columbia and Chesapeake Bay to Mexico; in British Isles,

Identification: A medium-size gray-brown Duck—length about 20 inches—with *large* white patch in *rear edge of wing*. On water, appears to have extremely thin neck. Much of the range of this bird

349. BLACK RAIL

(CRECISCUS JAMAICENSIS)

Range: Breeds from Kansas and Massachusetts to New Jersey, Virginia and Florida; Farallon race on California coast. Winters probably mainly south of the United States to Guatemala. *Habitat:* Grassy marshes. *Identification:* A tiny black chicken-like bird about 6 inches long—or not much bigger than a Sparrow. Sometimes confused with young of Virginia Rail. *Voice:* Said to resemble call of Yellow-billed Cuckoo (Wayne). *Breeding:* Six to ten eggs in ground nest, often in rather thin cover.

350. MOUNTAIN PLOVER

(EUPODA MONTANA)

Range: Breeds from Montana and Nebraska to New Mexico and Texas. Winters from California and Texas to Lower California and Mexico. *Habitat:* Prairies, deserts, grassy fields. *Identification:* May be recognizable in flight by the white under wing and the dark band. In breeding plumage, a dark line from bill to eye. Length, about 9 inches. *Breeding:* Three eggs, in hollow in ground, with little nesting material. Often far from water. *Food:* Insects. Even

351. GREAT GRAY OWL
(SCOTIAPTEX NEBULOSA)

Range: Breeds from Alaska and Mackenzie to California and Ontario. Southward in winter irregularly through southern Canadian provinces, and northern states. Other races are found in Europe and Asia. *Habitat:* Northern woodlands, especially along river-bottoms. *Identification:* Large size—length about 2½ feet, spread about 5—and absence of "ear-tufts." *Voice:* Said to give a musical whistle, and a deep hoot. *Breeding:* Three to four eggs, usually in old Hawk or Crow nest. *Food:* Small mammals, birds.

352. WHITE-TAILED KITE

(ELANUS LEUCURUS)

Range: California west of the desert divides; also in Texas, Oklahoma and Florida, south rarely to Guatemala. A closely allied race is found in South America. *Habitat:* Vicinity of fresh water—marshes and streams. *Identification:* A gull-like Hawk, very light, but with black "shoulders." Rounded white tail. Length, about 16 inches. *Voice:* "chicken-like *cheep, cheep, cheep, cheep*" (Pickwell). This exquisite bird is disappearing before the guns of those who ignorantly assume it takes chickens and game.

353. CHICKADEES AND BUSH-TIT

1, 2. Chestnut-backed Chickadee *(Penthestes rufescens),* from Prince William Sound, Alaska, and Montana, to California. Races: Nicasio and Barlow's Chickadees. 3, 4. Black-capped Chickadee *(Penthestes atricapillus)*—see Plate 160. 5, 6. Bush-Tit *(Psaltriparus minimus),* from British Columbia and Wyoming, to Lower California and Mexico. Races: Coast, California, Black-tailed, Grinda's, Lead-colored, and Lloyd's, Bush-Tits.

354. TWO TANAGERS

1, 2. Western Tanager *(Piranga ludoviciana)* breeds from British Columbia and South Dakota to Lower California, and Texas. Winters from Mexico to Costa Rica. 3, 4. Scarlet Tanager *(Piranga erythromelas)* breeds from Saskatchewan and Nova Scotia to Alabama and Georgia. Winters from Colombia to Bolivia and Peru.

355. MACGILLIVRAY'S SEASIDE SPARROW

(AMMOSPIZA MARITIMA)

This species (see Plate 93) has one of the longest, and narrowest, ranges of any of our birds. It is completely dependent upon the salt marsh. Recently the practice of draining coastal marshes in the name of mosquito control has become widespread, to the detriment of bird life such as this. Much of it has been unwarranted because of remoteness from towns; more has been inefficacious; most has been unnecessarily destructive of many forms of wild life. Marshes should be preserved where practicable, as wild-life habitats.

356. MARSH HAWK

(CIRCUS HUDSONIUS)

Range: Breeds from Alaska and Newfoundland to Lower California and Virginia. Winters from British Columbia and New Hampshire to Colombia. *Habitat:* Marshes and meadows. *Identification:* A long-winged, long-tailed Hawk with *white rump*. Habitually flies low, with wings canted upward. Length, about 2 feet; spread about 4. *Voice:* Varied, including *Kew-kew-kew-kew*. *Food:* Stoddard found remains of cotton-rats—a Quail enemy—in 925 out of 1,100 Marsh Hawk pellets he examined.

357. AMERICAN MAGPIE

(PICA PICA)

Range: From Alaska and Manitoba to Arizona and New Mexico. *Habitat:* More or less ubiquitous at various times of the year but more likely to be seen near conifers. *Identification:* Black and white coloration, large size—length, about 20 inches—long tail, black bill. Yellow-billed Magpie has yellow bill. (See Plate 362.) *Voice:* Cacks, whistles, gabbles, etc. *Breeding:* Six to nine eggs in bulky nest, two to sixty feet from ground. *Food:* Birds, eggs, carrion, insects, rodents.

358. PINE GROSBEAK

(PINICOLA ENUCLEATOR)

Range: Breeds from Alaska and Newfoundland to New Mexico (in the Rockies), British Columbia and Cape Breton Island. Winters to New Jersey, Minnesota, British Columbia, etc. Seven American races described, and another occurs in Europe. *Habitat:* North-ern and high coniferous forests. *Identification:* Large size—length, about 10 inches—rosy color of adult males. Females and young, grayish, with buffy on head and rump. *Voice:* A loud, mellifluous warble, suggestive of Purple Finch's song.

359. THREE TYRANT FLYCATCHERS

1, 2. Arkansas Kingbird. 4, 5. Say's Phoebe. 3. Scissor-tailed Fly-catcher *(Muscivora forficata),* breeds from Nebraska to Texas and Louisiana. Winters from Mexico to Panama. *Habitat:* Open country, where there are conspicuous perches. *Identification:* Long, forked tail, light head, red flanks. (See Plate 168 for only species that might be confused with it.) Length, about 14 inches. Spreads and closes tail, suggesting scissors. *Food:* Grasshoppers, crickets, and other insects.

360. TWO WRENS

1, 2, 3. Winter Wren *(Nannus hiemalis)*. 4. Rock Wren *(Salpinctes obsoletus)*. In the *Ranges* of many birds is indicated an extensive prolongation "in the mountains"; the Winter Wren is an example. The Red Crossbill (Plate 197) is equally at home in Alaska and northern Mackenzie—and in Guatemala. In low latitudes it finds the northern conditions it requires in high altitudes—8,000 to 13,000 feet. On the basis of plant and animal distribution, biologists have mapped the world's "life zones."

361. DUSKY GROUSE
(DENDRAGAPUS OBSCURUS)

Range: British Columbia, Yukon Territory and Mackenzie to New Mexico and Arizona in Rockies. Races: Richardson's and Fleming's Grouse. *Habitat:* In mountains, especially coniferous forests, up to timber-line. *Identification:* Length, about 20 inches. A Chicken-like bird, dark slate in coloration. *Voice:* A series of booming grunts. *Breeding:* Seven to ten eggs in ground nest. *Food:* Insects, seeds, etc.

362. FOUR WESTERN CORVIDS

1. Yellow-billed Magpie *(Pica nuttalli)*. 2. Steller's Jay *(Cyanocitta stelleri)*, ranges from Alaska, Wyoming and Utah to Mexico. Six races described. 3. California Jay *(Aphelocoma californica)*, ranges from Washington and Wyoming to Lower California and Texas.

Seven races, including Long-tailed and Woodhouse's Jays. 4, 5. Clark's Nutcracker *(Nucifraga columbiana)*, breeds from Alaska, Alberta and South Dakota to Lower California and New Mexico.

363. BOHEMIAN WAXWING

(BOMBYCILLA GARRULA)

Range: Breeds from Alaska and Manitoba to British Columbia and Alberta. Winters east to Nova Scotia and south irregularly to Pennsylvania. *Habitat:* Northern coniferous forests. *Identification:* Length, about 8 inches. Like Cedar Waxwing (See Plate 43) but with white and yellow in wing, and with long chestnut undertail coverts. *Breeding:* As in Cedar Waxwing. *Food:* Mountain-ash and other berries, fruits, insects, etc. Flocks of this bird rove the United States, sporadically, at irregular intervals.

364. WHITE-WINGED CROSSBILL
(LOXIA LEUCOPTERA)

Range: Breeds from Alaska and Quebec to British Columbia and Maine. Winters in much of its breeding area, and southward irregularly to Oregon, Illinois and North Carolina. *Habitat:* Northern coniferous forests. In winter, may appear wherever there is food—even at feeding stations. *Identification: Crossed mandibles.* Adult male, pink with white wing-bars. Length, about 6 inches. *Voice:* A characteristic rattling whistle. *Food:* Pine seeds, berries, etc. Very fond of salt.

365. LAPLAND LONGSPUR
(CALCARIUS LAPPONICUS)

Range: Breeds in Arctic America, Europe and Asia south to the Aleutians, Mackenzie and northern Quebec. Winters from Quebec and the north-central states irregularly south to Texas; in Europe and Asia to about latitude 30°. Race: Alaska Longspur. *Identifica-tion:* Length, about 6½ inches. "Alone, it appears a trifle like a House Sparrow, but *walks or creeps*, does not hop. Two white wing-bars . . . and a varying amount of reddish on the nape of the neck are distinctive." (Peterson.)

366. GYRFALCON

(FALCO RUSTICOLUS)

Range: Breeds in Arctic regions. Casual in winter south to Washington and Connecticut. Three races described. *Habitat:* Arctic cliffs, tundras, etc. *Identification:* Long tail and long-pointed wings of Falcons. Large size—length, about 2 feet, spread about 4. White birds as white as Snowy Owl, but the latter a chunky bird. Gray and Black Gyrfalcons like large Duck Hawks, but mostly larger and face not so contrastily marked. Except in pursuit, heavier in flight. See Plate 196.

367. BAND-TAILED PIGEON

(COLUMBA FASCIATA)

Range: Breeds from British Columbia and Montana to Guatemala and Lower California. Winters from the southwestern United States southward. *Habitat:* Widely distributed. *Identification:* Length, about 15 inches. A generally gray-blue Pigeon with a white crescent on back of head, and a broad, buffy band on end of *square* tail. *Voice:* A repeated and varied cooing. *Breeding:* One egg, usually in loose nest in an oak. *Food:* Nuts, berries, insects, etc. Wings make a noise "like escaping steam" in flight.

2

1

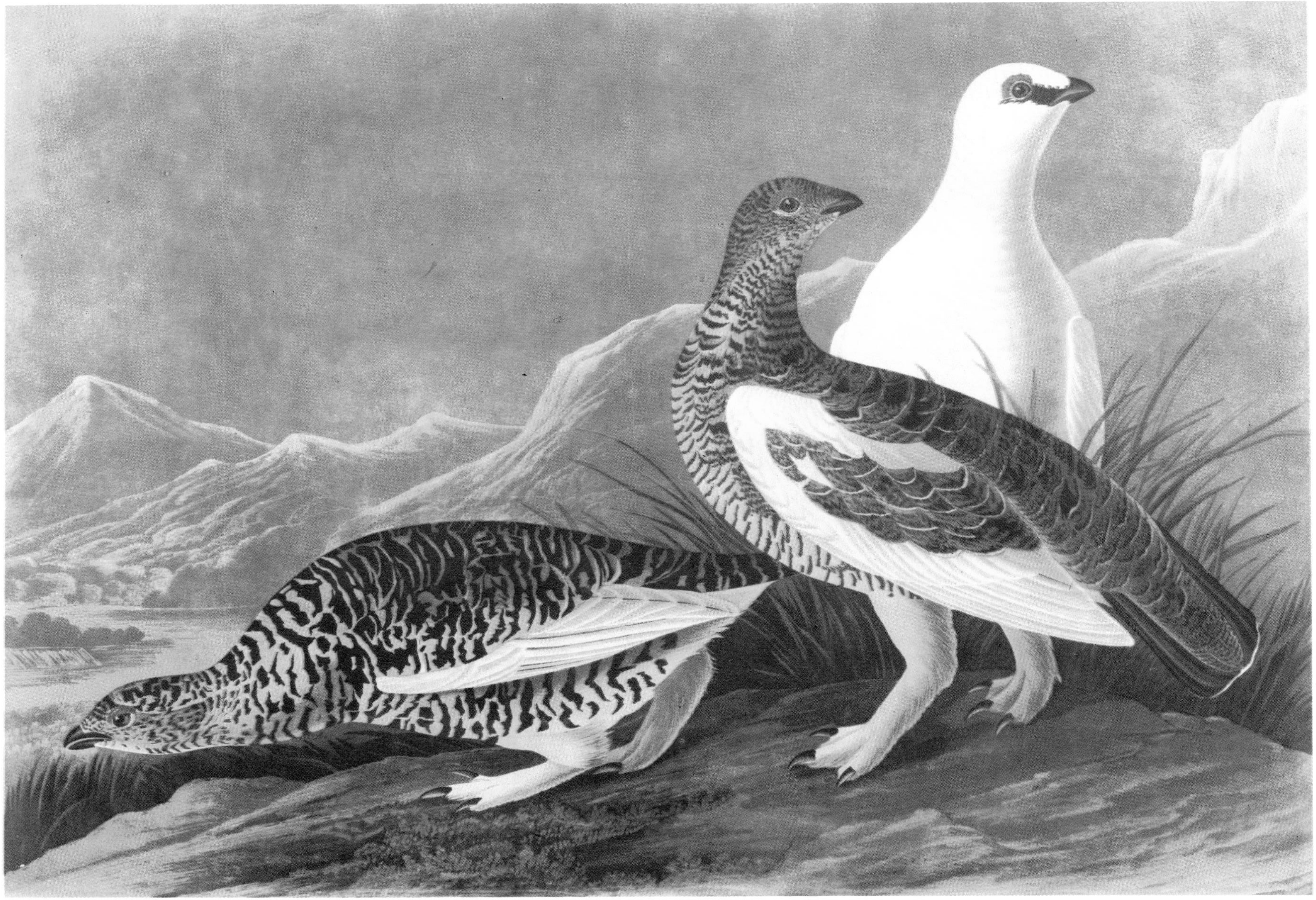

3

368. ROCK PTARMIGAN

(LAGOPUS RUPESTRIS)

Range: From Alaska, the Aleutian Islands and British Columbia, to Greenland. Races include: Reinhardt's, Welch's, Nelson's, Turner's, Chamberlain's, Sanford's, Townsend's, Evermann's, Kellogg's and Dixon's Ptarmigans. *Habitat:* Barren [illegible]en country. *Identification:* Small, brown, hen-like birds—length, about 15 inches—with white wings. Difficult to tell from Willow Ptarmigan in breeding plumage. In winter—white—plumage, however, this species has a Shrike-like mark through eye. *Food:* Insects, leaves, berries, etc.

369. THRASHER AND THRUSH

1. Sage Thrasher *(Oreoscoptes montanus)*, breeds from British Columbia and Nebraska to California and New Mexico. Winters from California and Texas to Mexico. A bird of the arid sagebrush. About 8½ inches long. At a distance, its gray-brown plumage appears almost uniform; at close view, the spotting underneath can be seen; sage-haunting habits; impetuous song (Dawson). 2, 3. Varied Thrush *(Ixoreus naevius)* breeds from Alaska and the Mackenzie Delta to Montana and California.

370. DIPPER
(CINCLUS MEXICANUS)

Range: From Alaska and Alberta to California and New Mexico. An allied race is found in Mexico, and Guatemala. *Habitat:* Mountain streams. *Identification:* Length, about 7 inches. Slate-colored, short tailed. Walks into water and wades in water. Very

"*jigic, jigic, jigic*" (Dawson). *Breeding:* Four to five eggs, in ball of moss, near water, often where it will be sprayed by waterfall. *Food:* Insects, small fishes. This delightful sprite of mountain tor-

371. SAGE GROUSE
(CENTROCERCUS UROPHASIANUS)

Range: Sagebrush plains from British Columbia (formerly), Saskatchewan and North Dakota to California, New Mexico and Nebraska. *Habitat:* As above. *Identification:* Great size—over 2 feet long—spiky tail, sagebrush habitat. *Voice:* Male, "a deep, guttural . . . *kuk, kuk, kuk, . . .* a cackling note of the female, like the cackle of a domestic hen" (Bent). *Breeding:* Seven to thirteen eggs, on ground, usually under sage bush. *Food:* "Leaves and tender shoots" (Judd). Also ants, grasshoppers, beetles, etc.

372. SWAINSON'S HAWK

(BUTEO SWAINSONI)

Range: Breeds from British Columbia and Manitoba to Mexico. Winters in southern South America, only occasionally north of the Equator. *Habitat:* Prairies, plains, deserts. *Identification:* Length, about 1½ feet. Characteristic individuals have white throat and belly, separated by broad band of dark brown. Gray tail is striped. Typical Buteo shape—broad wings and short tail. *Breeding:* Two to four eggs in bulky nest. *Food:* Habits highly beneficial to man, but is constantly shot.

373. TWO GROSBEAKS

1. Evening Grosbeak *(Hesperiphona vespertina)*, breeds from British Columbia and Michigan south, in the mountains, to southern Mexico. Winters from British Columbia, Saskatchewan and Quebec southward, to Mexico in the West, and Maryland in the East. (See Plate 424.) Most bird students know this bird only as an irregular winter visitant, likely to be found in a box-elder. About 8 inches long, its coloration and massive bill identify it. 2, 3, 4. Black-headed Grosbeak *(Hedymeles melanocephalus)*.

374. SHARP-SHINNED HAWK

(ACCIPITER VELOX)

Range: Breeds nearly throughout the United States and Canada south to California, Texas and Florida. Winters from Alaska and New Brunswick (casually) to Guatemala and Panama. *Habitat:* Woodlands. *Identification:* Small—length, about 1 foot. Typically accipitrine, *short, rounded* wings and *long* tail, the latter more or less square at end. Cooper's Hawk has *rounded* tail. These differences sometimes not apparent and a female Sharp-shin may appear as large as a male Cooper's. Crown color of back, darker in Cooper's.

375. COMMON REDPOLL

(ACANTHIS LINARIA)

Range: Breeds from Alaska and Quebec to Alberta and the Gulf of St. Lawrence; also through northern Europe and Asia. Winters in the northern United States, irregularly south to California and South Carolina. Also over the greater part of Europe. *Habitat:* When with us, in birch groves, weed patches, alders, etc. *Identification:* Length, about 5¼ inches. Small, streaked Sparrow with small bill and red cap. Males pink on breast and rump. Tree Sparrows have larger, *chestnut* cap, with breast clear except for central spot.

376. TRUMPETER SWAN
(CYGNUS BUCCINATOR)

Range: Now greatly restricted. Yellowstone Park region and Canada. Formerly as far south as Missouri. *Identification:* Length, about 6 feet. Spread 8 to 10 feet. No yellow spot in front of eye, as in Whistling Swan. Adult white; Audubon's bird immature. This bird was almost exterminated by the man with the gun. While few individuals would willingly kill a bird as rare as this, there is an unfortunate, widespread tendency to kill any large, unknown bird. Under protection this swan is increasing.

377. LIMPKIN

(ARAMUS PICTUS)

Range: Okefinokee Swamp, peninsular Florida west to the Wakulla River; in Cuba. *Habitat:* Swamps. *Identification:* Length, over 2 feet, spread over 3; Slightly decurved bill. Brown plumage, spotted with white. Weak flight, usually with legs dangling. *Voice:* A variety of wails that have given it the Florida name "Crying Bird." *Breeding:* Four to eight eggs, in low nest, often in colonies. *Food:* Mollusks, crustaceans, insects, lizards, etc. Drainage, by destroying its habitat, threatens to exterminate this bird.

378. HAWK OWL

(SURNIA ULULA)

Range: Breeds from Alaska and Hudson Strait to British Columbia and Ungava. Winters casually south to Washington, Nebraska, Michigan, Rhode Island, etc. *Habitat:* Woodlands. *Identification:* Length, about 16 inches. Spotted. Long tail. Often perches conspicuously in a tree-top. Hawk-like and diurnal in habit. *Breeding:* Three to seven eggs, in hollow trees, old Crow nests, etc. *Food:* Birds, and rodents, during winter; on breeding grounds, grasshoppers, beetles and other insects.

379. RUFOUS HUMMINGBIRD
(SELASPHORUS RUFUS)

Range: Breeds from Alaska and Alberta to Oregon and Montana. Winters in southern Mexico. *Habitat:* Mountain woodlands. *Identification:* Length, about 3¼ inches. "Abundant rufous of male distinctive" (Dawson). Female probably indistinguishable, in the field, from Allen's Hummingbird. *Voice:* A rattling note. *Breeding:* Two eggs in nest of plant down, moss, lichens and cobwebs.

1

2

380. RICHARDSON'S OWL

(CRYPTOGLAUX FUNEREA)

Range: Breeds from Alaska and the Magdalen Islands to northern British Columbia. In winter south to southern Canada and, casually, Oregon, Colorado, New England, etc. *Habitat:* Woodlands. *Identification:* Length about 10 inches. May be known from Screech Owl by absence of "ear-tufts"; Hawk Owl, by much smaller size. As a winter visitor, very tame. *Voice:* "a liquid note like dripping water." *Food:* Insects, mice. According to A. K. Fisher, beneficial in its diet!

381. BLUE AND SNOW GOOSE

(CHEN CAERULESCENS, C. HYPERBOREA)

1

2

Blue Goose: Breeds on Baffin and Southampton islands. Migrates though the Mississippi Valley and winters, principally, on the Louisiana marshes. It may be known by its blue-gray body and white head and neck. *Snow Goose:* Breeds from Alaska to Greenland.

Winters from California and Illinois (Lesser race) to Mexico; and on the Atlantic coast (Greater race) from Chesapeake Bay to Core Sound. A white Goose with *black* wing-tips. Audubon shared a general opinion in considering these as the same species.

1

382. SHARP-TAILED GROUSE

(PEDIOECETES PHASIANELLUS)

Range: From Alaska and Quebec to New Mexico, Wisconsin and Ontario. *Habitat:* Brushy areas, marshes, farms. *Identification:* Length, about 1½ feet. Tail largely white, and *pointed*. Lighter than Prairie Chicken. (See Plate 186.) *Voice:* Booming, clucking, cackling, crowing. *Breeding:* Ten to thirteen eggs in a barely lined hollow in the ground. *Food:* Insects, seeds, fruits, leaves, birds. This bird, like others in its family, is subject to marked fluctuations; peaks are said to occur at the time of grasshopper outbreaks.

383. LONG-EARED OWL
(ASIO WILSONIANUS)

Range: Breeds from British Columbia and Newfoundland to California and Virginia. Winters from southern Canada to Mexico and Florida. *Habitat:* Wooded swamps. *Identification:* Medium size—length about 14 inches. "Ear-tufts." Larger than Screech, smaller than Great Horned—the other two Owls with prominent "ear-tufts." *Voice:* A cat-like squall. *Breeding:* Four to six eggs, in old Crow or Hawk nest. *Food:* Largely destructive rodents. Small flocks of these Owls can often be found, in winter, in thick pine plantations.

384. DICKCISSEL

(SPIZA AMERICANA)

Range: Breeds from Wyoming and Ontario to Texas and Georgia (casually). From time to time irrupts into unwonted breeding territory. Winters from Guatemala to Colombia, Venezuela and Trinidad. *Habitat:* Fields, pastures, brushlands. *Identification:* Length, about 6½ inches. Rather like a tiny Meadowlark with a thick bill. Male has black breast patch, white throat and yellow belly. Female lacks black patch and has less yellow. *Voice:* A repetition of its name. *Breeding:* Three to five eggs in grass nest, often on ground.

385. TWO SWALLOWS

Bank Swallow *(Riparia riparia)*, breeds from Alaska and Quebec to California and Virginia; also in Europe, Asia and Africa. Migrates to Brazil and Peru; also to Africa and India. *Habitat:* Likely to be seen feeding over water, perching on telephone wires; nests in sand banks. Violet-green Swallow *(Tachycineta thalassina)*, breeds from Alaska and Alberta to Lower California and Mexico. *Habitat:* Feeding over water, perched on wires, etc. In nesting season, in the vicinity of cliffs.

386. AMERICAN EGRET
(CASMERODIUS ALBUS)

Range: Breeds from New Jersey, Ohio, Wisconsin, Utah, and Oregon south to Patagonia. Winters from Oregon and South Carolina and southward. Wanders, in late summer, as far north as prairie and maritime provinces. *Habitat:* Marshes, ponds. *Identification:* Large size—length over 3 feet, spread over 4. *White* plumage, yellow bill, black legs and feet. This bird is living proof that conservation *is* effective. Virtually wiped out a few years ago, by plume hunters, under protection it has become abundant.

387 · GLOSSY IBIS
(PLEGADIS FALCINELLUS)

Range: Florida, Haiti, Cuba, etc. Not infrequently seen as a casual in North, where it is probably carried by cyclones. An allied race in Java and Australia. *Habitat:* Marshes. *Identification:* Length, about 2 feet, spread, about 3. Obviously, by long decurved bill, an Ibis. Purplish and greenish coloration. Dark young White Ibises (Plate 222) have white underparts, which this bird does not. *Breeding:* Three to four eggs in low, colonial nests. *Food:* Crustaceans, insects, snakes, etc.

388. THREE ICTERIDS

1. Tricolored Red-wing *(Agelaius tricolor)*, valleys of northwestern Oregon (west of the Cascade Range) south through California (west of the Sierra Nevada) to northwestern Lower California. 2, 3, 4. Yellow-headed Blackbird *(Xanthocephalus xanthocephalus)*, breeds from British Columbia, Manitoba and Minnesota to Lower California, Mexico and Indiana. 5. Bullock's Oriole *(Icterus bullocki)*, breeds from British Columbia and Saskatchewan to Lower California and Texas; from the Pacific to South Dakota, Nebraska and Kansas. Winters in Mexico.

389. RED-COCKADED WOODPECKER

(DRYOBATES BOREALIS)

Range: South Atlantic and Gulf states north to Virginia, Tennessee, Kentucky and Missouri. *Habitat:* Woodlands, especially pineries. *Identification:* Length, about 7½ inches. Top of head *black*. Back crossed by *many transverse bars*. *Voice:* "a rather shrill, querulous *churr*" (Howell). *Breeding:* Three to four eggs in a hole in a pine, 20 to 70 feet high. *Food:* Ants, borers, and other insects; seeds.

390. THREE FINCHES

1. Lark Sparrow *(Chondestes grammacus)*, breeds from British Columbia and Ontario to Mexico, Alabama and Pennsylvania. Winters from California and Mississippi to Lower California and Mexico. 2, 3. Lark Bunting *(Calamospiza melanocorys)*, breeds from Alberta and Manitoba to New Mexico and Minnesota. Winters from Texas and Arizona to Mexico and Lower California. 4. Rusty Song Sparrow *(Melospiza melodia)*, Alaska, south to Washington and Oregon. (See Plate 25.)

391. AMERICAN BRANT

(BRANTA BERNICLA)

Range: Breeds in the Arctic regions of eastern North America, on both coasts of Greenland and, apparently, the Spitzbergen Archipelago. Winters on the Atlantic coast from New Jersey to North Carolina. Less frequently on the Pacific coast; and on the coasts of the British Isles. A related race occurs in the European and Asiatic Arctic. *Habitat:* Coastal bays. *Identification:* A small Goose—length, about 2 feet—lacking large white patch on black face. Short neck. Black breast. Light belly.

392. HARRIS'S HAWK
(PARABUTEO UNICINCTUS)

Range: From California and Texas to Argentina and Chile (Bent). *Habitat:* Prairies, chaparral, mesquite range. *Identification:* Length, about 1½ feet. Adult, dark brown with reddish on wings. White rump, and long tail, with white tip. "Its shape and flight are not unlike those of the marsh hawk" (Bent). *Breeding:* Three to five eggs, in nest in cactus, chaparral, etc. *Food:* Mice, lizards, birds, snakes, etc. This bird is said to be considerably reduced in numbers through wanton shooting.

393. WARBLER AND BLUEBIRDS

1. Townsend's Warbler *(Dendroica townsendi)*, breeds from Prince William Sound and the upper Yukon, Alaska, to Washington, Alberta and Montana. Winters from California to Nicaragua. 2, 3. Mountain Bluebird *(Sialia currucoides)*, breeds from Yukon and Manitoba to California and Chihuahua, and from Cascade Range and Sierra Nevada to North Dakota and Nebraska. Winters from California and Colorado to Lower California and Texas. 4, 5. Western Bluebird *(Sialia mexicana)* breeds from British Columbia and Colorado to Mexico. Winters from California and Utah south.

394. FOUR FRINGILLIDS

1. Chestnut-collared Longspur *(Calcarius ornatus)*, breeds from Montana and Manitoba to Wyoming, Kansas and Minnesota. Winters from Colorado, Nebraska and Iowa to Mexico. 2. Black-headed Goldfinch *(Spinus notatus)*. "Audubon's record of this Middle American species at Henderson, Kentucky, is not satisfactory and it is transferred to the Hypothetical List" (A.O.U. *Check-List*). 3. Golden-crowned Sparrow *(Zonotrichia coronata)*. 4. Arctic Towhee *(Pipilo maculatus)*, a northern and western species, may be known from the Red-eyed Towhee (Plate 29) by spots on wings and back.

395. THREE WESTERN WARBLERS

1, 2. Audubon's Warbler *(Dendroica auduboni)*, breeds from British Columbia and Saskatchewan to Guatemala. Winters from California and the Rio Grande, south. A subspecies is known as the Black-fronted Warbler. 3, 4. Hermit Warbler *(Dendroica occidentalis)*, breeds from Washington to the southern Sierra Nevada in California. Winters in Mexico, Guatemala and Nicaragua. 5, 6. Black-throated Gray Warbler *(Dendroica nigrescens)*, breeds from British Columbia and Utah to Lower California and New Mexico. Winters in Lower California and Mexico.

396. GLAUCOUS GULL
(LARUS HYPERBOREUS)

Range: Breeds from Alaska and Greenland to the Pribilof Islands and Labrador; also in the Arctic of the Eastern Hemisphere. Winters from the Aleutians and Greenland to California and New York; in the Old World to the Mediterranean and Japan. *Habitat:*

With us, likely to be seen among Herring Gulls. *Identification:* Large size—length, over two feet, about size of Great Black-backed Gull. *Heavy bill.* Absence of black in flight feathers. Light mantle. *Food:* "Almost any kind of animal food, fresh or carrion" (Bent).

397. SCARLET IBIS
(GUARA RUBRA)

Range: Tropical South America. Casual in the West Indies and Central America, and accidental in New Mexico, Texas, Louisiana and Florida. *Habitat:* Marshes. *Identification:* Size and shape of White Ibis (Plate 222) but of an intense red. *Breeding:* Two eggs, in colonial nestings. *Food:* Fishes, insects, mollusks, crustaceans, etc. These brilliant birds are shot from their nests by South American "natives," and salted down for sale in near-by markets. Bird protection laws are all but non-existent within their range.

398. THREE FRINGILLIDS

1. Lazuli Bunting *(Passerina amoena)* breeds from British Columbia and North Dakota to Lower California and Texas. Winters in Mexico. Length, about 5½ inches. The color-pattern of the male is diagnostic. Female may be known by warm buff of underparts and, usually, a suggestion of bluish on the back. Both sexes, of course, have thick bunting bills. (See Plates 74, 424.) 2. Clay-colored Sparrow *(Spizella pallida)*. 3. Oregon Junco *(Junco oreganus)*.

399. THREE WARBLERS

1, 2. Black-throated Green Warbler *(Dendroica virens)*. 3. Black-burnian Warbler *(Dendroica fusca)*. (See Plates 134, 135.) 4, 5. Macgillivray's Warbler *(Oporonis tolmiei)* breeds from Alaska and Saskatchewan to California and New Mexico. Winters from Lower California to Colombia. "Similar to the Connecticut and Mourning Warblers, the male possessing the distinctive features of both—the conspicuous *white eye-ring* of the Connecticut and the *black crape* of the Mourning" (Peterson).

400. FINCHES AND TANAGER

1. Arkansas Goldfinch (*Spinus psaltria*). 2. Hoary Redpoll (*Acanthis hornemanni*) breeds from Alaska to Ungava. Occasionally winters southward to northern United States. Likely to be seen feeding on weed seeds in wastelands. Distinguished from other Redpolls (see Plate 375) by unspotted or unstreaked rump. 3. Western Tanager (*Piranga ludoviciana*). 4. Townsend's Bunting (*Fringilla townsendi*); this bird, whose source is not given by Audubon in *The Birds of America*, is another of his unknown species. 5. Smith's Longspur (*Calcarius pictus*).

401. RED-BREASTED MERGANSER

(MERGUS SERRATOR)

Range: Breeds from Alaska and Greenland to British Columbia and Maine. Also in Iceland, Scandinavia, Siberia, etc. Winters, on the coast, from Maine to Texas, from Alaska to Lower California, and in the interior from the Great Lakes southward. Also from North Africa to Japan. *Habitat:* More likely to be seen on salt-water bays than is American Merganser. *Identification:* See Plates 232, 331. Male, *with green crest.* Female, *smudgy throat and breast, where that of American Merganser is patchy.*

1   2   3   4   5

402. FOUR ALCIDS

1, 2. Ancient Murrelet (*Synthliboramphus antiquus*) breeds on Forrester Island, Kodiak and Aleutian islands to Near Islands, and from Kamchatka to the Commander and Kurile islands and Japan. Winters from the Aleutians to Lower California and to Japan. May be known by the bluish black upper parts, and marked head pattern. Length, about 10 inches. (See Plate 430.) 3. Least Auklet (*Aethia pusilla*). 4. Crested Auklet (*Aethia cristatella*), from Kodiak through the Aleutian and Commander islands and north to Diomede Island; largely resident. 5. Rhinoceros Auklet (*Cerorhinca monocerata*).

403 · BARROW'S GOLDEN-EYE
(GLAUCIONETTA ISLANDICA)

Range: Breeds in Greenland, Iceland, and Labrador; also from Alaska and California to Montana and Colorado. Winters from Alaska and the Gulf of St. Lawrence to California, Colorado and Massachusetts. *Habitat:* Mountain lakes; rivers; in winter, coastal waters. *Identification:* Male may be told from Golden-eye (see Plate 342) by *crescentic spot* before eye and by black and white spotting of wings. *Breeding:* Six to fifteen eggs, in hollow trees. *Food:* Fishes, mollusks, amphibians, crustaceans, water weeds.

1

2

404. EARED GREBE
(COLYMBUS NIGRICOLLIS)

Range: Breeds from British Columbia and Manitoba to Lower California and Iowa. Winters from Washington to Guatemala. *Habitat:* Lakes; coastal waters in winter. *Identification:* Length, about 12 inches. Small size and Grebe habit of carrying neck erect distinguish

from Loons. Black neck, as indicated by specific name, identifies it in breeding plumage. In winter, difficult to tell from Horned Grebe. (See Plate 259.) *Voice:* "*poo-eep, poo-eep*" (Saunders). *Breeding:*

405. SEMIPALMATED SANDPIPER

(EREUNETES PUSILLUS)

Range: Breeds from Siberia and Baffin Island to Hudson Bay and Labrador. Winters from South Carolina and the Gulf of Mexico to Patagonia. Migrates mainly east of the Rocky Mountains. *Habitat:* In winter and on migration, mud-flats, shallow pools, etc. *Identification:* One of the common "Peep." Length, about 6 inches. Fairly stocky bill, feet and legs *black*. (See Plate 320.) *Voice:* A whistle that suggests the whinnying of a horse. *Food:* Insects, mollusks, worms, crustaceans, etc.

406. TRUMPETER SWAN
(CYGNUS BUCCINATOR)

The history of our water-fowl may be well shown by two graphs, starting at the same point, one indicating habitats, and the other water-fowl populations when America was settled. Both graphs fall slowly until the late 1800's, when drainage and overshooting send them tobogganing. The population curve drops much more rapidly—there are not enough water-fowl left to fill available marshes. The conservationist's job is to halt the decline of the habitat curve, and bring the water-fowl curve up to it. (See Plate 376.)

407 . AMERICAN SOOTY ALBATROSS

(PHOEBETRIA PALPEBRATA)

"Audubon's record of specimens supposed to have been taken by Townsend off the coast of Oregon regarded as not satisfactory . . . Appeared in the third edition as *P. palpebrata*; now transferred to the Hypothetical List." (A.O.U. *Check-List*.) This species breeds on South Georgia and Kerguelen islands, and near New Zealand, and ranges widely through southern oceans. Most interesting accounts of birds of this group are given in Robert Cushman Murphy's *Oceanic Birds of South America*.

408. AMERICAN SCOTER
(OIDEMIA AMERICANA)

Range: Breeds from Siberia to James Bay and Newfoundland. Winters, on the coasts, from Maine to New Jersey, from the Aleutians to southern California; in the interior to the Great Lakes. *Habitat:* Lakes, oceans offshore. *Identification:* Length, about 1½ feet. Male, a chunky, *all black* Duck. Female, brown, with single broad light area on face—other female Scoters have spots on face. *Breeding:* Six to ten eggs in grassy, ground nest. *Food:* Mussels, clams, scallops, fishes, insects, etc.

409. FORSTER'S AND TRUDEAU'S TERNS

Predatory birds have been judged by findings as to what they eat. Do they eat man's "enemies"? Then they are "beneficial." Do they eat what he eats—or wants to kill for sport? Then they are "harmful"—and should be "controlled." Recent ecological investigations have demonstrated, however, that stomach contents tell only part of the story. The presence of Quail in a Great Horned Owl's pellets show it has been eating birds—but more important, it may be evidence of poor cover and food for the Quail.

410. GULL-BILLED TERN
(GELOCHELIDON NILOTICA)

Range: Breeds on the Atlantic coast from Virginia to Georgia; on the Gulf coast from Mississippi to Texas; Salton Sea, California; in the Bahamas, West Indies and South America. Winters from Texas and Louisiana to Patagonia. *Habitat:* Coast, marshes. *Identification:* Length, about 14 inches. Black bill, heavy, suggesting that of Gulls, whence name. Tail not deeply forked. *Voice:* A laughing note, *"af, af, af,* like a gull"* (Yarrell). *Breeding:* Two to three eggs in ground nest on beach or marsh. *Food:* Mostly insects.

411. WHISTLING SWAN
(CYGNUS COLUMBIANUS)

Range: Breeds, mainly north of the Arctic Circle, from Alaska to Baffin Island. Winters from the Great Lakes to North Carolina and from Alaska to Lower California. *Habitat:* Coastal bays, as Currituck Sound; Back Bay, Virginia, etc. *Identification:* On the Atlantic coast the introduced Mute Swan is confused with this species. At close range the knobbed bill of the former may be seen. It also carries its neck in a graceful curve whereas the Whistling Swan carries it nearly straight, as it floats in the water.

2

1

412. TWO CORMORANTS

1. Baird's Cormorant (*Phalacrocorax pelagicus*), breeds from Siberia and coasts of the Bering Sea, to Japan and Lower California. Win-ters from the Aleutian Islal ᵃⁿᵈ Commander Islands to China.

feet—white flank patches in breeding season, and lustrous green and violet coloration. 2. Brandt's Cormorant (*Phalacrocorax pencil-*

413. VALLEY QUAIL
(LOPHORTYX CALIFORNICA)

Range: From Oregon and Nevada to Lower California; Catalina Island. Races include California Quail. *Habitat:* Gardens, farms, scrub—widely distributed. *Identification:* Length, about 10 inches—Robin size. Recurved crest. Black throat of male. Scaled appearance of belly. Desert Quail unscaled below and male has bright chestnut crown. *Voice:* "Some of the notes . . . suggest the familiar *bob-white* of our eastern Quail" (Bent). *Food:* Fruit, grain, grass, seeds and insects.

414. TWO WARBLERS

1, 2. Golden-winged Warbler *(Vermivora chrysoptera)*, breeds from Minnesota and Massachusetts to Iowa and, in the mountains, Georgia. Winters from Guatemala to Colombia and Venezuela. (See Plate 479.) 3, 4. Cape May Warbler *(Dendroica tigrina)*, breeds from Mackenzie and Nova Scotia to Manitoba and Maine. Winters in the Bahamas and West Indies to Tobago. (See Plate 462.) The Golden-wing is as common, on migration, in many areas, as the Cape May is rare.

415. TWO BARK FEEDERS

1, 2. Brown Creeper *(Certhia familiaris)*. Breeds from Alaska and Quebec to Mexico and North Carolina. A woodland bird that may come to suet at winter feeding stations. Known by its bark-like coloration and habit of spiralling upward around trees as it seeks insects and their eggs on the bark. 3, 4. Pygmy Nuthatch *(Sitta pygmaea)*. From British Columbia and Idaho to Mexico and Lower California. Known by its small size—length about 4 inches—tree-creeping habit, and gray-brown head contrasting with leaden back.

416. FIVE WOODPECKERS

1, 2. Hairy Woodpecker *(Dryobates villosus)*, from Alaska and Newfoundland, to Central America (See Plate 417.) 3, 4. Red-bellied Woodpecker *(Centurus carolinus)*, from South Dakota and Delaware to Florida and Texas. Identified by red cap and cross-barring of back. 5, 6. Red-shafted Flicker *(Colaptes cafer)*, from Alaska and Saskatchewan to Texas and Lower California. 7, 8. Lewis's Woodpecker *(Asyndesmus lewisi)*, from British Columbia and Alberta to Colorado and Arizona. Color pattern distinctive. Blacker back than in Audubon's plate. 9, 10. Red-breasted Sapsucker *(Sphyrapicus varius)*. (See Plate 190.)

417. TWO WOODPECKERS

3, 4. Three-toed Woodpecker *(Picoides tridactylus)*. Hairy Wood-pecker *(Dryobates villosus)*—various races shown. See Plate 416. *Habitat:* Woodlands. *Identification:* Length, about 9 inches. Black and white coloration, white back. Pattern identical with smaller

Downy's (Plate 112) except that latter has black spots on white outer tail feathers. Hairy, however, has *much heavier bill* and its *kick-kick* notes are repeated on one pitch, instead of descending as in the Downy's call.

1. Rock Ptarmigan (*Lagopus rupestris*)—see Plate 368. 2. White-tailed Ptarmigan (*Lagopus leucurus*), Alaska and Mackenzie, through the mountains to British Columbia, the Cascades, and the Rockies from Montana to New Mexico. Found above timberline.

Length, about 12½ inches. In winter, may be known by its complete whiteness; in summer, by its white wings, tail, and body patches (Taverner). It lays six to eight eggs—occasionally fifteen—in shallow depression in grass. It eats insects, buds, flowers, seeds, etc.

418. TWO PTARMIGAN

419. THRUSH, SOLITAIRE, AND JAY

1. Dwarf Hermit Thrush *(Hylocichla guttata nanus)*. Breeds from Cross Sound, Alaska, to the coast region of southern British Columbia. Winters south to California, Lower California, Arizona and New Mexico. A race of the Hermit Thrush. (See Plate 58.) 2. Townsend's Solitaire *(Myadestes townsendi)*. (See Plate 460.) 3. Canada Jay *(Perisoreus canadensis)*. This bird is discussed on Plate 107.

420. BICOLORED RED-WING

(AGELAIUS PHOENICEUS)

Range: Sacramento and San Joaquin valleys, California. The A.O.U. *Check-List* includes fourteen subspecies of the Red-wing, five of them from California alone. Most people who watch birds as a hobby are not interested in subspecies, except to find out whether or not field identification is possible. The sparseness, or absence, of the buffy wing marking identifies this race. See Plate 67.

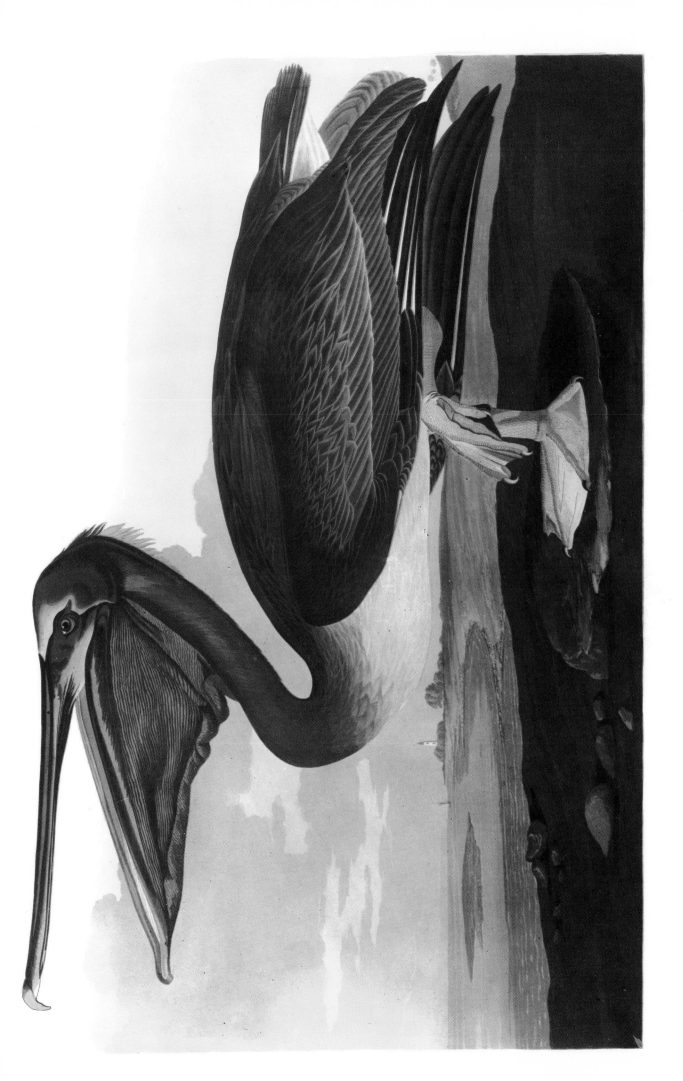

421. BROWN PELICAN
(PELECANUS OCCIDENTALIS)

Florida and southern California, with their strong subtropical character, are Meccas for northern bird students. (Exact directions for finding characteristic birds in these states were published in *Bird-Lore* magazine, October, 1937, and December, 1935.) No birds seem more typical of these southern coasts than the Brown Pelicans. They fly with ponderous gravity and superb mastery of the air over bays and harbors, and plunge, with great splashes, for their food. They dive down-wind and rise up-wind. See Plate 251.

422. ROUGH-LEGGED HAWK

(BUTEO LAGOPUS)

One of the principal claims to superiority of bird-study as a hobby, is the fact that it is not seasonal. In all months, in all weathers, the field-glass brigade tramps the marshes, fields, woods, and shores, enjoying commonplace species, on watch for rarities. Winter, the season when this bird appears, not only presents a galaxy of northern Finches, Ducks, Alcids, and predators, it tries human endurance, and adds, to the satisfaction of "good lists," a sense of triumphing over cold, snow and sleet. (See Plate 166.)

423. TWO QUAIL

1. *Colinus cristatus*, supposed by Audubon to have been taken on our northwest coast, actually is found in Panama, Colombia, Venezuela, the Guianas and Brazil. 2, 3. Mountain Quail (*Oreortyx picta*), from Vancouver Island and Nevada to Lower California. A bird of the western mountains. Length, about 10 inches. Long, straight crest and chestnut throat diagnostic. Dawson writes its note as *toó-wook*, etc. It lays five to fifteen eggs in a shallow depression in the ground.

424. FRINGILLIDS AND ICTERID

1. Lazuli Bunting *(Passerina amoena)*—see Plate 398. 2. House Finch *(Carpodacus mexicanus)*. 3. Rosy Finch *(Leucosticte tephrocotis)*. 4. Cowbird *(Molothrus ater)*—see Plate 99. 5, 6. Evening Grosbeak *(Hesperiphona vespertina)*—see Plate 373. 7. Townsend's Fox Sparrow *(Passerella iliaca)*—see Plate 108.

425. ANNA'S HUMMINGBIRD
(CALYPTE ANNA)

Range: California and Lower California. In migration casually to Arizona, Mexico, etc. Habitat: Gardens, woodlands, etc. Identification: Length, about 4 inches. Red hood in male. Female, nondescript and difficult to determine. Large size and spotted throat indicative. Voice: Compared by Dawson to snipping note made by barber's shears. Breeding: Two eggs in nest in bush or tree.

426. CALIFORNIA CONDOR

(GYMNOGYPS CALIFORNICANUS)

Range: Now confined to southern California, formerly also in northwestern Lower California. *Habitat:* Undisturbed mountains. *Identification:* Immense size—spread 9 or 10 feet. Soars with wingtips curved upward. White patches under wings. *Breeding:* One egg, in cave or crevice, on ground. Does not lay every year. *Food:* Carrion. This magnificent bird is one of the rarest in the world, and is in grave danger of extermination. It has frequently been shot and has succumbed to poison distributed by governmental agencies.

427. OYSTER-CATCHERS

These birds might be called the North American Black Oyster-catcher (1) and the South American Black Oyster-catcher (2—*Haematopus ater*). The latter species ranges, according to Murphy's *Oceanic Birds of South America*, "from islands in the estuary of the Rio de la Plata southward to the Falkland Islands and Cape Horn, and northward along the Pacific coast at least to latitude 7° S. in Peru." The specimen on which Audubon based his description and painting, was sent him from California.

428. SURF-BIRD

(APHRIZA VIRGATA)

Range: Breeds on the Alaska mountains in south-central Alaska. Winters more or less regularly on the Queen Charlotte Islands, Vancouver Island, and the coast of southern Alaska, and thence south to the Straits of Magellan. *Habitat:* Surf-line, on rocky coasts.

Identification: Length, about 11 inches. Short bill, white rump, and white patch in wing. *Voice:* A whistled *teu, teu, teu. Breeding:* Four eggs, in ground nest, above timber line. First discovered in 1926 by the late George M. Wright.

429. STELLER'S EIDER
(POLYSTICTA STELLERI)

Range: Breeds on the Arctic coasts of Siberia and Alaska from the Taimyr Peninsula and Point Barrow to Kamchatka and perhaps the Aleutian and Shumagin islands. Winters in the vicinity of the Aleutian Islands. The bird student who would enjoy the sight of this beautiful Duck in life, must journey to northern regions of fog and ice. Here, in a latitude inhospitable to man, avian life teems.

430. **MARBLED MURRELET**
(BRACHYRAMPHUS MARMORATUS)

Range: Breeds in the Queen Charlotte Islands and summers to California. Winters from the Pribilof Islands to southern California. *Habitat:* Sounds, bays and channels. *Identification:* Length, about 10 inches—Robin-size. In winter, resembles a miniature California Murre. (See Plate 218.) Black and white coloration; sharp tapering bill with long, sloping forehead. Chin white, nape more narrowly sooty, bill longer and more uniformly black, as compared with Ancient Murrelet (Plate 402).

431. FLAMINGO

(PHOENICOPTERUS RUBER)

Range: Atlantic coast of subtropical and tropical America. Breeds from the Bahamas to Guiana and Peru; formerly a regular visitor near the southern tip of the Florida Peninsula; now of casual occurrence on the Florida coast. *Habitat:* Shallow coastal waters. *Iden-*tification: Large size—length about 4 feet, spread about 5½. Pink coloration. In flight, neck extended, slightly downward. *Breeding:* One egg in mud nest. For a fascinating account of the Flamingo, see Chapman's *Camps and Cruises of an Ornithologist.*

432. FOUR OWLS

1, 2. Burrowing Owl (*Speotyto cunicularia*). 3. European Little Owl (*Carine noctua*), the bird that, for more than 2,000 years, has been associated with Pallas Athene, goddess of wisdom. 4, 5. Pygmy Owl (*Glaucidium gnoma*). 6. Short-eared Owl (*Asio flammeus*),

breeds from Alaska and Greenland to California and New Jersey; also over much of rest of world. A bird of the marshes, diurnal in habit. Food habits make it highly valuable to man.

433. A FEATHERED POT-POURRI

1, 2. Bullock's Oriole *(Icterus bullocki)*. 3. Baltimore Oriole *(Icterus galbula)*. (See Plate 12.) 4, 5. Mexican Goldfinch *(Carduelis mexicanus* Swainson) is, according to Ridgway, found in Mexico in general, southern Texas, and is accidental in Colorado. 6. Varied Thrush *(Ixoreus naevius)*. 7. Northern Water-Thrush *(Seiurus noveboracensis)*.

434. FLYCATCHERS AND VIREO

1. Least Flycatcher *(Empidonax minimus)*. 2. Small-headed Fly-catcher *(Musicapa minuta)* is "known only from the works of Wilson and Audubon whose specimens came from New Jersey and Kentucky respectively." (A.O.U. *Check-List.*) The real identity of the bird has never been determined. 3. Blue Mountain Warbler *(Dendroica montana)*—another unknown. 4. Bartram's Vireo. 5. Western Wood Pewee *(Myiochanes richardsoni)*. 6. Black Phoebe.

435. DIPPER

(CINCLUS MEXICANUS)

Since this bird has been discussed on Plate 370, it may be well to mention, here, a threat to American birdlife—the fisherman who, unlike Izaak Walton, would kill all creatures that take fish he—the fisherman—wants to kill. American courts have decided that our wild life belongs to all the people until it has ben legally "reduced to possession." Thus, in the Dipper, the Merganser, the Tern and the Kingfisher, the bird lover has a joint interest, and he may justly protest their slaughter.

TRANSCRIPT OF THE LEGENDS

ON THE ORIGINAL PLATES

and

INDEX OF COMMON NAMES

TRANSCRIPT

OF THE LEGENDS ON THE ORIGINAL PLATES

WITH A NOTE CONCERNING THEM

NOTE ON THE ORIGINAL PLATES

THE ORIGINAL EDITION of *The Birds of America* was published by Audubon in London during the years 1827–1838. Each plate reproduced an original water-color painting by the naturalist, and was a hand-colored impression from a copperplate. These plates were aquatint engravings, and were printed on double elephant folio Whatman paper, each sheet measuring 39½ x 26½ inches before trimming. The first plate was made late in 1826; the first part, containing the first five plates, was published in 1827; while the last plate was finished in 1838.

There were 435 plates in all, issued in 87 parts of five plates each. Although subscriptions were taken for parts as issued (as well as for complete sets) the plates are generally found bound into four volumes, each with an engraved title page. There are one hundred plates in each of the first three volumes, and 135 in the fourth. The set from which the present reproductions are made is uncut and unbound, but contains the title-page sheets.

The first ten plates were engraved by William H. Lizars of Edinburgh; they were retouched and reprinted later by Robert Havell and Son (Robert Havell, Jr.) in London. For a time the Havells worked together producing the remaining plates; then the son engraved independently, his father printing and coloring; after 1830 the son did all the work under his own name, and, after the death of his father in 1832, dropped the "Jr." from his name.

The plates were published at two guineas the part, or £182/14s. the set ($1,000 in America); and it is believed that fewer than 200 complete bound sets were made up. There were, however, some unbound sets; and since there were more than a hundred subscribers who paid for the earlier parts but defaulted before the publication was completed, there were perhaps as many as 300 impressions taken of the earlier plates. In all, Audubon had received 279 subscriptions, but only 161 names remained on his list in 1838.

Subscriptions were received throughout the eleven years of publication, so presumably sets of prints were printed and colored at various times. We know that this was true of the earlier plates, a fact which explains the variations to be found not only in the subjects themselves, but in legends and dates, and even in the numbers. In Plate I, for example, the famous Wild Turkey, there are at least three states of the engraved legend. In the first state (as in the present set) the common name is given as "Great American Cock" and the engraver's imprint is "Engraved by W. H. Lizars"; in the second state the common name remains the same but "Retouched by R. Havell Jr." is added below the original imprint; in the third state the common name is changed to "Wild Turkey" while the double imprint remains.

In the present volume no exhaustive collation of these variations has been possible. In the Transcript below, the plates used in making the reproductions have been followed. Since this set is complete and in pristine uncut condition, with the earlier plates in the first known state, it is a reasonable assumption that the plates are in the earliest state throughout.

The octavo edition of *The Birds of America* was first published by Audubon in New York (and J. B. Chevalier in Philadelphia) in 1840–1844. There were seven volumes, this time with text. There were 500 plates in this edition, lithographed and hand-colored—mostly by J. T. Bowen of Philadelphia.

The legends appearing on the original plates consist of the following items, not all of which are on every plate: *part number; plate number,* in Roman numerals (except for plates 11–14 and 16–55 inclusive, and all those from the octavo edition, which appear in Arabic numerals); *common name* and *scientific name* (see note at head of the *Index of Common Names* on page xxv); *identification* by number of the various birds in the plate (these identifications are occasionally incorrect, as indicated in the accompanying text; and the identification numbers sometimes appear in the legend but not with the subject itself);

plant, tree and *reptile names*, etc.; *Drawn from Nature by John J. Audubon, F.R.S., M.W.S.* or some similar inscription; and the *engraver's name*, etc., with the *date*.

In the Transcript which follows, only the *plate numbers*, the *common* and *scientific names*, the *identifications*, the *plant names*, etc., and the *dates* are reprinted. Audubon's spellings of bird and plant names, even where occasionally incorrect or inconsistent, have been retained; but the original variegated punctuation, abbreviation, style of lettering, order of items, capitalization, etc., have been made consistent. The plate numbers are all given in Arabic numerals.

TRANSCRIPT OF THE LEGENDS ON THE ORIGINAL PLATES

ELEPHANT FOLIO · VOLUME I

(1). Great American Cock, Meleagris Gallopavo, Male. Vulgo Wild Turkey.

(2). Yellow-billed Cuckoo, Coccyzus Carolinensis. Plant, Popaw, Porcelia Triloba.

(3). Prothonotary Warbler, Dacnis Protonotarius. Plant, Vulgo Cane Vine.

(4). Purple Finch, Fringilla Purpurea. Plant, Pinus Pendula, Vulgo Black Larch.

(5). Bonaparte Flycatcher, Muscicapa Bonapartii. Plant, seed pud Magnolia Grandiflora.

(6). Great American Hen and Young, Meleagris Gallopavo, Female. Vulgo Wild Turkey.

(7). Purple Grackle, Quiscalus Versicolor, 1 Male, 2 Female. Plant, Vulgo Indian Corn.

(8). White-throated Sparrow, Fringilla Pensylvanica, 1 Male, 2 Female. Plant, Cornus Florida, Vulgo Dog Wood.

(9). Selby's Flycatcher, Muscicapa Selbii. Plant, Vulgo Pheasant's Eye.

(10). Brown Lark, Anthus Aquaticus, 1 Male, 2 Female.

(11). Bird of Washington or Great American Sea Eagle, Falco Washingtoniensis, Male.

(12). Baltimore Oriole, Icterus Baltimore, 1 and 2 Males, 3 Female and nest. Plant, Liriodendron Tulipifera, Vulgo Yellow Poplar.

(13). Snow Bird, Fringilla Nivalis, 1 Male, 2 Female. Plant, Vulgo Great Swamp Ash.

(14). Prairie Warbler, Sylvia Discolor, 1 Male, 2 Female. Plant, Vulgo Buffaloe Grass.

(15). Blue Yellow-back Warbler, Sylvia Americana, 1 Male, 2 Female. Plant, Vulgo Louisiana Flag.

(16). Great-footed Hawk, Falco Peregrinus, 1 Male, 2 Female.

(17). Carolina Pigeon or Turtle Dove, Columba Carolinensis, 1 Male, 2 Female. Plant, Steuartia Malacodrendron.

(18). Bewick's Long-tailed Wren, Troglodytes Bewickii. Plant, Vulgo Iron Wood.

(19). Louisiana Water Thrush, Turdus Aquaticus. Plant, Vulgo Indian Turnip.

(20). Blue-winged Yellow Warbler, Dacnis Solitaria, 1 Male, 2 Female. Plant, Vulgo Wild Althea.

(21). Mocking Bird, Turdus Polyglottus, 1 Male, 2 Female. Plant, Vulgo Yellow Jessamin. Rattlesnake, Crotalis Horridus.

(22). Purple Martin, Hirundo Purpurea, 1 Male, 2 Female. Nest, a Gourd.

(23). Maryland Yellow Throat, Sylvia Trichas, 1 Male, 2 Female. Plant, Vulgo 1 Wild Olive, 2 Bitter Wood.

(24). Roscoe's Yellow-throat, Sylvia Rosco. Plant, Vulgo Swamp Oak.

(25). Song Sparrow, Fringilla Melodia, 1 Male, 2 Female. Plant, Vulgo Wortle Berry.

(26). Carolina Parrot, Psitacus Carolinensis, 1 Male, 2 Female, 3 Young. Plant, Vulgo Cockle Burr.

(27). Red-headed Woodpecker, Picus Erythrocephalus, 1 Male, 2 Female, 3, 4, 5 Young.

(28). Solitary Flycatcher, Vireo Solitarius, 1 Male, 2 Female. Plant, Vulgo Cane.

(29). Towee Bunting, Fringilla Erythropthalma, 1 Male, 2 Female. Plant, Vulgo Black-berry.

(30). Vigors Vireo, Vireo Vigorsii, Male. Plant, Tradescantia Virginica.

(31). White-headed Eagle, Falco Leucocephalus, Male. Fish, Vulgo Yellow Mud Cat. 1828.

(32). Black-billed Cuckoo, Coccyzus Erythrophthalmus, 1 Male, 2 Female. Plant, Magnolia Grandiflora. 1828.

(33). Yellow Bird or American Goldfinch, Carduelis Americana, 1 Male, 2 Female. Plant, Cnicus Lanceolatus, Vulgo Common Thistle. 1828.

(34). Worm-eating Warbler, Dacnis Vermivora, 1 Male, 2 Female. Plant, Phytolacca Decandra, Vulgo Poke-berry. 1828.

(35). Children's Warbler, Silvia Childreni, 1 Male, 2 Female. Plant, Cassia Occidentalis, Vulgo Spanish Coffee. 1828.

(36). Stanley Hawk, Astur Stanleii, 1 Male, 2 Female. 1828.

(37). Gold-winged Woodpecker, Picus Auratus, 1 Male, 2 Female. 1828.

(38). Kentucky Warbler, Sylvia Formosa, 1 Male, 2 Female. Plant, Magnolia Auriculata. 1828.

(39). Crested Titmouse, Parus Bicolor, 1 Male, 2 Female. Plant, Pinus Strobus. 1828.

(40). American Redstart, Muscicapa Ruticilla, 1 Male, 2 Female. Plant, Ostrya Virginica, Vulgo Scrub Elm. 1828.

(41). Ruffed Grous, Tetrao Umbellus, 1 and 2 Male, 3 Female. Vulgo Pheasant, 1828.

(42). Orchard Oriole, Icterus Spurius, 1 and 2 Male, 3 and 4 Adult, 2nd and 3d Year, 5 Female. Plant, Vulgo Honey Locust, Gleditschia Triacanthos. 1828.

(43). Cedar Bird, Bombycilla Carolinensis, 1 Male, 2 Female. Plant, Vulgo Red Cedar, Juniper Virginiana. 1828.

(44). Summer Red Bird, Tanagra Aestiva, 1 Old Male, 2 Young, 3 Female. Plant, Vulgo Wild Muscadine, Vitis Rotundifolia. 1828.

(45). Traill's Flycatcher, Muscicapa Trailli. Plant, Vulgo Sweet Gum, Liquidamber Styraciflua. 1828.

(46). Barred Owl, Strix Nebulosa, Adult Male. Grey Squirrel, Scurius Cinereus. 1828.

(47). Ruby-throated Humming Bird, Trochilus Colubris, 1 Male, 2 Female, 3 Young. Plant, Bignania Radicans, Vulgo Trumpet Flower. 1828.

(48). Cerulean Warbler, Sylvia Azurea, 1 Male, 2 Female. Plant, Vulgo Bear-berry, Ilex Dahon. 1828.

(49). Blue-green Warbler, Sylvia Rara. Plant, Vulgo Spanish Mulberry, Callicarpa Americana. 1828.

(50). Swainson's Warbler [sic], Sylvicola Swainsonia, Male. Tree, Vulgo White Oak. 1828.

(51). Red-tailed Hawk, Falco Borealis, 1 Male, 2 Female. 1829.

(52). Chuck Will's Widow, Caprimulgus Carolinensis, 1 Male, 2 Female. Plant, Bignonia Capreolata. 1829.

(53). Painted Bunting, Fringilla Ciris, 1 and 2 Old Males, 3 Male of 1st Year, 4 2nd Year, 5 Female. Plant, Prunus Chicasa. 1829.

(54). Rice Bunting, Icterus Agripennis, 1 Male, 2 Female. Plant, Acer Rubrum. 1829.

(55). Cuvier's Wren, Regulus Cuvieri, Male. Plant, Kalmia Latifolia. 1829.

(56). Red-shouldered Hawk, Falco Lineatus, Gmelin, 1 Male, 2 Female.

(57). Loggerhead Shrike, Lanius Ludovicianus, Linnaeus, 1 Male, 2 Female. Green Briar or Round-leaved Smilax, Smilax Rotundifolia.

(58). Hermit Thrush, Turdus Minor, Gmel., 1 Male, 2 Female.

(59). Chestnut-sided Warbler, Sylvia Icterocephala, Latham, 1 Male, 2 Female. Moth Mullein, Verbascum Blattaria.

(60). Carbonated Warbler, Sylvia Carbonata, Male. Maybush or Service, Pyrus Botryapium.

(61). Great Horned Owl, Strix Virginiana, Gmel., 1 Male, 2 Female.

(62). Passenger Pigeon, Columba Migratoria, Linn., 1 Male, 2 Female.

(63). White-eyed Flycatcher or Vireo, Vireo Noveboracensis, Bonaparte, Male. Pride of China or Bead-tree, Melia Azedarach.

(64). Swamp Sparrow, Fringilla Palustris, Wilson, Male. May-apple, Podophyllum Peltatum.

(65). Rathbone Warbler, Sylvia Rathbonia, 1 Male, 2 Female. Ramping Trumpet-flower, Bignonia Capreolata.

(66). Ivory-billed Woodpecker, Picus Principalis, 1 Male, 2 and 3 Female. 1829.

(67). Red-winged Starling, Icterus Phoeniceus, 1 Adult Male, 2 Young Male, 3 Old Female, 4 Young. Plant, Acer Rubrum, Vulgo Swamp Maple. 1829.

(68). Republican Cliff Swallow, Hirundo Fulva, 1 Male, 2 Female, 3 Eggs, 4 Nests. 1829.

(69). Bay-breasted Warbler, Sylvia Castanea, 1 Male, 2 Female. Plant, Vulgo Highland Cotton, Gossipium Herbaceum. 1829.

(70). Henslow's Bunting, Ammodramus Henslowii. 1 Spigelia Marilandiea, 2 Phlox Aristata. 1829.

(71). Winter Hawk, Circus Hyemalis, Adult Male. Bull Frog. 1829.

(72). Swallow-tailed Hawk, Falco Furcatus, 1 Male, Female the Same. Reptile, Vulgo Garter Snake. 1829.

(73). Wood Thrush, Turdus Mustelinus, 1 Male, 2 Female. Plant, Cornus Florida, Vulgo Dogwood. 1829.

(74). Indigo Bird, Fringilla Cyanea, 1 Adult Male, 2 Male first year, 3 2nd year, 4 Female. Plant, Schisandra Coccinea, Vulgo Salsparilla. 1829.

(75). Le Petit Caporal, Falco Temerarius, Male. 1829.

(76). Virginian Partridge, Perdix Virginiana, 1 Adult Male, 2 Young, 3 Adult Female, 4 Young, 5 Very Young Birds. 1830.

(77). Belted Kingfisher, Alcedo Alcyon, 1 and 2 Male, 3 Female. 1830.

(78). Great Carolina Wren, Troglodytes Ludovicianus, 1 Male, 2 Female. Plant, Vulgo Dwarf Horse Chestnut, Aesculus Pavia. 1830.

(79). Tyrant Flycatcher, Muscicapa Tyrannus, 1 Male, 2 Female. Plant, Cotton Wood, Populus Candicans. 1830.

(80). Anthus Hypogaeus. Phlox Subulata. 1830.

(81). Fish Hawk, Falco Haliaetus, Male. Vulgo Weak Fish. 1830.

(82). Whip-poor-will, Caprimulgus Vociferus, 1 Male, 2 and 3 Female. Quercus Tinctoria, Vulgo Black Oak. 1830.

(83). House Wren, Troglodytes Aedon, 1 Male, 2 Female, 3, 4, 5, Young. 1830.

(84). Blue-grey Flycatcher, Sylvia Coerula, 1 Male, 2 Female. Plant, Juglans Nigra, Vulgo Black Walnut. 1830.

(85). Yellow-throat Warbler, Sylvia Pensilis, Male. Plant, Castanea Pumila, Vulgo Chink-apin. 1830.

(86). Black Warrior, Falco Harlani, 1 Male, 2 Female. 1830.

(87). Florida Jay, Garrulus Floridanus, 1 Male, 2 Female. Diospyros Virginiana, Vulgo Persimon. 1830.

(88). Autumnal Warbler, Sylvia Autumnalis, 1 Male, 2 Female. Plant, Betula Papyrifera, Vulgo Canoe Birch. 1830.

(89). Nashville Warbler, Sylvia Rubricapilla, 1 Male, 2 Female. Plant, Ilex, Vulgo Spice-wood. 1830.

(90). Black and White Creeper, Sylvia Varia. Pinus Pendula, Vulgo Black Larch. 1830.

(91). Broad-winged Hawk, Falco Pennsylvanicus, 1 Male, 2 Female. Plant, Juglans Porcina, Vulgo Pig-nut. 1830.

(92). Pigeon Hawk, Falco Columbarius, 1 Male, 2 Female. 1830.

(93). Sea-side Finch, Fringilla Maritima, 1 Male, 2 Female. Plant, Rosa Carolina, Vulgo Wild Rose. 1830.

(94). Bay-winged Bunting, Fringilla Graminea, Male. Plant, Cactus Opuntia, Vulgo Prickly Pear. 1830.

(95). Blue-eyed Yellow Warbler, Sylvia Aestiva. Plant, Wisterea. 1830.

(96). Columbia Jay, Garrulus Ultramarinus, 1 Male, 2 Female. 1830.

(97). Mottled Owl, Strix Asio, 1 Adult, 2 and 3 Young. Plant, Pinus Inops, Vulgo Jersey Pine. 1830.

(98). Marsh Wren, Troglodytes Palustris, 1 Male, 2 and 3 Female, 4 Nest. 1830.

(99). Cow Bunting, Icterus Pecoris, 1 Male, 2 Female. 1830.

(100). Green-blue, or White-bellied Swallow, Hirundo Bicolor, 1 Male, 2 Female. 1830.

ELEPHANT FOLIO · VOLUME II

(101). Raven, Corvus Corax, Male. Thick Shell-bark Hickory, Juglans Laciniosa.

(102). Blue Jay, Corvus Cristatus, 1 Male, 2 and 3 Female.

(103). Canada Warbler, Sylvia Pardalina, 1 Male, 2 Female. Plant, Big Laurel, Rhododendron Maximum.

(104). Chipping Sparrow, Fringilla Socialis, Male. Black Locust, Robinia Pseudacacia.

(105). Red-breasted Nuthatch, Sitta Canadensis, 1 Male, 2 Female.

(106). Black Vulture or Carrion Crow, Cathartes Atratus, 1 Male, 2 Female. American Deer, Cervus Virginianus. 1831.

(107). Canada Jay, Corvus Canadensis, Linn., 1 Male, 2 Female. White Oak, Quercus Alba. 1831.

(108). Fox-coloured Sparrow, Fringilla Iliaca, 1 Male, 2 Female. 1831.

(109). Savannah Finch, Fringilla Savanna, 1 Male, 2 Female. 1 Spigelia Marilandiea, 2 Phlox Aristata. 1831.

(110). Hooded Warbler, Sylvia Mitrata, 1 Male, 2 Female. 1831.

(111). Pileated Woodpecker, Picus Pileatus, Linn., 1 Adult Male, 2 Adult Female, 3 and 4 Young Males. Racoon Grape, Vitis Aestivalis.

(112). Downy Woodpecker, Picus Pubescens, 1 Male, 2 Female. Bignonia Capreolata. 1831.

(113). Blue-bird, Sylvia Sialis, 1 Male, 2 Female, 3 Young. Great Mullein, Verbascum Thapsus. 1831.

(114). White-crowned Sparrow, Fringilla Leucophrys. 1 Male, 2 Female. Summer Grape, Vitis Aestivalis. 1831.

(115). Wood Pewee, Muscicapa Virens, Male. Swamp Honeysuckle, Azalea Biscosa. 1831.

(116). Ferruginous Thrush, Turdus Rufus, Linn., 1 Male, 2 Female. Black-jack Oak, Quercus Nigra. Black Snake.

(117). Mississippi Kite, Falco Plumbeus, Gmel., 1 Male, 2 Female.

(118). Warbling Flycatcher, Muscicapa Gilva, Vieillot, 1 Male, 2 Female. Swamp Magnolia, Magnolia Glauca.

(119). Yellow-throated Vireo, Vireo Flavifrons, Vieill., Male. Swamp Snow-ball, Hydrangea Quercifolia.

(120). Pewit Flycatcher, Muscicapa Fusca, Gmel., 1 Male, 2 Female. Cotton Plant, Gossypium.

(121). Snowy Owl, Strix Nyctea, Linn., 1 Male, 2 Female.

(122). Blue Grosbeak, Fringilla Corulea, Bonap., 1 Male, 2 Female, 3 Young. Dog-wood, Cornus Florida.

(123). Black & Yellow Warbler, Sylvia Maculosa, Lath., 1 Male, 2 Female. Flowering Raspberry, Rubus Odoratus.

(124). Green Black-capt Flycatcher, Muscicapa Pusilla, Wils., 1 Male, 2 Female. Snake's-head, Chelone Glabra.

(125). Brown-headed Nuthatch, Sitta Pusilla, Lath., 1 Male, 2 Female.

(126). White-headed Eagle, Falco Leucocephalus, Linn., Young.

(127). Rose-breasted Grosbeak, Fringilla Ludoviciana, Bonap., 1 Male, 2 Female, 3 Young in autumn, 4 Young. Ground Hemlock, Taxus Canadensis.

(128). Cat Bird, Turdus Felivox, Vieill., 1 Male, 2 Female. Black-berry, Rubus Villosus.

(129). Great Crested Flycatcher, Muscicapa Crinita, Linn., Males.

(130). Yellow-winged Sparrow, Fringilla Passerina, Wils., Male. Phlox Subulata.

(131). American Robin, Turdus Migratorius, 1 Male, 2 Female, 3 Young. Chestnut Oak, Quercus Prinus. 1832.

(132). Three-toed Woodpecker, Picus Tridactylus, Linn., 1 Males, 2 Female. 1832.

(133). Black-poll Warbler, Sylvia Striata, Lath., 1 Males, 2 Female. Black Gum Tree, Nyssa Aquatica. 1832.

(134). Hemlock Warbler, Sylvia Parus, Wils., 1 Male, 2 Female. Dwarf Maple, Acer Spicatum. 1832.

(135). Blackburnian Warbler, Sylvia Blackburnia, Male. Phlox Maculata. 1832.

(136). Meadow Lark, Sturnus Ludovicianus, Linn., 1 Males, 2 Females. Gerardia Flava. 1832.

(137). Yellow-breasted Chat, Icteria Viridis, Bonap., 1 Males, 2 Female. Sweet Briar, Rosa Rubiginosa. 1832.

(138). Connecticut Warbler, Sylvia Agilis, Wils., 1 Male, 2 Female. Gentiana Saponaria. 1832.

(139). Field Sparrow, Fringilla Pusilla, Wils., Male. Calopogon Pulchellum and Vaccinium Tenellum. 1832.

(140). Pine Creeping Warbler, Sylvia Pinus, Lath., 1 Male, 2 Female. Yellow Pine. 1832.

(141). Goshawk, Falco Palumbarius, Linn., 1 Adult Male, 2 Young. Stanley Hawk, Falco Stanleii, Audubon, 3 Adult.

(142). American Sparrow Hawk, Falco Sparverius, Linn., 1 Male, 2 Female. Butter-nut or White Walnut, Juglans Cinerea.

(143). Golden-crowned Thrush, Turdus Aurocapillus, Wils., 1 Male, 2 Female. Woody Nightshade, Solanum Dulcamara.

(144). Small Green-crested Flycatcher, Muscicapa Acadica, Gmel., 1 Male, 2 Female. Sassafras, Laurus Sassafras. 1832.

(145). Yellow Red-poll Warbler, Sylvia Petechia, Lath., 1 Male, 2 Female. Helenium Quadridentatum. 1832.

(146). Fish Crow, Corvus Ossifragus, Wils., 1 Male, 2 Female. Vulgo Honey Locust, Gleditschia Triacanthos. 1832.

(147). Night Hawk, Caprimulgus Virginianus, Brisson, 1 Male, 2 Female. White Oak, Quercus Alba. 1832.

(148). Pine Swamp Warbler, Sylvia Sphagnosa, Bonap., 1 Male, 2 Female. Hobble Bush, Viburnum Tantanoides. 1832.

(149). Sharp-tailed Finch, Fringilla Caudacuta, Wils., 1 Male, 2 Female. 1832.

(150). Red-eyed Vireo, Vireo Olivaceus, Bonap., Male. Honey Locust, Gleditschia Triacanthos. 1832.

(151). Turkey Buzzard, Cathartes Atratus, 1 Male, 2 Young. 1832.

(152). White-breasted Black-capped Nuthatch, Sitta Carolinensis, Briss., 1 Male, 2 Female. 1832.

(153). Yellow-crown Warbler, Sylvia Coronata, Lath., 1 Male, 2 Young. Iris Versicolor. 1832.

(154). Tennessee Warbler, Sylvia Peregrina, Wils., Male. Prunus Sp. 1832.

(155). Black-throated Blue Warbler, Sylvia Canadensis, Lath., Male. Canadian Columbine, Aquilegia Canadensis. 1832.

(156). American Crow, Corvus Americanus, Male. Black Walnut, Corvus Americanus [sic]. Nest of the Ruby-throated Humming Bird. 1833.

(157). Rusty Grakle, Quiscalus Ferrugineus, Bonap., 1 Male, 2 Female, 3 Young. Black Haw. 1833.

(158). American Swift, Cypselus Pelasgius, Temminck, 1 Male, 2 Female. Nests. 1833.

(159). Cardinal Grosbeak, Fringilla Cardinalis, Bonap., 1 Male, 2 Female. Wild Almond. 1833.

(160). Black-capped Titmouse, Parus Atricapillus, Linn., 1 Male, 2 Female. Supple-jack. 1833.

(161). Brasilian Caracara Eagle, Polyborus Vulgaris. 1833.

(162). Zenaida Dove, Columba Zenaida, 1 Male, 2 Female. Anona. 1833.

(163). Palm Warbler, Sylvia Palmarum, 1 Male, 2 Young. Wild Orange. 1833.

(164). Tawny Thrush, Turdus Wilsonii, Male. Habenaria Lacera, Cornus Canadensis. 1833.

(165). Bachman's Finch, Fringilla Bachmani, Male. Pinckneya Pubens. 1833.

(166). Rough-legged Falcon, Falco Lagopus, Male. 1833.

(167). Key-west Dove, Columba Montana, 1 Male, 2 Female. 1833.

(168). Forked-tailed Flycatcher, Muscicapa Savana, Male. Gordonia Lasianthus. 1833.

(169). Mangrove Cuckoo, Coccyzus Seniculus, Male. 1833.

(170). Gray Tyrant, Tyrannus Grisens. Agati Grandiflora. 1833.

(171). Barn Owl, Strix Flammea, 1 Male, 2 Female. Ground Squirrel, Sciurus Striatus. 1833.

(172). Blue-headed Pigeon, Columba Cyanocephala, 1 Male, 2 Female. 1833.

(173). Barn Swallow, Hirundo Americana, 1 Male, 2 Female. 1833.

(174). Olive-sided Flycatcher, Muscicapa Inornata, 1 Male, 2 Female. Pinus Balsamea, Fir Balsam. 1833.

(175). Nuttall's Lesser Marsh Wren, Troglodites Brevirostris, 1 Male, 2 Female. 1833.

(176). Spotted Grous, Tetrao Canadensis, 1 Males, 2 Females. 3 Trillium Pictum, 4 Streptopus Distortus. 1833.

(177). White-crowned Pigeon, Columba Leucocephala, 1 Male, 2 Female. Cordia Sebestena. 1833.

(178). Orange-crowned Warbler, Sylvia Celata, 1 Male, 2 Female. Vaccinium.

(179). Wood Wren, Troglodytes Americana, Male. Smilacina Borealis. 1833.

(180). Pine Finch, Fringilla Pinus, 1 Male, 2 Female. Pinus Pendula. Black Larch. 1833.

(181). Golden Eagle, Aquila Chrysaetos, Adult Female. Northern Hare. 1833.

(182). Ground Dove, Columba Passerina, Linn., 1, 2, 3 Males, 4 Female, 5 Young. Wild Orange. 1833.

(183). Golden-crester Wren, Regulus Cristatus, Vieill., 1 Male, 2 Female. Thalia Dealbata.

(184). Mangrove Humming Bird, Trochilus Mango, 1, 2, 3 Males, 4 and 5 Females. Tecoma Grandiflora. 1833.

(185). Bachman's Warbler, Sylvia Bachmanii, Aud., 1 Male, 2 Female. Gordonia Pubescens. 1833.

(186). Pinnated Grous, Tetrao Cupido, Linn., 1 and 2 Males, 3 Female. Lilium Superbum. 1834.

(187). Boat-tailed Grackle, Quiscalus Major, Vieill., 1 Male, 2 Female. Live Oak, Quercus Virens.

(188). Tree Sparrow, Fringilla Canadensis, Lath., 1 Male, 2 Female. Berberis Canadensis. 1834.

(189). Snow Bunting, Emberiza Nivalis, Linn., 1 and 2 Adult, 3 Young. 1834.

(190). Yellow-bellied Woodpecker, Picus Varius, Linn., 1 Male, 2 Female. Prunus Caroliniana. 1834.

(191). Willow Grous or Large Ptarmigan, Tetrao Saliceti, Temm., 1 Male, 2 Female, and Young. Plants, 1 Labrador Tea, 2 Sea Pea. 1834.

(192). Great American Shrike or Butcher Bird, Lanius Septentuonalis, 1 Male, 2 Female, 3 Female Summer plumage, 4 Young or Female Winter plumage. Crataequs Apiifolia. 1834.

(193). Lincoln Finch, Fringilla Lincolnii, 1 Male, 2 Female. Plants, Cornus Suissica, 2 Rubus Chamoerus, 3 Kalmia Glauca. 1834.

(194). Canadian Titmouse, Parus Hudsonicus, 1 Male, 2 Female, 3 Young. 1834.

(195). Ruby-crowned Wren, Regulus Calendula, Stephens, 1 Male, 2 Female, Summer plumage. Kalmia Angustifolia.

(196). Labrador Falcon, Falco Labradora, 1 Male, 2 Adult Female. 1834.

(197). American Crossbill, Loxia Curvirostra, Linn., 1 Adult Male, 2, 3 Young Male, 4 Adult Female, 5 Young Female. Hemlock. 1834.

(198). Brown-headed Worm-eating Warbler, Sylvia Swainsonii. Azalia Calendula, Orange Coloured Azalia. 1834.

(199). Little Owl, Strix Acadica, Gmel., 1 Male, 2 Female. Common Mouse. 1834.

(200). Shore Lark, Alauda Alpestris, Z., 1 Adult Male Summer plumage, 2 Female, 3 Male Winter plumage, 4, 5, 6 Young.

ELEPHANT FOLIO · VOLUME III

(201). Canada Goose, Anser Canadensis, Vieill., 1 Male, 2 Female.

(202). Red-throated Diver, Colymbus Septentrionalis, 1 Adult Male Summer plumage, 2 Adult Male Winter plumage, 3 Adult Female, 4 Young. 1834.

(203). Fresh-water Marsh Hen, Rallus Elegans, Aud., 1 Male Spring plumage, 2 Young Autumnal plumage. 1834.

(204). Salt-water Marsh Hen, Rallus Crepitans, Gmel., 1 Adult Male Spring plumage, 2 Female. 1834.

(205). Virginia Rail, Rallus Virginianus, Linn., 1 Male, 2 Female, 3 Young Autumnal plumage. 1834.

(206). Summer or Wood Duck, Anas Sponsa, Linn., 1 and 2 Males, 3 and 4 Females. Platanus Occidentalis, Button Wood Tree. 1834.

(207). Booby Gannet, Sula Fusca. 1834.

(208). Esquimaux Curlew, Numenius Borealis, Lath., 1 Male, 2 Female. 1834.

(209). Wilson's Plover, Charadrius Wilsonius, 1 Male, 2 Female. 1834.

(210). Least Bittern, Ardea Exilis, Gmel., 1 Male, 2 Female, 3 Young. 1834.

(211). Great Blue Heron, Ardea Herodias, Male. 1834.

(212). Common Gull, Larus Canus, Linn., 1 Adult, 2 Young. 1834.

(213). Puffin, Mormon Arctictus, 1 Male, 2 Female. 1834.

(214). Razor Bill, Alca Torda, 1 Male, 2 Female. 1834.

(215). Hyperborean Phalarope, Phalaropus Hyperboreus, Lath., 1 Adult Male Spring plumage, 2 Adult Female, 3 Young Autumnal plumage. 1834.

(216). Wood Ibis, Tantalus Loculator. 1834.

(217). Louisiana Heron, Ardea Ludoviciana, Wils., Adult Male. 1834.

(218). Foolish Guillemot, Uria Troile, Lath., 1 Adult Male Summer plumage, 2 Female. 1834.

(219). Black Guillemot, Uria Grylle, Lath., 1 Adult Summer plumage, 2 Adult Winter plumage, 3 Young. 1834.

(220). Piping Plover, Charadrius Melodus, 1 Male, 2 Female. 1834.

(221). Mallard Duck, Anas Boschas, Linn., 1 Males, 2 Females. 1834.

(222). White Ibis, Ibis Alba, 1 Adult, 2 Young in Autumn. 1834.

(223). Pied Oyster-catcher, Haematopus Ostralegus, Linn. 1834.

(224). Kittiwake Gull, Larus Tridactylus, Linn., 1 Adult, 2 Young. 1834.

(225). Kildeer Plover, Charadrius Rociferus, 1 Male, 2 Female. 1834.

(226). Hooping Crane, Grus Americana, Adult Male. 1834.

(227). Pin-tailed Duck, Anas Acuta. 1834.

(228). American Green-winged Teal, Anas Carolinensis, Lath., 1 Male, 2 Female. 1834.

(229). Scaup Duck, Fuligula Marila, 1 Male, 2 Female. 1834.

(230). Ruddy Plover, Tringa Arenaria, 1 Male, 2 Female. 1834.

(231). Long-billed Curlew, Numenius Longirostris, 1 Male, 2 Female. City of Charleston. 1834.

(232). Hooded Merganser, Mergus Cucullatus, 1 Male, 2 Female. 1834.

(233). Sora or Rail, Rallus Carolinus, Linn., 1 Male, 2 Female. 3 Young. 1834.

(234). Tufted Duck, Fuligula Rufitorques, Bonap., 1 Male, 2 Female. 1834.

(235). Sooty Tern, Sterna Fuliginosa. 1834.

(236). Night Heron or Qua Bird, Ardea Nycticorax, Linn., 1 Adult, 2 Young. 1835.

(237). Great Esquimaux Curlew, Numenius Hudsonicus, Lath. 1835.

(238). Great Marbled Godwit, Limosa Fedoa, Vieill., 1 Male, 2 Female. 1835.

(239). American Coot, Fulica Americana, Gmel. 1835.

(240). Roseate Tern, Sterna Dougalii, Mont. 1835.

(241). Black-backed Gull, Larus Marinus. 1835.

(242). Snowy Heron or White Egret, Ardea Candidissima, Gmel., Adult Male Spring plumage. Rice Plantation, South Carolina. 1835.

(243). American Snipe, Scolopax Wilsonii, 1 Male, 2 and 3 Female. South Carolina Plantation near Charleston. 1835.

(244). Common Gallinule, Gallinula Chloropus, Adult Male. 1835.

(245). Uria Brunnichii. 1835.

(246). Eider Duck, Fuligula Mollissima, 1 Male, 2 Female. 1835.

(247). Velvet Duck, Fuligula Fusca, 1 Male, 2 Female. 1835.

(248). American Pied-bill Dobchick, Podiceps Carolinensis. 1835.

(249). Tufted Auk, Mormon Cirrhatus, Lath., 1 Male, 2 Female. 1835.

(250). Arctic Tern, Sterna Arctica. 1835.

(251). Brown Pelican, Pelicanus Fuscus, Adult Male. 1835.

(252). Florida Cormorant, Carbo Floridanus, Adult Male, Spring Dress. View, Florida Keys. 1835.

(253). Jager, Lestris Pomarina, Temm. 1835.

(254). Wilson's Phalarope, Phalaropus Wilsonii, Sabine, 1 Adult Male, 2 Female. 1835.

(255). Red Phalarope, Phalaropus Platyrhynchus, Temm., 1 Adult Male, 2 Adult Female, 3 Winter plumage. 1835.

(256). Purple Heron, Ardea Rufescens, Buffon, 1 Adult full Spring plumage, 2 Young two years old, in Spring plumage. 1835.

(257). Double-crested Cormorant, Phalacrocorax Dilophus, Swainson & Richardson, Adult Male Spring plumage.

(258). Hudsonian Godwit, Limosa Hudsonica, Swain. & Richards., 1 Male, 2 Young Female, Summer plumage 1835.

(259). Horned Grebe, Podiceps Cornutus, Lath., 1 Adult Male, 2 Female Winter plumage. 1835.

(260). Fork-tail Petrel, Thalassidroma Leachii, 1 Male, 2 Female. 1835.

(261). Hooping Crane, Grus Americana, Young. View in the interior of the Floridas with sand hills in the distance. 1835.

(262). Tropic Bird, Phaeton Aethereus, Linn., 1 Male, 2 Female. 1835.

(263). Pigmy Curlew, Tringa Subarquata, Temm., 1 Adult Male, 2 Young. 1835.

(264). Fulmar Petrel, Procellaria Glacialis, Linn., Adult Male Summer plumage. 1835.

(265). Buff-breasted Sandpiper, Tringa Rufescens, Vieill., 1 Male, 2 Female. 1835.

(266). Common Cormorant, Phalacrocorax Carbo, Dumont, 1 Adult Male Spring plumage, 2 Female, 3 Young. 1835.

(267). Arctic Yager, Lestris Parasitica. 1835.

(268). American Woodcock, Scolopax Minor, Gmel., 1 Male, 2 Female, 3 Young in Autumn. 1835.

(269). Greenshank, Totanus Glottis, Temm. View of St. Augustine and Spanish Fort, East Florida. 1835.

(270). Stormy Petrel, Thalassidroma Wilsonii, 1 Male, 2 Female. 1835.

(271). Frigate Pelican, Tachypetes Aquilus, Vieill., Adult Male. 1835.

(272). Richardson's Jager, Lestris Richardsonii, 1 Adult Male, 2 Young in September. 1835.

(273). Cayenne Tern, Sterna Cayana, Lath., Adult Male, Spring plumage. 1835.

(274). Semipalmated Snipe or Willet, Totanus Semipalmatus, Temm., 1 Adult Male Spring plumage, 2 Adult Female Winter plumage. 1835.

(275). Noddy Tern, Sterna Stolida, Linn., Adult Male. 1835.

(276). King Duck, Fuligula Spectabilis, Lath., 1 Male, 2 Female. 1835.

(277). Hutchins's Barnacle Goose, Anser Hutchinsii, Richards. & Swain. 1835.

(278). Schinz's Sandpiper, Tringa Schinzii, Brehm. View on the East Coast of Florida.

(279). Sandwich Tern, Sterna Boyssii, Lath. Florida Cray Fish. 1835.

(280). Black Tern, Sterna Nigri, Linn., 1 Adult, 2 Young in Autumn. 1835.

(281). Great White Heron, Ardea Occidentalis, Adult Male Spring plumage. View Key-West. 1835.

(282). White-winged Silvery Gull, Larus Leucopterus, Bonap., 1 Male Summer plumage, 2 Young in Winter. 1835.

(283). Wandering Shearwater, Puffinus Cinereus, Bonap., Male. 1835.

(284). Purple Sandpiper, Tringa Maritima, Bonap., 1 Male Summer plumage, 2 Female Winter, 3 Charadrius Wilsonius. 1835.

(285). Fork-tailed Gull, Larus Sabini, Swain. & Richards., 1 Male Summer plumage, 2 Tringa Arenaria, Male Spring plumage. 1835.

(286). White-fronted Goose, Lath., Anser Albifrons, Bechstein, 1 Male, 2 Female. 1836.

(287). Ivory Gull, Lath., Larus Eburneus, Gmel., 1 Adult Male, 2 Young Second Autumn. 1835.

(288). Yellow Shank, Totanus Flavipes, Vieill., Male Summer plumage. View in South Carolina. 1836.

(289). Solitary Sandpiper, Totanus Chloropygius, Vieill., 1 Male, 2 Female. 1835.

(290). Red-backed Sandpiper, Tringa Alpina, Linn., 1 Summer plumage, 2 Winter plumage. 1835.

(291). Herring Gull, Larus Argentatus, Brunnich, 1 Adult Male Spring plumage. 2 Young in November. Raccoon Oysters and view of the entrance into St. Augustine. 1836.

(292). Crested Grebe, Podiceps Cristatus, Lath., 1 Adult Male Spring plumage, 2 Young first Winter. 1836.

(293). Large-billed Puffin, Mormon Glacialis, Leach, 1 Male, 2 Female. 1836.

(294). Pectoral Sandpiper, Tringa Pectoralis, 1 Male, 2 Female. 1836.

(295). Manx Shearwater, Puffinus Anglorum, Ray, Male. 1836.

(296). Barnacle Goose, Anser Leucopsis, 1 Male, 2 Female. 1836.

(297). Harlequin Duck, Fuligula Histrionica, Bonap., 1 Old Male, 2 Female, 3 Young Male third Year. 1836.

(298). Red-necked Grebe, Podiceps Rubricollis, Lath., 1 Adult Male Spring plumage, 2 Winter plumage. 1836.

(299). Dusky Petrel, Lath., Puffinus Obscurus, Cuvier, Male in Spring. 1836.

(300). Golden Plover, Charadrius Pluvialis, Linn., 1 Summer plumage, 2 Winter, 3 Variety in March. 1836.

E L E P H A N T F O L I O · V O L U M E I V

(301). Canvas-backed Duck, Fuligula Vallisneria, Steph., 1 and 2 Male, 3 Female. View of Baltimore. 1836.

(302). Dusky Duck, Anas Obscura, Gmel., 1 Male, 2 Female. 1836.

(303). Bartram Sandpiper, Totanus Bartramius, Temm., 1 Male, 2 Female. 1836.

(304). Turn-stone, Strepsilas Interpres, Illiger, 1 Summer plumage, 2 Winter. 1836.

(305). Purple Gallinule, Gallinula Martinica, Gmel., Adult Male Spring plumage. 1836.

(306). Great Northern Diver or Loon, Colymbus Glacialis, Linn., 1 Adult, 2 Young in Winter. 1836.

(307). Blue Crane or Heron, Ardea Coerulea, 1 Adult Male Spring plumage, 2 Young second year. View near Charleston, S. C. 1836.

(308). Tell-tale Godwit or Snipe, Totanus Melanoleucus, Vieill., 1 Male, 2 Female. View in East Florida. 1836.

(309). Great Tern, Sterna Hirundo, Linn., Male Spring plumage. 1836.

(310). Spotted Sandpiper, Totanus Macularius, 1 Adult Male, 2 Female. View on Bayou Sarah, Louisiana. 1836.

(311). American White Pelican, Pelicanus Americanus, Aud., Male Adult. 1836.

(312). Long-tailed Duck, Fuligula Glacialis, 1 Male Summer plumage, 2 Male Winter, 3 Young Female. 1836.

(313). Blue-winged Teal, Anas Discors, Linn., 1 Male, 2 Female. 1836.

(314). Black-headed Gull, Larus Atricilla, Linn., 1 Adult Male Spring plumage, 2 Young first Autumn. 1836.

(315). Red-breasted Sandpiper, Tringa Islandica, Linn., 1 Summer plumage, 2 Winter. 1836.

(316). Black-bellied Darter, Plotus Anhinga, Linn., 1836.

(317). Black or Surf Duck, Fuligula Perspicillata, 1 Adult Male, 2 Female. 1836.

(318). American Avocet, Recurvirostra Americana, 1 Young in first Winter plumage, 2 Adult. 1836.

(319). Lesser Tern, Sterna Minuta, Linn., 1 Adult Spring plumage, 2 Young in September.

(320). Little Sandpiper, Tringa Pusilla, Wils., 1 Adult Male Summer plumage, 2 Female. 1836.

(321). Roseate Spoonbill, Platalea Ajaja, Linn., Male Adult. 1836.

(322). Red-headed Duck, Fuligula Ferina, Steph., 1 Male, 2 Female. 1836.

(323). Black Skimmer or Shearwater, Rhincops Nigra, Linn., Male. 1836.

(324). Bonapartian Gull, Larus Bonapartii, Swain. and Richards., 1 Male Spring plumage, 2 Female, 3 Young first Autumn. 1836.

(325). Buffel-headed Duck, Fuligula Albeola, 1 Male, 2 Female. 1836.

(326). Gannet, Sula Bassana, Lacep., 1 Adult Male, 2 Young, first Winter. Gannet Rock, Gulph of St. Lawrence. 1836.

(327). Shoveller Duck, Anas Clypeata, Linn., 1 Male, 2 Female. 1836.

(328). Long-legged Avocet, Himantopus Nigricollis, Vieill., Male. 1836.

(329). Yellow-breasted Rail, Rallus Noveboracencis, Bonap., Adult Male Spring. 1836.

(330). Ring Plover, Charadrius Semipalmatus, 1 Adult Male, 2 Young in August. 1836.

(331). Goosander, Mergus Merganser, Linn., 1 Male, 2 Female. Cohoes Falls, State of New York. 1836.

(332). Pied Duck, Fuligula Labradora, 1 Adult Male, 2 Female. 1836.

(333). Green Heron, Ardea Virescens, Linn., 1 Adult Male, 2 Young in September. 1836.

(334). Black-bellied Plover, Charadrius Helveticus, 1 Adult Male, Spring plumage, 2 Young in Autumn, 3 Nestling. 1836.

(335). Red-breasted Snipe, Scolopax Grisea, Gmel., 1 Spring plumage, 2 Winter. 1836.

(336). Yellow-crowned Heron, Ardea Violacea, Linn., 1 Adult Male Spring plumage, 2 Young in October. 1836.

(337). American Bittern, Ardea Minor, 1 Male, 2 Female. 1836.

(338). Bemaculated Duck, Anas Glocitans, Young Male in December. 1836.

(339). Little Auk, Uria Alle, Temm., 1 Male, 2 Female. 1836.

(340). Least Stormy Petrel, Thalassidroma Pelagica, 1 Male, 2 Female. 1836.

(341). Great Auk, Alca Impennis, Linn. 1836.

(342). Golden-eye Duck, Fuligula Clangula, 1 Male, 2 Female. 1836.

(343). Ruddy Duck, Fuligula Rubida, 1 Adult Male, 2 Adult Female, 3 Young Male second Spring, 4 Young first Autumn. 1836.

(344). Long-legged Sandpiper, Tringa Himantopus, 1 Spring plumage, 2 Winter. 1836.

(345). American Widgeon, Anas Americana, Gmel., 1 Male, 2 Female. 1836.

(346). Black-throated Diver, Colymbus Arcticus, Linn., 1 Male, 2 Female, 3 Young in October. 1836.

(347). Smew or White Nun, Mergus Albellus, Linn., 1 Male, 2 Female. 1836.

(348). Gadwall Duck, Anas Strepera, Linn., 1 Male, 2 Female. 1836.

(349). Least Water-hen, Edwards, Rallus Jamaicensis, Gmel., 1 Male, 2 Young Adult. 1836.

(350). Rocky Mountain Plover, Charadrius Montanus, Townsend, Adult Female. 1836.

(351). Great Cinereous Owl, Strix Cinerea, Gmel., Adult Female. 1837.

(352). Black-winged Hawk, Falco Dispar, Temm., 1 Male, 2 Female. 1837.

(353). Chestnut-backed Titmouse, Parus Rufescens, Towns., 1 Male, 2 Female. Black-capt Titmouse, Parus Atricapillus, Wils., 3 Male, 4 Female. Chestnut-crowned Titmouse, Parus Minimus, Towns., 5 Male, 6 Female and Nest. Willow Oak, Quercus Phelloes, Linn. 1837.

(354). Louisiana Tanager, Tanagra Ludoviciana, Wils., 1 and 2 Males Spring plumage. Scarlet Tanager, Tanagra Rubra, Linn., 3 Old Male Spring plumage, 4 Old Female Spring plumage. Plant, Laurus Carolinensis. 1837.

(355). MacGillivray's Finch, Fringilla MacGillivraii, 1 Male, 2 Female. 1837.

(356). Marsh Hawk, Falco Cyaneus, 1 Adult Male, 2 Adult Female, 3 Young Male. 1837.

(357). American Magpie, Corvus Pica, 1 Male, 2 Female. 1837.

(358). Pine Grosbeak, Pyrrhula Enucleator, 1 Male Adult Spring plumage, 2 Female, 3 Young first Winter. 1837.

(359). Arkansaw Flycatcher, Muscicapa Verticalis, Bonap., 1 Male, 2 Female. Swallow-tailed Flycatcher, Muscicapa Forficata, Gmel., 3 Male. Say's Flycatcher, Muscicapa Saya, Bonap., 4 Male, 5 Female. 1837.

(360). Winter Wren, Sylvia Troglodytes, 1 Male, 2 Female, 3 Young in Autumn. Rock Wren, Troglodytes Obselata, Say, 4 Female. 1837.

(361). Long-tailed or Dusky Grous, Tetrao Obscurus, 1 Male, 2 Female. 1837.

(362). 1 Yellow-billed Magpie, Corvus Nutalleii, Aud. 2 Steller's Jay, Corvus Stellerii. 3 Ultramarine Jay, Corvus Ultramarinus. 4 and 5 Clark's Crow, Corvus Columbianus, Wils. Plant, Platanus Racemosus, Nuttall, Acorn of Quercus Macrocarpa, Mich. 1837.

(363). Bohemian Chatterer, Bombycilla Garrula, 1 Male, 2 Female. Pyrus Americanus, Canadian Service Tree. 1837.

(364). White-winged Crossbill, Loxia Leucoptera, Gmel., 1 and 2 Adult Male, 3 Adult Female, 4 Young Female. New Foundland Alder. 1837.

(365). Lapland Longspur, Fringilla Laponica, 1 Male Spring plumage, 2 Male in Winter, 3 Female. 1837.

(366). Iceland or Jer Falcon, Falco Islandicus, Lath., Female Birds. 1837.

(367). Band-tailed Pigeon, Columba Fasciata, Say, 1 Male, 2 Female. Plant, Nuttall Cornel, Cornus Nuttalli, Aud. 1837.

(368). Rock Grous, Tetrao Rupestris, Leach, 1 Male in Winter, 2 Female Summer plumage, 3 Young in August. 1837.

(369). Mountain Mocking Bird, Orpheus Montanus, Towns., 1 Male. Varied Thrush, Turdus Naevius, Gmel., 2 and 3 Male and Female. Plant, Mistletoe, Viscum Verticillatum. 1837.

(370). American Water Ouzel, Cinclus Americanus, 1 Male, 2 Female. 1837.

(371). Cock of the Plains, Tetrao Urophasianus, 1 Male, 2 Female. 1837.

(372). Common Buzzard, Buteo Vulgaris, Female. Marsh Hare, Lepus Palustris, Bachman, Female. 1837.

(373). Evening Grosbeak, Fringilla Vespertina, Cooper, 1 Old Male. Spotted Grosbeak, Fringilla Maculata, 2 and 3 Male, 4 Female. 1837.

(374). Sharp-shinned Hawk, Falco Velox, Wils., 1 Male, 2 Female. 1837.

(375). Lesser Red-poll, Fringilla Linaria, Linn., 1 Male, 2 Female. Plant, Snow Berry, Symphoricarpos Racemosus. 1837.

(376). Trumpeter Swan, Cygnus Buccinator, Young. 1837.

(377)). Scolopaceus Courlan, Aramus Scolopaceus, Vieill. 1837.

(378). Hawk Owl, Strix Funerea, 1 Male, 2 Female. 1837.

(379). Ruff-necked Humming-bird, Trochilus Rufus, Lath., 1 and 2 Males, 3 Female and Nest. Plant, Cleome Heptaphylla. 1837.

(380). Tengmalm's Owl, Strix Tengmalmi, 1 Male, 2 Female. 1837.

(381). Snow Goose, Anser Hyperboreus, Pallas, 1 Adult Male, 2 Young Female first Winter. 1837.

(382). Sharp-tailed Grous, Tetrao Phasianellus, 1 Male, 2 Female. 1837.

(383). Long-eared Owl, Strix Otus, Male. 1837.

(384). Black-throated Bunting, Fringilla Americana, 1 Male, 2 Female. 1837.

(385). Bank Swallow, Hirundo Viparia, 1 Male, 2 Female, 3 Young. Violet-green Swallow, Hirundo Malassinus, Swain., 4 Male, 5 Female.

(386). White Heron, Ardea Alba, Linn., Male Spring Plumage. Horned Agama, Tapayaxin of Hernandes. 1837.

(387). Glossy Ibis, Ibis Falcinellus, Adult Male. 1837.

(388). Nuttall's Starling, Icterus Tricolor, Aud., 1 Adult Male. Yellow-headed Troopial, Icterus Xanthocephalus, Bonap., 2 Adult Male, 3 Adult Female, 4 Head of Young Male. Bullock's Oriole, Icterus Bullockii, 5 Adult Male. 1837.

(389). Red-cockaded Woodpecker, Picus Querulus, Wils., 1 Males, 2 Female. 1837.

(390). Lark Finch, Fringilla Grammaca, Say, 1 Male. Prairie Finch, Fringilla Bicolor, Towns., 2 Male, 3 Female. Brown Song Sparrow, Fringilla Cinerea, Gmel., 4 Male. 1837.

(391). Brant Goose, Anser Bernicla, 1 Male, 2 Female. 1837.

(392). Louisiana Hawk, Buteo Harrisi, Aud., Adult Female. 1837.

(393). Townsend's Warbler, Sylvia Townsendi, Nuttall, 1 Male. Arctic Blue Bird, Sialia Arctica, Swain., 2 Male, 3 Female. Western Blue Bird, Sialia Occidentalis, Towns., 4 Male, 5 Female. Plant, Carolina Allspice, Calycanthus Floridus. 1837.

(394). Chestnut-coloured Finch, Plectrophanes Ornata, **Towns., 1 Male Spring.** Black-headed Siskin, Fringilla

Magellanica, Vieill., 2 Old Male. Black Crown Bunting, Lath., Emberiza Atricapilla, Gmel., 3 Adult Male. Arctic Ground Finch, Pipilo Arctica, Swain., 4 Male, 5 Female. 1837.

(395). Audubon's Warbler, Sylvia Auduboni, Towns., 1 Male, 2 Female. Hermit Warbler, Sylvia Occidentalis, Towns., 3 Male, 4 Female. Black-throated Gray Warbler, Sylvia Nigrescens, Towns., 5 and 6 Males. Plant, Strawberry Tree, Euyonumus Americana. 1837.

(396). Burgomaster Gull, Larus Glaucus, Brunn., 1 Adult Male, 2 Young, first Autumn. 1837.

(397). Scarlet Ibis, Ibis Rubra, Vieill., 1 Adult Male, 2 Young second Autumn. 1837.

(398). Lazuli Finch, Fringilla Amoena, 1 Male Spring plumage. Clay-coloured Finch, Emberiza Pallida, Swain., 2 Male. Oregon Snow Finch, Fringilla Oregona, Towns., 3 Male, 4 Female. Plant, Liberty Bush, Azalea Nudiflora. 1837.

(399). Black-throated Green Warbler, Sylvia Virens, 1 Male, 2 Female. Blackburnian Warbler, Sylvia Blackburniae, 3 Female. Mourning Warbler, Sylvia Philadelphia, 4 Male, 5 Female. 1837.

(400). Arkansaw Siskin, Fringilla Spaltria, 1 Male. Mealy Red-poll, Linota Borealis, 2 Male. Louisiana Tanager, Tanagra Ludoviciana, 3 Female. Townsend's Finch, Emberiza Townsendi, 4 Male. Buff-breasted Finch, Emberiza Picta, 5 Male. 1837.

(401). Red-breasted Merganser, Mergus Serrator, Linn., 1 Male, 2 Female. Plant, Sarracenia Fiava. 1838.

(402). Black-throated Guillemot, Mergulus Antiquus, Bonap., 1 Adult, 2 Young. Nobbed-billed Auk, Phaleris Nodirostris, Bonap., 3. Curled-crested Auk, Phaleris Superciliata, 4. Horned-billed Guillemot, Ceratorrhina Occidentalis, Bonap., [5]. 1838.

(403). Golden-eye Duck, Clangula Vulgaris, Male Summer plumage. 1838.

(404). Eared Grebe, Podiceps Auritus, 1 Adult, 2 Young first Winter. 1838.

(405). Semipalmated Sandpiper, Tringa Semipalmata, Wils. 1838.

(406). Trumpeter Swan, Cygnus Buccinator, Richards., Adult. 1838.

(407). Dusky Albatros, Diomedea Fusca. 1838.

(408). American Scoter Duck, Fuligula Americana, 1 Male, 2 Female. 1838.

(409). 1 Havell's Tern, Sterna Havelli, Aud. 2 Trudeau's Tern, Sterna Trudeaui, Aud. 1838.

(410). Marsh Tern, Sterna Anglica, Montagu, Male Summer plumage. 1838.

(411). Common American Swan, Cygnus Americanus, Sharpless. Nymphea Flava, Leitner.

(412). Violet-green Cormorant, Phalacrocorax Resplendens, Aud., Female in Winter. Townsend's Cormorant, Phalacrocorax Townsendi, Aud. 1838.

(413). Californian Partridge, Perdix Californica, Lath., 1 Male, 2 Female. 1838.

(414). Golden-winged Warbler, Sylvia Chrysoptera, Lath., 1 Male, 2 Female. Cape May Warbler, Sylvia Maritima, Wils., 3 Male, 4 Female. 1838.

(415). Brown Creeper, Certhia Familiaris, Linn., 1 Male, 2 Female. 3, 4 Californian Nuthatch, Sitta Pygmea, Vigors. 1838.

(416). Hairy Woodpecker, Picus Villosus, Linn., 1 Male, 2 Female. Red-bellied Woodpecker, Picus Carolinus, Linn.,

3 Male 4 Female. Red-shafted Woodpecker, Picus Mexicanus, Aud., 5 Male, 6 Female. Lewis Woodpecker, Picus Torquatus, Wils., 7 Male, 8 Female. Red-breasted Woodpecker, Picus Ruber, Lath., 9 Male, 10 Female.

(417). Maria's Woodpecker, Picus Martini, Aud., 1 Male, 2 Female. Three-toed Woodpecker, Picus Hirsitus, Vieill., 3 Male, 4 Female. Phillips' Woodpecker, Picus Phillipsi, Aud., 5 and 6 Males. Canadian Woodpecker, Picus Canadensis, Buff., 7 Male. Harris's Woodpecker, Picus Harrisi, Aud., 8 Male, 9 Female. Audubon's Woodpecker, Picus Auduboni, Trudeau, 10 Male. 1838.

(418). American Ptarmigan, Tetrao Mutus, Leach, 1 Male Spring plumage. White-tailed Grous, Tetrao Leucurus, Swain., 2 Winter plumage.

(419). Little Tawny Thrush, Turdus Minor, Gmel., 1 Male. Ptiliogonys Townsendi, Aud., 2 Female. Canada Jay, Corvus Canadensis, Linn., 3 Young Male.

(420). Prairie Starling, Icterus Gubernator, Aud., 1 Male, 2 Female. 1838.

(421). Brown Pelican, Pelicanus Fuscus, Young first Winter. 1838.

(422). Rough-legged Falcon, Buteo Lagopus, 1 Old Male, 2 Young first Winter.

(423). Plumed Partridge, Perdix Plumifera, Gould, 2 Male, 3 Female. Thick-legged Partridge, Perdix Neoxenus, Aud., 1 Supposed Young Male. 1838.

(424). Lazuli Finch, Fringilla Amoena, Say, 1 Female. Crimson-necked Bull-finch, Pyrrhula Frontalis, Bonap., 2 Male. Grey-crowned Linnet, Linaria Tephrocotis, Swain., 3 Male. Cow-pen Bird Icterus Pecoris, Bonap., 4 Young Male. Evening Grosbeak, Fringilla Vespertina, Coop., 5 Female, 6 Young Male. Brown Longspur, Plectrophanes Townsendi, Aud., 7 Female. 1838.

(425). Columbian Humming Bird, Trochilus Anna, Lesson, 1, 2, 3, 4 Male, 5 Female and Nest. Plant Hibiscus Virginicus. 1838.

(426). Californian Vulture, Cathartes Californianus, Ill., Old Male. 1838.

(427). White-legged Oyster-catcher, Hoematopus Bachmani, Aud., 1 Male. Slender-billed Oyster-catcher, Hoematopus Townsendi, Aud., 2 Female. 1838.

(428). Townsend's Sandpiper, Frinca Townsendi, Aud., Females. 1838.

(429). Western Duck, Fuligula Stelleri, Bonap. 1838.

(430). Slender-billed Guillemot, Uria Townsendi, Aud., 1 Male, 2 Female. 1838.

(431). American Flamingo, Phoenicopterus Ruber, Linn., Old Male. 1 Profile view of Bill at its greatest extension, 2 Superior front view of upper Mandible, 3 Interior front view of upper Mandible, 4 Inferior front view of lower Mandible, 5 Interior front view of lower Mandible with the Tongue in, 6 Profile view of Tongue, 7 Superior front view of Tongue, 8 Inferior front view of Tongue, 9 Perpendicular front view of the foot fully expanded. 1838.

(432). Burrowing Owl, Strix Cunicularia, 1 Male. Large-headed Burrowing Owl, Strix Californica, 2 Male. Little Night Owl, Strix Noctua, Lath., 3 Female. Columbian Owl, Strix Passerinoides, Temm., 4 and 5 Males. Short-eared Owl, Strix Brachyotus, Wils., 6 Male. 1838.

(433). Bullock's Oriole, Icterus Bullocki, Swain., 1 Young Male, 2 Old Female. Baltimore Oriole, Icterus Baltimore, Bonap., 3 Old Female. Mexican Goldfinch, Carduellis Mexicanus, Swain., 4 Male, 5 Female. Varied Thrush, Turdus Noevius, Lath., 6 Female. Common Water Thrush, Turdus Aquaticus, Wils., 7 Male. 1838.

(434). Little Tyrant Flycatcher, Tyrannula Pusilla, Swain., Small-headed Flycatcher, Muscicapa Minuta, Wils., 2 Male. Blue Mountain Warbler, Sylvia Montana, Wils., 3 Male. Bartram's Vireo, Vireo Bartrami, Swain., 4 Male. Short-legged Pewee, Muscicapa Phoebe, Lath., 5

Male. Rocky Mountain Flycatcher, Tyrannula Nigricans, Swain., 6 Male. 1838.

(435). Columbian Water Ouzel, Cinclus Townsendi, Aud., 1 Female. Arctic Water Ouzel, Cinclus Mortoni, Towns., 2 Male. 1838.

INDEX OF COMMON NAMES

IN THE PRESENT TEXT AND ON THE ORIGINAL PLATES

Note: 1. The common names of birds as given in this book are those in current usage, as adopted in the *Check-List* of the American Ornithologists' Union. These names appear in roman type in the following *Index*. 2. The common names of birds as given by Audubon on his original plates frequently differ from those given in the A.O.U. *Check-List*. Where they differ to a considerable degree, Audubon's original names appear in *italic* type in the following *Index*.

Albatross, American Sooty, 407; *Dusky*, 407.

Auk, *Curled-crested*, 402; Great, 341; *Little*, 339; *Nobbed-billed*, 402; Razor-billed, 214, 218, 245; *Tufted*, 249.

Auklet, Crested, 402; Least, 402; Rhinoceros, 402.

Avocet, 318; *American*, 318; *Long-legged*, 328.

Baldpate, 345.

Bird, Cow-pen, 424; *Yellow*, 33.

Bittern, American, 337; Least, 210.

Blackbird, Brewer's, 157; Rusty, 157; Yellow-headed, 388.

Black Warrior, 86.

Bluebird, 113; *Arctic*, 393; Azure, 113; Mountain, 393; Western, 393.

Bobolink, 54.

Bob-white, 76.

Booby, White-bellied, 207.

Brant, 286; American, 391.

Bufflehead, 325.

Bull-finch, Crimson-necked, 424.

Bunting, *Bay-winged*, 94; *Black Crown*, 394; *Black-throated*, 384; *Cow*, 99; *Henslow's*, 70; Indigo, 74; Lark, 390; Lazuli, 398, 424; Painted, 53; *Rice*, 54; Snow, 189; Townsend's, 400; *Towee*, 29.

Bush-Tit, 353.

Butcher Bird, 192.

Buzzard, Common, 372; *Turkey*, 151.

Canvasback, 301, 322.

Caracara, Audubon's, 161.

Cardinal, 159; Florida, 159; Gray-tailed, 159; Louisiana, 159.

Catbird, 128.

Cedar Bird, 43.

Chat, Yellow-breasted, 137; Long-tailed, 137.

Chatterer, Bohemian, 363.

Chickadee, Acadian, 194; Black-capped, 160, 353, 194; Brown-headed, 160; Chestnut-backed, 353; Columbian, 194; Hudsonian, 194; Long-tailed, 160; Nicasio and Barlow's, 353; Oregon, 160.

Chicken, Prairie, 186, 382.

Chuck-will's-widow, 52.

Cock, Great American, 1.

Cock of the Plains, 371.

Colinus cristatus, 423.

Condor, California, 426.

Coot, 239; *American*, 239.

Cormorant, Baird's, 412; Brandt's, 412; *Common*, 266; Double-crested, 252, 257, 266; Farallon, 252; Florida, 252; *Townsend's*, 412; *Violet-green*, 412; White-crested, 252; European, 266.

Courlan, Scolopaceus, 377.

Cowbird, 99, 424.

Crane, *Blue*, 307; Florida, 261; *Hooping*, 226, 261; Little Brown, 261; Sandhill, 261; Whooping, 226.

Creeper, *Black and White*, 90; Brown, 415.

Crossbill, *American*, 197; Red, 197; White-winged, 364.

Crow, 156, 101; *American*, 156; *Carrion*, 106; *Clark's*, 362; Eastern, 146, 156; Fish, 146; Florida, 156; Northwestern, 156; Southern, 156; Western, 156.

Cuckoo, Black-billed, 32, 2; Mangrove, 169; Maynard's, 169; Yellow-billed, 2, 32, 169.

Curlew, Eskimo, 208; *Great Esquimaux*, 237; Hudsonian, 237; Long-billed, 231; *Pigmy*, 263.

Cuvier's Regulus, 55.

Darter, Black-bellied, 316.

Dickcissel, 384.

Dipper, 370, 435.

Diver, Black-throated, 346; *Great Northern*, 306; *Red-throated*, 202.

Dobchick, American Pied-bill, 248.

Dove, Ground, 182; *Key-west*, 167; Mourning, 17; *Turtle*, 17; Zenaida, 162.

Dovekie, 339.

Dowitcher, 335, 263, 315; Long-billed, 335.

Duck, *American Scoter*, 408; Bemaculated, 338; Black, 302, 317; *Buffel-headed*, 325; *Canvas-backed*, 301; *Dusky*, 302; Eider, 246; *Gadwall*, 348; *Golden-eye*, 342, 403; Greater Scaup, 229; Harlequin, 297; King, 276; Labrador, 332; Lesser Scaup, 229; *Long-tailed*, 312; *Pied*, 332; *Pin-tailed*, 227; *Red-headed*, 322; Ring-necked, 234; Ruddy, 343; *Scaup*, 229; *Shoveller*, 327; *Summer*, 206; *Surf*, 317; *Tufted*, 234; *Velvet*, 247; *Western*, 429; Wood, 206, 232.

Eagle, Bald, 11, 31, 126; *Brasilian Caracara*, 161; Golden, 181, 11; *Great American Sea*, 11; *White-headed*, 31, 126.

Egret, American, 386, 281; Brewster's, 242; Dickey's, 256; Reddish, 256; Snowy, 242, 307; *White,* 242.

Eider, American, 246, 276; King, 276, 246; Steller's, 429.

Falcon, Iceland, 366; *Jer,* 366; *Labrador,* 196; *Rough-legged,* 166, 422.

Finch, *Arctic Ground,* 394; *Bachman's,* 165; *Buff-breasted,* 400; *Chestnut-coloured,* 394; *Clay-coloured,* 398; *Lark,* 390; *Lazuli,* 398, 424; *Lincoln,* 193; *MacGillivray's,* 355; *Oregon Snow,* 398; *Pine,* 180; *Prairie,* 390; Purple, 4, 122; *Savannah,* 109; *Sea-side,* 93; *Sharp-tailed,* 149; *Townsend's,* 400.

Flamingo, 431, 321.

Flicker, 37; Red-shafted, 416.

Flycatcher, Acadian, 144; Alder, 45, 144; *Arkansaw,* 359, *Blue-grey,* 84; *Bonaparte,* 5; Crested, 129; Fork-tailed, 168; *Great Crested,* 129; *Green Black-capt,* 124; Least, 434, 144; Little, 45; *Little Tyrant,* 434; *Olive-sided,* 174; *Pewit,* 120; *Rocky Mountain,* 434; Say's, 359; Scissor-tailed, 359, 168; *Selby's,* 9; *Small Green-crested,* 144; Small-headed, 434; Solitary, 28; *Swallow-tailed,* 359; *Traill's,* 45; *Tyrant,* 79; *Warbling,* 118; *White-eyed,* 63; Yellow-bellied, 144.

Fulmar, 264.

Gadwall, 348.

Gallinule, *Common,* 244; Florida, 244, 305; Purple, 305.

Gannet, 326; *Booby,* 207.

Gnatcatcher, Blue-gray, 84; Western, 84.

Godwit, *Great Marbled,* 238; Hudsonian, 258; Marbled, 238; *Tell-tale,* 308.

Golden-eye, American, 342; Barrow's, 403.

Goldfinch, 33, 180; Arkansas, 400; Black-headed, 394; Mexican, 433.

Goose, Barnacle, 296; Blue, 381, 286; *Brant,* 391; Cackling, 201; Canada, 201, 277, 286; Hutchins's, 277, 201; *Hutchins's Barnacle,* 277; Lesser Canada, 201; Snow, 381, 296; White-cheeked, 201; White-fronted, 286.

Goosander, 331.

Goshawk, 141.

Grackle, Boat-tailed, 187, 87; Bronzed, 7; Purple, 7; *Rusty,* 157.

Grebe, Eared, 404, 259, 298; Great-crested, 292; Holboell's, 298; Horned, 259, 298, 404; Pied-billed, 248; *Red-necked,* 298; Western, 298.

Green-shank, 269.

Grosbeak, Black-headed, 373; Blue, 122; *Cardinal,* 159; Evening, 373, 424; Pine, 358, 4; Rose-breasted, 127; *Spotted,* 373.

Grouse, Dusky, 361; Fleming's, 361; *Long-tailed,* 361; *Pinnated,* 186; Richardson's, 361; *Rock,* 368; Ruffed, 41, 176; *Spotted,* 176; Spruce, 176; Sage, 371; Sharp-tailed, 382, 186; *White-tailed,* 418; *Willow,* 191.

Guillemot, Black, 219; *Black-throated,* 402; Mandt's, 219; *Foolish,* 218; *Horned-billed,* 402; *Slender-billed,* 430.

Gull, *Black-headed,* 314; Bonaparte's, 324, 285, 314; *Burgomaster,* 396; California, 212; *Common,* 212; *Fork-tailed,* 285; Franklin's, 324; Glaucous, 396, 287; Glaucous-winged, 291; Great Black-backed, 241; Herring, 291, 264, 282; Iceland, 282, 287; Ivory, 287; *Kittiwake,* 224; Laughing, 314, 285; Ring-billed, 212, 282, 291; Sabine's, 285; Short-billed, 212; Thayer's, 291; Vega, 291; *White-winged Silvery,* 282.

Gyrfalcon, 196, 366.

Hawk, *Black-winged,* 352; Broad-winged, 91; Cooper's, 36, 374; Duck, 16; *Fish,* 81; *Great-footed,* 16; Harlan's, 86, 51; Harris's, 392; Krider's, 51; *Louisiana,* 392; Marsh, 356, 166; Pigeon, 75, 92; Red-bellied, 56; Red-shouldered, 56, 71; Red-tailed, 51, 56, 86; Rough-legged, 166, 422; Sharp-shinned, 374; Sparrow, 142; *Stanley,* 36, 141; Swainson's, 372; *Swallow-tailed,* 72; *Winter,* 71.

Hen, *Great American,* 6; Heath, 186.

Heron, Black-crowned Night, 236, 386; California, 211; Great Blue, 211; Great White, 281; Green, 333, 307; Anthony's Green, 333; Frazar's Green, 333; Little Blue, 307; *Louisiana,* 256; *Night,* 236; Northwest Coast, 211; *Purple,* 256; Snowy, 242; Treganza's, 211; Ward's, 211; *Yellow-crowned,* 336; Yellow-crowned Night, 386.

Hummingbird, Allen's, 379; Anna's, 425; *Columbian,* 425; *Mangrove,* 184; Ruby-throated, 47; *Ruff-necked,* 379; Rufous, 379.

Ibis, Glossy, 387; Scarlet, 397; White, 222; Wood, 216.

Indigo Bird, 74.

Jaeger, 253; Long-tailed, 267; Parasitic, 272; Pomarine, 253; *Richardson's,* 272.

Jay, Blue, 102; California, 362; Canada, 107, 419; *Columbia,* 96; Florida, 87; Long-tailed, 362; *Steller's,* 362; *Ultramarine,* 362; Woodhouse's, 362.

Junco, Oregon, 398; Slate-colored, 13.

Killdeer, 225, 330.

Kingbird, 79, 170; Arkansas, 359; Gray, 170.

Kingfisher, Belted, 77.

Kinglet, Golden-crowned, 183, 195; Ruby-crowned, 195, 55.

Kite, Mississippi, 117; Swallow-tailed, 72; White-tailed, 352.

Kittiwake, 224.

Knot, 315.

Lark, *Brown,* 10; Horned, 200; *Shore,* 200.

Le Petit Caporal, 75.

Limpkin, 377.

Linnet, Grey-crowned, 424.

Longspur, Alaska, 365; *Brown,* 424; Chestnut-collared, 394; Lapland, 365.

Loon, 306; Common, 306; Pacific, 346; Red-throated, 202.

Magpie, American, 357; Yellow-billed, 357, 362.

Magpie-Jay, Collie's, 96.

Mallard, 221.

Mango, Black-throated, 184.

Man-o'-war-bird, 271.

Marsh Hen, Fresh-water, 203; *Salt-water,* 204.

Martin, Purple, 22.

Meadowlark, 136; *Western,* 136.

Merganser, American, 331; Hooded, 232, 325; Red-breasted, 401, 331.

Mockingbird, 21; *Mountain,* 369.

Murre, Atlantic, 218, 245; California, 218, 430; Pallas's, 245; Brünnich's, 245.

Murrelet, Ancient, 402, 430; Marbled, 430.

Nighthawk, 147, 82.

Nutcracker, Clark's, 362.

Nuthatch, Brown-headed, 125; *Californian*, 415; Florida, 152; Gray-headed, 125; Pygmy, 415; Red-breasted, 105; Rocky Mountain, 152; Slender-billed, 152; White-breasted, 152; *White-breasted Black-capped*, 152.

Old-squaw, 312.
Oriole, Baltimore, 12, 42, 433; Bullock's, 433, 388; Orchard, 42, 12.
Osprey, 81.
Ouzel, American Water, 370; *Arctic Water*, 435; *Columbian Water*, 435.
Oven-bird, 143.
Owl, Barn, 171; Barred, 46; Burrowing, 432; *Columbian*, 432; *European Little*, 432; *Great Cinereous*, 351; Great Gray, 351; Great Horned, 61, 383; Hawk, 378, 380; *Little*, 199; *Little Night*, 432; Long-eared, 383; *Mottled*, 97; Pygmy, 432, 199; Richardson's, 380, 199; Saw-whet, 199, 380; Screech, 97, 380, 383; Short-eared, 432; Snowy, 121, 366; *Tengmalm's*, 380.
Oyster-catcher, 223; Black, 427, 223; *Pied*, 223; *Slender-billed*, 427; *White-legged*, 427.

Paroquet, Carolina, 26.
Parrot, Carolina, 26.
Partridge, *Californian*, 413; Hungarian, 76; *Plumed*, 423; *Thick-legged*, 423; *Virginian*, 76.
Pelican, Brown, 251, 421; *Frigate*, 271; White, 311.
Petrel, *Dusky*, 299; *Fork-tail*, 260; *Fulmar*, 264; Leach's 260; *Least Stormy*, 340; Storm, 340; *Stormy*, 270; Wilson's, 270, 260.
Pewee, *Short-legged*, 434; Wood, 115; Western Wood, 434.
Phalarope, *Hyperborean*, 215; Northern, 215, 255; Red, 255; Wilson's, 254, 255.
Phoebe, 120; Black, 434.
Pigeon, Band-tailed, 367; *Blue-headed*, 172; *Carolina*, 17; Passenger, 62; White-crowned, 177.
Pintail, 227.
Pipit, American, 10, 80.
Plover, Black-bellied, 334, 300; Golden, 300, 334; *Kildeer*, 225; Mountain, 350; Piping, 220, 230; *Ring*, 330; *Rocky Mountain*, 350; *Ruddy*, 230; Semipalmated, 330, 209; Snowy, 209, 220, 330; Upland, 303; Wilson's, 209, 330.
Ptarmigan, *American*, 418; Chamberlain's, 368; Dixon's, 368; Evermann's, 368; Kellogg's, 368; Nelson's, 368; Reinhardt's, 368; Rock, 368, 418; Sanford's, 368; Townsend's, 368; Welch's, 368; Willow, 368; *Large*, 191; Willow, 191; White-tailed, 418.
Ptiliogonys, Townsend's, 419.
Puffin, Atlantic, 213; Horned, 293; Large-billed, 293; Tufted, 249.

Qua Bird, 236.
Quail, Mountain, 423; Valley, 413.
Quail-Dove, Blue-headed, 172; Key West, 167.

Rail, 233; Black, 349; Clapper, 204, 203; King, 203; Virginia, 205; Yellow, 329; *Yellow-breasted*, 329.
Raven, 101.
Razor Bill, 214.
Red Bird, Summer, 44.

Redhead, 322.
Redpoll, Common, 375; Hoary, 400; *Lesser*, 375; *Mealy*, 400.
Redstart, American, 40.
Red-wing, 67; Bicolored, 420; Tricolored, 388.
Robin, 131.

Sanderling, 230, 285.
Sandpiper, Baird's, 320; *Bartram*, 303; Buff-breasted, 265; Curlew, 263; Least, 320, 278; *Little*, 320; *Long-legged*, 344; Pectoral, 294; Purple, 284; Red-backed, 290, 263; *Red-breasted*, 315; *Schinz's*, 278; Semipalmated, 405, 278, 320; Solitary, 289; Spotted, 310, 289; Stilt, 344; *Townsend's*, 428; Western, 320; White-rumped, 278, 320.
Sapsucker, Red-breasted, 190, 416; Red-naped, 190; Yellow-bellied, 190.
Scoter, American, 408; Surf, 317; White-winged, 247, 219.
Shearwater, 323; Audubon's, 299; Greater, 283, 299; Manx, 295; Sooty, 264; *Wandering*, 283.
Shoveller, 327, 313.
Shrike, California, 57; *Great American*, 192; Loggerhead, 57; Migrant, 57; Northern, 192; White-rumped, 57.
Siskin, Arkansaw, 400; *Black-headed*, 394; *Pine*, 180.
Skimmer, Black, 235, 323.
Smew, 347.
Snipe, 308; *American*, 243; *Red-breasted*, 335; *Semipalmated*, 274; Wilson's, 243.
Snow Bird, 13.
Solitaire, Townsend's, 419.
Sora, 237, 233.
Sparrow, Bachman's, 165; *Brown Song*, 390; Bryant's, 109; Chipping, 104, 139; Clay-colored, 398; Field, 139; Fox, 108, 424; *Fox-coloured*, 108; Gambel's, 114; Golden-crowned, 394; Grasshopper, 130; Henslow's, 70, 130; House, 113, 365; Lark, 390; Lincoln's, 193; Nelson's, 149; Nuttall's, 114; Pine-woods, 165; Puget Sound, 114; Rusty Song, 390; Savannah, 109; Seaside, 93; Macgillivray's Seaside, 355; Sharp-tailed, 149; Song, 25; Swamp, 64; Tree, 188, 375; Vesper, 94; White-crowned, 114; White-throated, 8; *Yellow-winged*, 130.
Spoonbill, Roseate, 321.
Starling, Nuttall's, 388; *Prairie*, 420; *Red-winged*, 67.
Stilt, Black-necked, 328.
Surf-bird, 428.
Swallow, Bank, 385; Barn, 173; Cliff, 68; *Green-blue*, 100; *Republican Cliff*, 68; Tree, 100; Violet-green, 385; *White-bellied*, 100.
Swan, *Common American*, 411; *Trumpeter*, 376, 406; Whistling, 411.
Swift, *American*, 158; Chimney, 158.

Tanager, *Louisiana*, 354, 400; Scarlet, 354; Summer, 44; Western, 354, 400.
Teal, Blue-winged, 313; Green-winged, 228.
Tern, Arctic, 250, 309; Black, 280; Cabot's, 279; Caspian, 273; *Cayenne*, 273; Common, 309, 250; Forster's, 409, 309; *Great*, 309; Gull-billed, 410; *Havell's*, 409; Least, 319; *Lesser*, 319; *Marsh*, 410; Noddy, 275; Roseate, 240, 309; Royal, 273; *Sandwich*, 279; Sooty, 235; Trudeau's, 409.
Thrasher, Brown, 116; **Sage**, 369.

Thrush, *Ferruginous,* 116; *Golden-crowned,* 143; Hermit, 58; Alaska Hermit, 58; Audubon's Hermit, 58; Dwarf Hermit, 58; Eastern Hermit, 58; Mono Hermit, 58; Monterey Hermit, 58; Northern Water, 433; *Little Tawny,* 419; *Tawny,* 164; Varied, 369, 433; Willow, 164; Wood, 73.

Titmouse, *Black-capped,* 160; *Black-capt,* 353; *Canadian,* 194; *Chestnut-backed,* 353; *Chestnut-crowned,* 353; *Crested,* 39; Tufted, 39.

Towhee, 29; Arctic, 394, 29; White-eyed, 29.

Tropic-bird, Red-billed, 262; Yellow-billed, 262.

Turkey, Wild, 1, 6.

Turnstone, Ruddy, 304.

Tyrant, Gray, 170.

Uria Brunnichii, 245.

Veery, 164.

Vireo, Bartram's, 434; Blue-headed, 28; Cassin's, 28; Mountain, 28; Plumbeous, 28; San Lucas, 28; Red-eyed, 150, 154; *Vigors,* 30; Warbling, 118; White-eyed, 63; Yellow-throated, 119.

Vulture, Black, 106, 151; *Californian,* 426; Turkey, 151, 106.

Warbler, Audubon's, 395; *Autumnal,* 88; Bachman's, 185; Bay-breasted, 69, 88, 133; Black and White, 90; *Black and Yellow,* 123; Blackburnian, 134, 135, 399; Blackpoll, 133, 88, 90; Black-throated Blue, 148, 155; Black-throated Gray, 395; Black-throated Green, 399; *Blue-eyed Yellow,* 95; *Blue-green,* 49; Blue Mountain, 434; Blue-winged, 20; Blue-winged Yellow, 20; *Blue Yellowback,* 15; *Brown-headed Worm-eating,* 198; Cairns's, 155; Canada, 5, 103, 53; Cape May, 414; Carbonated, 60; Cerulean, 48, 49; Chestnut-sided, 59; *Children's,* 35; Connecticut, 138; Dusky, 178; Golden Pileolated, 124; Golden-winged, 414; *Hemlock,* 134; Hermit, 395; Hooded, 9, 110; Kentucky, 38, 78; Lutescent, 178; Macgillivray's, 399; Magnolia, 50, 123; Mourning, 399; Myrtle, 153; Nashville, 89; Orange-crowned, 178; Parula, 15; Pileolated, 124; Pine, 30, 140; *Pine Creeping,* 140; *Pine Swamp,* 148; *Prairie,* 14; Prothonotary, 3; *Rathbone,* 65; Sycamore, 85; Swainson's, 198; Tennessee, 154; Townsend's, 393; Western Palm, 145; Wilson's, 124, 110; Worm-eating, 34, 198; Yellow, 35, 65, 95; *Yellow-crown,* 153; Yellow Palm, 145, 163; *Yellow Red-poll,* 145; Yellow-throated, 85.

Washington, Bird of, 11.

Water-hen, Least, 349.

Water Thrush, *Common,* 433; Louisiana, 19; Northern, 433, 19.

Water-turkey, 316.

Waxwing, Cedar, 43, 363; Bohemian, 363, 43.

Whip-poor-will, 82, 52, 147.

White Nun, 347.

Widgeon, American, 345.

Willet, 274.

Woodcock, American, 268.

Woodpecker, 417; American Three-toed, 132; Arctic Three-toed, 132; *Audubon's,* 417; Batchelder's, 112; *Canadian,* 417; *Downy,* 112; Gairdner's, 112; *Gold-winged,* 37; *Hairy,* 416, 417; *Harris's,* 417; Ivory-billed, 66, 111; Lewis', 416; *Maria's,* 417; *Phillips',* 417; Pileated, 111; *Red-bellied,* 416; *Red-breasted,* 416; Red-cockaded, 389; Red-headed, 27; *Red-shafted,* 416; *Three-toed,* 132, 417; Willow, 112; *Yellow-bellied,* 190.

Wren, Baird's, 18; Bewick's, 18; Cuvier's, 55; Carolina, 78; *Golden-crester,* 183; *Great Carolina,* 78; *House,* 83, 179; Long-billed Marsh, 98, 175; Marian's Marsh, 98; *Nuttall's Lesser Marsh,* 175; Prairie Marsh, 98; Rock, 360; *Ruby-crowned,* 195; *San Diego,* 18; Short-billed Marsh, 175; Texas, 18; Tule Marsh, 98; Vigors's, 18; Winter, 360; *Wood,* 179; Worthington's Marsh, 98.

Yager, Arctic, 267.

Yellow-legs, Greater, 308, 288; Lesser, 288, 254, 308, 344.

Yellow Shank, 288.

Yellow-throat, Florida, 24; Maryland, 23, 24; Northern, 24; *Roscoe's,* 24; Salt Marsh, 24; Tule, 24; Western, 24.